Managing
Systems
Maintenance

Managing Systems Maintenance

William E. Perry

QED® Information Sciences, Inc.
Wellesley, MA. 02181

MANAGING SYSTEMS MAINTENANCE

Printed in the United States of America

First Printing: July 1981   Second Printing: May 1983

Library of Congress Catalog Card Number: 81-51630

International Standard Book Number: 0-89435-046-3

Contents

Preface

There are three types of people involved in data processing: those who make things happen, those who watch things happen, and those who don't know what's happening. Too frequently the people involved with new systems development are considered to be those who make things happen, while the people involved with systems maintenance are considered to be those who watch things happen. In some organizations, to be assigned to systems maintenance means to be categorized as a second-class citizen.

The facts of life dispute this philosophy. Many organizations expend the majority of their data processing resources on performing systems maintenance. In addition, many think it requires more skill to be a successful systems maintenance analyst than it does to be a successful systems analyst who successfully develops a new application system. This book is dedicated to the many unsung heroes of data processing who fight a daily battle to keep production systems functioning.

Research in systems analysis, training courses, and most publications deal exclusively with new systems development. Only minimal effort has gone into developing effective methods for performing systems maintenance. This trend has continued even though the amount of effort and resources going into new systems development has continued to decrease during the last decade. As more parts of an organization become computerized, the opportunities for developing new applications will decrease while maintaining existing applications will consume an increasing percentage of the data processing budget.

This book is based upon the author's personal experience as a maintenance systems analyst and on the experiences of others with similar responsibilities. The processes and forms presented in this book are a composite of the practices utilized by many data processing organizations. The author has attempted to incorporate good maintenance practices while eliminating ineffective practices. By utilizing the recommended procedures, organizations will significantly reduce the cost of maintenance. At the same time, data processing management will be able to monitor and adjust the process to gain even greater efficiency.

The maintenance process cannot be changed quickly. However, without action nothing will ever happen. An organization's poor maintenance practices are like a jar filled with bad water. You can wish that the bad water were not in the jar, but frustration, wishing, and expletives will not eliminate the bad water. However, a single stone thrown into the jar will cause some of the water to overflow out of the jar. A few improved maintenance practices have the same impact on a data processing department. As more stones are thrown into the jar more bad water is discharged. Over a period of time the stones will slowly displace all of the bad practices. The same philosophy needs to be used to incorporate effective systems maintenance practices. The road to effective maintenance is reached by taking a single step at a time.

The practices in this book may appear to be time consuming, but they work. It takes time to read a map and plot a course, but using a map gets you to your destination. The maintenance destination is more effective maintenance at a reduced cost. This book provides you the map and the direction. May you use them with success.

Chapter 1
The Systems Maintenance Dilemma

CHAPTER OVERVIEW

As the data processing industry has matured, systems maintenance has come to consume an ever increasing share of the data processing resources. The term "maintenance" has multiple implications for the data processing community. Some people view maintenance as a negative function involving error correction; others view maintenance as a highly creative and challenging aspect of data processing.

As the number and complexity of computerized applications increase, so does the demand for maintenance. Computerized applications must reflect the changing methods of conducting business by organizations. Any change that occurs within or outside the data processing function can necessitate systems maintenance.

Systems maintenance includes any activity needed to ensure that application programs remain in satisfactory working condition. This encompasses a broad range of activities involving error correction, need specification, system and program design, coding, testing, training, and monitoring the implementation of change. The management of maintenance is the management of change.

The broad interpretation of the maintenance function has resulted in the term being modified to indicate specific aspects of maintenance. For example, the following definitions of maintenance exist:

o   Corrective maintenance - Maintenance that is conducted for the purpose of eliminating an existing error or problem.

o   Deferred maintenance - Maintenance that is needed but is postponed until appropriate resources are available.

o   Preventive maintenance - Maintenance that occurs in anticipation of problems. For example, an application may install a fix to prevent a problem that has already occurred in another application.

o   Emergency maintenance - Unscheduled maintenance that is designed to eliminate a current problem situation which has stopped or otherwise affected successful operation of the application.

o   File maintenance - The addition, modification, or deletion of systems specifications.

o   Program maintenance - The addition, modification, or deletion of program instructions.

o   Scheduled maintenance - Maintenance that occurs at a predetermined time.

For the purpose of this book, systems maintenance is defined as all of the activities involved in keeping application systems working in a condition satisfactory to all involved parties.

The increasing need for data processing services directly affects the maintenance effort. Much of the demand placed upon data processing involves changing the existing computerized applications. Problems associated with controlling change place additional pressures upon data processing management to satisfy user needs on a timely basis.

SYSTEMS MAINTENANCE PRESSURES

The systems maintenance environment is not always a controlled environment. Data processing departments have more difficulty in scheduling maintenance than they do in scheduling new systems development. This is because many of the systems maintenance requests (as the multiple definitions of maintenance imply) do not take place under the direction of the data processing department. Also, maintenance requests do not flow in an even stream, but usually in bunches, often at inopportune times.

Managing the maintenance function is tantamount to managing change. The process of managing change is subject to the following pressures (See Figure 1-1):

o   Uncontrolled operating environment - The operating environment includes all of the vendor-supplied software utilized to support applications systems. This includes programs, and so forth. Controls are necessary in this environment to ensure that the right version of the program is placed into operation at the proper time and to ensure that it interfaces with the proper files and other applications systems. The less controlled this environment is, the more responsibility the applications systems/programmers will have for maintaining the integrity of the operating environment. Insufficient controls in the operating environment can lead to applications systems problems as well as ineffective application performance.

o   Insufficient maintenance program - Maintenance, like many other segments of data processing, has grown rapidly in size and scope. What a few years ago appeared not to be a problem has grown in many organizations to be a function that consumes most of the data processing resources. Many organizations are experiencing problems in controlling maintenance efforts. The result is the data processing function is sometimes directed by forces other than the management of the function.

o   Poorly-designed systems and programs - Maintaining well-designed application systems is a challenge for most systems analysts/programmers. As systems become more integrated and more complex, maintenance in one area of an application is more likely to impact another area. Many organizations still operate computerized applications developed during the 1960's. Many of these do not have today's structured systems design and extensive systems documentation. Maintaining these poorly-designed programs and systems is not only more time consuming, but also is more problematic.

o   Extensive user change requirements - Many users are unfamiliar with the systems maintenance process. They neither understand the cost and effort required to make the requested changes nor do they know how to modify the change requests to make them more feasible. Without this type of understanding, many users issue a continual stream of change requests to the data processing department. If maintenance personnel do not have these requests, if they are late in honoring them, users become vocally discontent with the data processing function.

Data processing management must address these pressures in establishing an ongoing effective maintenance program. The methods and procedures outlined in this book are designed to help data processing management and systems analysts/programmers perform maintenance more effectively. The key to success is in understanding the maintenance pressures and then in developing solutions that permit the maintenance process to function in an orderly fashion.

FIGURE 1-1

SYSTEMS MAINTENANCE PRESSURES

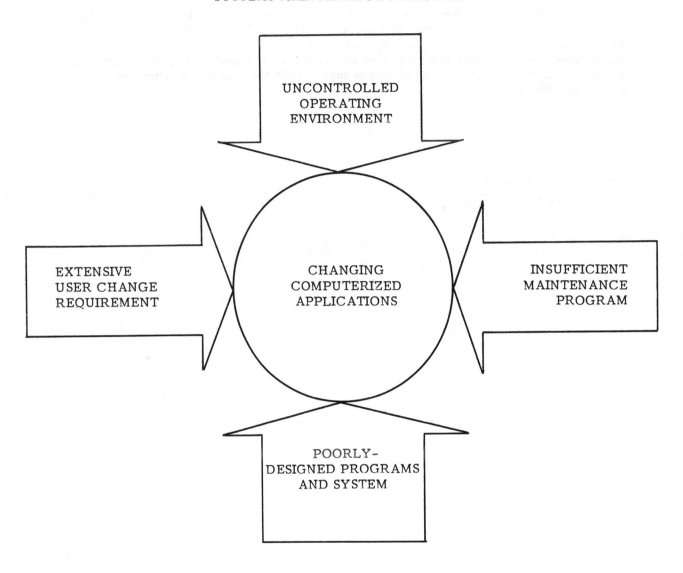

COST OF SYSTEMS MAINTENANCE

When data processing is first introduced into an organization, maintenance is only a minor aspect of the data processing effort. However, as the number of systems grow, maintenance becomes an increasingly greater part of the total EDP systems effort. In many organizations the cost of maintenance far exceeds the cost of new systems development.

Many large organizations obtained their first computer in the late 1950's or early 1960's. By 1970 many of these organizations had reached the point where they were expending as much on maintenance as they were on new systems development. By 1980 many of those same organizations reported that over 80% of the data processing resources are consumed by the systems maintenance function. Figure 1-2 illustrates this phenomenon.

Organizations which have only recently begun to use computers may appear at various points on the maintenance cost continuum illustrated in Figure 1-2. Also, the point on this maintenance continuum where your organization falls may be dependent upon how you define what is systems development effort and what is maintenance.

Organizations can anticipate that during the next few years their expenditure for systems maintenance will increase because:

o   Fewer new application systems are being developed.

o   Most new hardware provides application system compatibility enabling old systems to operate on the new hardware.

o   New technology and increased competition force organizations to change their methods of conducting business more frequently, thus requiring more changes to computerized application systems.

IMPEDIMENTS TO EFFECTIVE SYSTEMS MAINTENANCE

All data processing organizations strive to develop and operate an effective systems maintenance function. Sound policies and procedures are necessary components of an effective maintenance function. Unfortunately, many factors make it difficult to organize the maintenance function.

The maintenance environment varies from organization to organization. In some organizations, maintenance is decentralized, leaving it up to the project manager to establish controls. Other organizations have a highly centralized maintenance function stringently regulated by policies and procedures. Most organizations fall somewhere between the two extremes. Most organizations attempt to centralize the procedures but decentralize the actual performance of the maintenance.

The same analysis techniques that are effective in designing computer systems are effective in designing maintenance systems. The initial step in both procedures is to conduct a needs analysis in order to identify impediments to effective systems maintenance. The impediments are discussed below and are summarized in Figure 1-3.

FIGURE 1-2

COST OF SYSTEMS MAINTENANCE
AS A PERCENT OF EDP SYSTEMS EFFORT

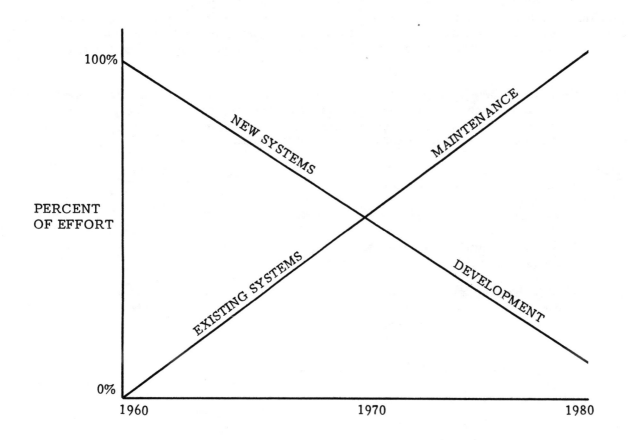

FIGURE 1-3

AREAS OF SYSTEMS MAINTENANCE REQUIRING MAINTENANCE ATTENTION

IMPEDIMENT	SOLUTION
1. Lack of maintenance information	1. Develop procedures to collect maintenance statistics.
2. Unapproved changes made	2. Develop maintenance approval procedures
3. Inconsistent approach to implementing system changes	3. Develop standardized method for installing changes
4. Users dissatisfied with implementation schedule	4. Develop a priority system for implementing changes
5. Repetition of same errors in multiple system	5. Develop method of informing all systems and programming personnel of common problems
6. System difficult to maintain	6. Replace or retrofit difficult-to-maintain system
7. Inadequate controls over installing, operating and deleting different version of systems	7. Develop controlled operating environment for installing changes
8. Problems occur when changes are installed	8. a. Perform regression testing b. Train users c. Monitor the change process

Impediment #1

o   Impediment - Lack of maintenance information: Before they can effectively manage maintenance, organizations must have sufficient information about the function to establish effective solutions.

o   Solution - Develop information collection procedures: Procedures need to be developed to collect information about the maintenance function. The accumulation of this information into maintenance statistics will enable management to track the function and make necessary adjustments.

Impediment #2

o   Impediment - Unapproved changes made: Without proper controls, changes can be implemented through the request of users, management, and/or programmers. Any request may be honored.

o   Solution - Develop maintenance approval procedures: Procedures need to be developed that ensure that no changes are made to application systems until those changes have been approved.

Impediment #3

o   Impediment - Inconsistent approach to implementing system changes: Individual projects should not be permitted to establish their own methods of implementing changes.

o   Solution - Develop standardized methods for installing changes: Procedures should be developed that provide a step-by-step standard approach for accepting, implementing, and placing changes into production.

Impediment #4

o   Impediment - Users dissatisfied with implementation schedule: The timeliness of installing changes or the priority of installing changes proves unsatisfactory to users.

o   Solution - Develop a priority system for implementing changes: The data processing project team in conjunction with the users should regularly review system changes and establish a priority for implementing those changes. Priorities may change, but the user will always be a major voice in establishing priorities.

Impediment #5

o   Impediment - Repetition of the same error in multiple systems: A Type X error occurs in one system, only to be followed a short time later by the occurrence of the same error in another application.

o   Solution - Develop a method of informing all systems and programming personnel of common errors. Analyze each error to determine whether it is unique to a specific application system or whether that type of error may be encountered in other applications. If the error could be common to many applications, inform systems programming personnel who will be affected.

Impediment #6

o   Impediment - System difficult to maintain: The structure of the system and/or programs, or the lack of documentation make it difficult for the systems analyst/programmer to determine how and where to implement a needed change.

o   Solution - Replace or retrofit difficult-to-maintain systems: The only solution to a poorly structured or documented application system is to redesign or retrofit that system so that it meets the current systems, programming, and documentation standards.

Impediment #7

o   Impediment - Unable to adequately control the installing, operating, and deleting of different versions of application systems: The current method of assigning system and programming version numbers may make it difficult to perform maintenance. This also leads to a lot of "dead wood" in the source and object program libraries.

o   Solution - Develop a controlled operating environment for installing changes: The source libraries should establish an efficient method for labeling different versions of the same program or system and for placing that into production at the required time while deleting obsolete versions.

Impediment #8

o   Impediment - Problems occur when changes are installed: Changes cannot be installed without causing problems for users or operating personnel. Changes installed in one part of the system cause problems in another part or in another system.

o   Solution - Perform regression testing, train users, and monitor the change process: Implementation problems are frequently associated with inadequate testing, training, and monitoring procedures. A successful maintenance function spends the time and effort required to assure that installation problems are minimal.

The maintenance guidleines presented in this book are designed to overcome impediments to good maintenance. These procedures will be outlined step by step so that you can understand and implement them.

SCOPE OF SYSTEMS MAINTENANCE

The self-assessment questionnaire provides an overview of the scope of activities included in the maintenance function. Systems maintenance does not often have the same excitement as developing new applications. Newer systems are based on newer technology, thus they appear to provide the major data processing challenge. On the other hand, people concerned with systems maintenance may be using twenty-year-old technology, but it can be as challenging or more challenging as attempting to master new technology.

FIGURE 1-4

OVERLAPPING CATEGORIES OF SYSTEMS MAINTENANCE

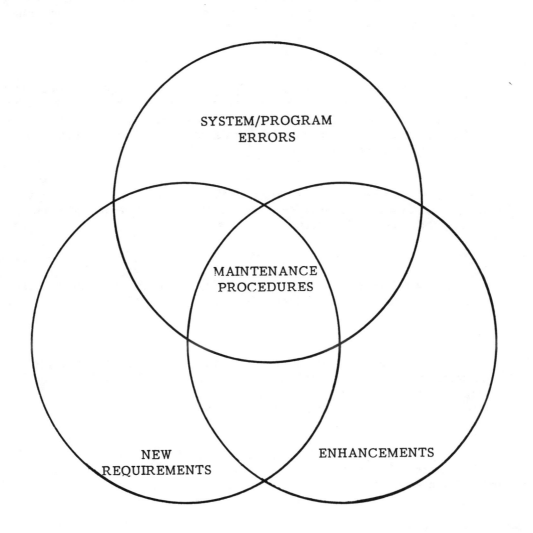

SYSTEM/PROGRAM
ERRORS

MAINTENANCE
PROCEDURES

NEW
REQUIREMENTS

ENHANCEMENTS

Put in its proper perspective, the scope of systems maintenance is extensive. Using our definition, it encompasses all activities needed to keep application systems in satisfactory working condition. These activities can be divided into the following three categories of systems maintenance (See Figure 1-4):

o   <u>System/program errors</u> - Systems errors include anything causing a program to fail to meet the users' needs. These errors include data errors, programming and systems errors, operating software interface errors, incorrect reports, and abnormal program terminations. This category includes both errors and omissions. An omission is the failure to perform a necessary action.

o   <u>New requirements</u> - As organization requirements change, so must application systems change. These needs can be small (the change in a column name on a report) or large (additions requiring several years of systems and programming effort to implement).

o   <u>Enhancements</u> - Changes that improve the economy, effectiveness, or efficiency of the application system. These types of changes affect how the application system performs during operation. Changes can be made to accomodate new hardware and software, as well as to develop better ways to perform the existing functions.

These three categories are easy to conceptualize, but difficult to address individually, as they overlap. (See Figure 1-4.) For example, in correcting an error, a programmer may also enhance operating performance. However, all three should be governed by the organization's maintenance procedures. Good maintenance procedures should reduce the time and effort expended on maintenance.

SUMMARY

As the data processing function becomes more successful, there are fewer new applications to computerize. The trend is clear. The data processing function will be devoting an ever increasing portion of their resources and effort on systems maintenance.

Systems maintenance does not appear to provide the same interest and challenge to many data processing professionals as does the development and implementation of new applications using new technology. Therefore, in many data processing organizations systems maintenance has received too little attention. Management has not devoted the same time and effort to systems maintenance as they have to new systems development and software acquisition.

Chapter 2
Building An Effective Systems Maintenance Policy

CHAPTER OVERVIEW

The first step in building an effective systems maintenance policy is a self-assessment of the maintenance function. This process is similar to the initial step undertaken by a systems analyst when designing a new application. Once an organization understands the problems, it should address systems maintenance using the same tools and techniques that the systems analyst uses in solving any other business problem. Most organizations can substantially reduce maintenance costs while greatly increasing user satisfaction.

Building an effective maintenance policy is a four-step process. The first step establishes maintenance policies and procedures, while the second step seeks feedback on these policies and procedures. Without good feedback, data processing management cannot be sure if their policies and procedures are effective or if they are being followed. The third step is the analysis of that feedback data. This involves considering factors external to the maintenance cycle. The last step is recommending and installing changes to the process in order to improve the process.

SYSTEMS MAINTENANCE SELF-ASSESSMENT EXERCISE

The maintenance function self-evaluation exercise is designed to provide data processing management with an assessment of their organization's systems maintenance function. The questionnaire is based upon the experiences of organizations with effective maintenance functions.

Each question addresses a different area of systems maintenance. "Always" indicates that the probability of serious maintenance problems is minimal. "Rarely" indicates that the organization is subject to a greater systems maintenance risk than the assessor feels is warranted. However, the answer may be "don't know" because the maintenance area has not yet been addressed, or the necessary type of information is unavailable. For example, if the question asks about maintenance statistics, and no statistics are available, then the self-assessment answer should be "don't know."

The assessor's answer to the adequacy or inadequacy of a maintenance area should be based upon the policies, procedures, and practices for that specific area. All assessors must ask themselves if their procedures, policies, and practices would encourage and lead to effective systems maintenance. They should judge whether or not the systems maintenance itself is effective. For example, if an organization establishes a policy for approving program changes, develops a form, writes procedures, distributes them to the appropriate people, and then establishes a monitoring system which ensures that only approved changes are installed, it could be assumed that the controls were "always adequate." The assessor should not be asked to determine whether or not some unapproved changes were made. That is a very time-consuming process, and the enforcement of procedures is a management responsibility.

The questionnaire is designed to expose symptoms, not causes. The answers provide a general overview of the maintenance area. The completed questionnaire can indicate how much effort, if any, should be expended on modifying or extending the maintenance function. If an organization can achieve a rating of "always" or "usually" for all the questions, its maintenance function is probably sufficient to meet the organization's needs. However, if some "rarely" assessments are given, or the assessor does not know the answer, further investigation or changes are warranted.

The questionnaire should be completed by a member of data processing management familiar with the organization's maintenance function. If the person knows the function, management will only need to allocate minimal time for fact gathering. The remaining chapters of the book cover recommended solutions for the problems that this self-assessment questionnaire may uncover.

Completing the Systems Maintenance Self-Assessment Questionnaire

The systems maintenance questionnaire includes many areas within the maintenance function which are representative of key control points within the maintenance function. They are not meant to be exhaustive but, rather, representative of the type of impediments that may exist in building and operating an adequate systems maintenance function.

The questions to be answered in the self-assessment questionnaire are briefly explained below:

Question 1: Is systems maintenance categorized by type of maintenance?

Explanation: Many categories of maintenance, such as critical maintenance, must be done immediately even though other maintenance requests are pending. Each category requires different planning and controls. However, unless maintenance projects are categorized by type, they will all be given the same priority.

Question 2: Are pertinent statistics kept for each maintenance effort (i.e., frequency, type, systems/programming effort, number of tests, computer resources consumed, and total cost of satisfying maintenance requests)?

Explanation: Management analysis of the use of data processing resources into different types of maintenance and application areas cannot be effectively achieved without proper feedback statistics. Systems maintenance tasks should be individually budgeted and monitored. Effective budgeting is a strong control. Traditionally, systems maintenance has been poorly controlled; frequently, budgets and plans are ignored. If management fails to monitor the budgetary process, management may lose control of its maintenance resources.

Question 3: Is the maintenance budget established using "zero-based budgeting" so that each year all maintenance tasks must be justified?

Explanation: When projects must rejustify the total maintenance budget each year, they must undertake a more thorough investigation to establish the need for maintenance. This should have the effect of improving maintenance management. When maintenance projects are carefully budgeted and monitored, then variations from the plan must be explained and justified.

Question 4: Is there a formal procedure for requesting changes to application systems? (Note: A formal system should include a formal method for approving changes.)

Explanation: In a formal system, the individual initiating the change must document not only the change but also the reason for the change. Using this system permits the data processing department to assign a control number to each request with the result that the department can monitor each request individually. This process makes it harder both to initiate changes, eliminating some of the unnecessary requests, and to lose change requests because they are not formally documented.

Question 5: Are changes initiated by the data processing systems analysts/programmers subject to the same formal change control procedure as the application users must follow?

Explanation: Data processing management will lose control over the application change process if they allow systems analysts/programmers to "piggyback" their changes in user-requested changes. Systems personnel frequently install their own changes to correct what they believe to be potential flaws in the system, to improve operational efficiency, or just to add some niceties to the output report. However, these types of changes can be costly and time consuming, and at the same time may cause other problems in the system.

Question 6: When changes are initiated, is regression testing employed?

Explanation: Regression testing tests the unchanged portions of the system. Without regression testing, the systems personnel do not know if the installation of a change in one part of the system is adversely affected by another unrelated part of the system. Although this testing can be expensive, it provides insurance against unexpected problems.

Question 7: Are load modules permitted to be changed through the entry of new source code?

Explanation: If organizations allow utility programs (e.g., SUPER ZAP) to change load modules while avoiding many of the audit trail controls, the result may be both unauthorized load module manipulation and system problems caused by changes which were improperly entered to the load modules.

Question 8: Are all load modules connected through naming contentions to their creating source module?

Explanation: If special unnamed or numbered load modules can be created to handle unique situations, the system change audit trail will be broken. When this happens, it is difficult to relate source code to load modules.

Question 9: Is maintenance of application programs restricted to the application programming staff who initiated and entered those program?

Explanation: Changes to an application system should be restricted to the application systems staff. This ensures that personnel follow normal procedures and that the application system project team remains in control of their own application. The most common types of violations of normal maintenance procedures happen when changes occurring in the organization's hardware and software result in changes to application systems.

Question 10: Does management have a complete knowledge of all program activities?

Explanation: Many maintenance changes are installed as favors to users of the application. Programmers frequently make these changes in conjunction with other changes. Even though the amount of effort is small, the authorization procedures are violated. This occurs in many organizations because management has not stated strongly enough that these types of changes should not be made.

Question 11: Are programs protected in accordance with their respective security needs?

Explanation: Most organizations treat all application source and load programs with the same level of security. These organizations do not take into account that some programs may not require any security measures, while others are highly sensitive and require extensive security.

Question 12: Is written documentation required for changes which were made verbally to save time?

Explanation: In many instances, the original requests, verbal or written change requests, are verbally modified. In some instances, documentation is promised, but it never arrives because no one established follow-up procedures. An effective procedure may not be to install changes until the formal written documentation has arrived.

Question 13: Are procedures established to ensure that programmers comply with the source code naming conventions?

Explanation: In an effort to get changes installed quickly, programmers may violate the source code naming conventions as well as other procedures.

Question 14: Are procedures established so that only authorized load modules can be executed?

Explanation: Programmers frequently find situations which they think require them to employ extraordinary means to satisfy a specific need. Their solution is to install a special, but unauthorized, load module to correct a situation which may have been caused by the application programmer. Installing load modules without following the normal procedures should be prohibited.

Question 15: Are guidelines established to determine when a program should be rewritten instead of maintained?

Explanation: Many programs are maintained in a patchwork fashion when it would be more economical to operate, more responsive to operate, and easier to maintain if programmers rewrote it. However, when guidelines are lacking as to how much time to spend rewriting a program, systems analysts and programmers may believe it is cheaper to make that one more change than to rewrite the program.

Question 16: Do maintenance procedures require that documentation be updated when changes are made?

Explanation: When systems first become operational, documentation is normally up to date. As systems maintenance continues, however, the documentation often falls behind. This may occur because changes are minor and documentation does not seem that important or because programmers may want to wait until a series of changes is in before they bring documentation up to date. In addition, programmers occasionally pencil changes into the margin on documentation sheets rather than wholly updating that documentation. Without strong management backing, documentation will not be kept current.

Question 17: Do program maintenance procedures specify which of the available program maintenance software systems commands programmers can use?

Explanation: Some of the software systems used for systems maintenance contain some very powerful systems maintenance commands. The more powerful commands permit manipulation which does not leave a trail indicating that changes had been entered. Management should only allow certain key personnel to use the more powerful systems maintenance commands; in addition, they should establish procedures to monitor the use of those commands.

Question 18: Are procedures established to purge the source code library of obsolete programs?

Explanation: Special one-time programs and numerous variations of existing source programs often remain on the source code library unless procedures are established to purge that library. When a source program is no longer useful, delete it from the source code library.

Question 19: Are programs deleted from the load module library when their useful life is complete?

Explanation: The load module library is subject to the same problem as the source code library. The same procedures pertaining to purging a source code library apply to the load module library. In addition, whenever a program is deleted from one library, check whether an equivalent version of the program is in the other library. If so, then issue a message suggesting that it, too, be purged.

Question 20: Are procedures established to ensure that changes to applications systems will be properly billed to users?

Explanation: Without proper data, management may find it difficult to develop good systems maintenance policies and procedures. One of the key elements of success is accurate information about the systems maintenance process. Thus, programmers and systems analysts should be discouraged from inaccurate or improper reporting costs associated with systems maintenance.

Question 21: Are procedures established to require the systems analysts/programmers to consider the impact a systems maintenance change may have on other related programs and systems?

Explanation: When new systems are installed, sufficient time and effort is usually expended to determine how the system interrelates with other systems. However, the same detailed procedure may not be followed during this systems maintenance process. Without this type of analysis, a change installed to fix one problem may result in many other new problems.

Question 22: Are procedures established so that the systems analysts/programmers will consider whether an error uncovered in their system may be common to many systems? (If so, they should make other projects aware of the problem.)

Explanation: Many systems and programming problems are related to software system features and programming language instruction usage. When these types of problems cause errors, the programmers should alert other programmers to the type of circumstances which caused the problem. This communication may enable other projects to uncover problems before they become serious, or advise them to avoid the combination of circumstances which can cause such problems.

Question 23: Do procedures require that backup source code be retained during systems maintenance?

Explanation: It may become necessary to reconstruct programs in the object code library. This requires that a version of the source code be retained to support each version of the program in the object code library. If this policy is violated and source code is updated without the creation of a new version, it would be extremely difficult and costly to reconstruct a lost or inoperative object program.

Question 24: Are procedures established for defining the scope of testing for each system and program change?

Explanation: Programmers are normally optimistic about their ability to design, implement, and install changes. Some believe the risk associated with making a change is very low and thus conduct no testing at all; others, pressured because of time schedules, minimize tests. However, when management establishes testing criteria these decisions are no longer programmer decisions.

Question 25: Are procedures established to forewarn all affected individuals or groups of changes in the production version of the system?

Explanation: Users of application systems should not be surprised by the introduction of changes. Frequently overzealous programmers implement and install anticipated rather than authorized requests. It is important to alert users that a change is being installed so that they are aware that other parts of the system may be inadvertently affected. Sometimes this extra checking makes it possible for programmers to anticipate and correct problems before they become serious.

Question 26: Are procedures established to permit the identification of multiple versions of source and load programs?

Explanation: In complex systems, multiple changes can occur at any point. To effectively utilize systems analysts and programmers and control what and when changes go into production, it may be necessary to have the capability to identify multiple versions of a single program through a naming convention.

Question 27: Are procedures established to collect systems maintenance statistics from systems maintenance software?

Explanation: Systems maintenance software can provide data processing management with statistics about the maintenance environment. Data processing management should take advantage of these capabilities and have reports prepared based upon systems maintenance software statistics.

You should now complete the systems maintenance self-assessment questionnaire which is given in Figure 2-1.

FIGURE 2-1

SYSTEMS MAINTENANCE SELF-ASSESSMENT QUESTIONNAIRE

#	MAINTENANCE GUIDELINE	ASSESSMENT OF GUIDELINES				
		ALWAYS	USUALLY	RARELY	DON'T KNOW	COMMENTS
1.	Is systems maintenance categorized by type of maintenance?					
2.	Are pertinent statistics kept for each maintenance effort (i.e., frequency, type, systems/programming effort, number of tests, computer resources consumed, and total cost of satisfying maintenance requests)?					
3.	Is the maintenance budget established using "zero-based budgeting" so that each year all maintenance tasks must be justified?					
4.	Is there a formal procedure for requesting changes to application systems? (Note: A formal system should include a formal method for approving changes.)					
5.	Are changes initiated by the data processing systems analysts/programmers subject to the same formal change control procedure as the application users must follow?					
6.	When changes are initiated, is regression testing employed?					
7.	Are load modules permitted to be changed through the entry of new source code?					
8.	Are all load modules connected through naming contentions to their creating source module?					
9.	Is maintenance of application programs restricted to the application programming staff who initiated and entered those programs?					

FIGURE 2-1

SYSTEMS MAINTENANCE SELF-ASSESSMENT QUESTIONNAIRE

#	MAINTENANCE GUIDELINE	ASSESSMENT OF GUIDELINE				
		ALWAYS	USUALLY	RARELY	DON'T KNOW	COMMENTS
10.	Does management have a complete knowledge of all program activities?					
11.	Are programs protected in accordance with their respective security needs?					
12.	Is written documentation required for changes which were made verbally to save time?					
13.	Are procedures established to ensure that programmers comply with the source code naming conventions?					
14.	Are procedures established so that only authorized load modules can be executed?					
15.	Are guidelines established to determine when a program should be rewritten instead of maintained?					
16.	Do maintenance procedures require that documentation be updated when changes are made?					
17.	Do program maintenance procedures specify which of the available program maintenance software systems commands programmers can use?					
18.	Are procedures established to purge the source code library of obsolete programs?					
19.	Are programs deleted from the load module library when their useful life is complete?					
20.	Are procedures established to ensure that changes to applications systems will be properly billed to users?					

FIGURE 2-1.

SYSTEMS MAINTENANCE SELF-ASSESSMENT QUESTIONNAIRE

#	MAINTENANCE GUIDELINE	ASSESSMENT OF GUIDELINE				
		ALWAYS	USUALLY	RARELY	DON'T KNOW	COMMENTS
21.	Are procedures established to require the systems analysts/programmers to consider the impact a systems maintenance change may have on other related programs and systems?					
22.	Are procedures established so that the systems analysts/programmers will consider whether an error uncovered in their system may be common to many systems? (If so, they should make other projects aware of the problem.)					
23.	Do procedures require that backup source code be retained during systems maintenance?					
24.	Are procedures established for defining the scope of testing for each system and program change?					
25.	Are procedures established to forewarn all affected individuals or groups of changes in the production version of the system?					
26.	Are procedures established to permit the identification of multiple versions of source and load programs?					
27.	Are procedures established to collect systems maintenance statistics from systems maintenance software?					

USING THE ASSESSMENT RESULTS

The objective of the systems maintenance self-assessment questionnaire is to provide a preliminary assessment of the adequacy of your maintenance function. Based on that preliminary assessment, management can initiate studies and investigations to determine the seriousness of a potential weakness and the type of procedures that you should incorporate to correct the weakness.

At the completion of the self-assessment questionnaire, you should total the number of maintenance areas that you checked either "rarely" or "don't know." These are the areas which potentially may have systems maintenance weaknesses. These are the important maintenance areas.

Figure 2-2 provides a guideline for assessing the maintenance function in your organization. The assessment is based on the total number of "rarely" and "don't know" checks. After you have accumulated the number of "rarely" and "don't know" answers on your self-assessment questionnaire, compare the total number with the appropriate category in Figure 2-2. The chart recommends an action to be taken based upon your assessment.

The remaining material in this book will provide direction and guidance on establishing and operating an effective systems maintenance function.

FIGURE 2-2

EXPLANATION OF SELF-ASSESSMENT QUESTIONNAIRE RESULTS

NUMBER OF "RARELY" OR "DON'T KNOW" ANSWERS	ACTION TO BE TAKEN BASED ON ASSESSMENT
0-3	On-line systems maintenance appears to be adequate. No additional assessment appears to be warranted.
4-8	Potential systems maintenance weaknesses may exist. Management should appoint a task force to review systems maintenance and to recommend improvements.
9-14	Systems maintenance appears to have weaknesses. Management should initiate a detailed study of the systems maintenance function and should be prepared to commit substantial resources to correct the weaknesses.
15-27	Systems maintenance weaknesses appear to be extremely serious. Management should give a very high priority to improvement in this systems maintenance area.

BUILDING A MAINTENANCE POLICY

The systems maintenance policies and procedures are the general controls established by the data processing department. General controls govern how the personnel in the data processing department are to perform their work. General controls govern such things as the forms and procedures people use, the computer language in which programs are written, the methods for both documenting and maintaining application systems.

Some organizations rigidly control systems maintenance, while others leave it to the systems analysts/programmers to use their discretion as to how they maintain their systems. The amount of control exercised by an organization is dependent upon the philosophy of the maintenance procedures such as the turnover of people and the need for application systems to continue to be responsive to user needs.

The major argument people give for minimizing systems maintenance controls is that they inhibit programmer creativity. It has been argued that creative programmers are more productive programmers. Whatever inhibits creativity inhibits productivity. Experience has shown that having good standards encourages creativity because the standards provide programmers with good practices and allow them to be creative in those areas where creativity really improves productivity.

Poor systems maintenance policies and procedures can affect productivity -- both in data processing and other controlled situations. For example, well-coordinated traffic lights move traffic through congested areas quickly. On the other hand, poorly timed traffic lights can cause traffic to move more slowly than if there were no traffic lights at all.

The key to good maintenance procedures and standards is that they should help systems analysts/programmers perform their function. Each procedure or standard should have one of the following effects:

1. <u>Compliance with requirements</u> - Requires the process to proceed in accordance with organizational industrial and/or governmental policies, procedures, laws, or regulations. For example, many states prohibit banks from keeping fictitious accounts on their books for test purposes. Procedures enforcing compliance with laws and regulations are good procedures.

2. <u>Eliminate bad practices</u> - Good procedures and standards would prohibit systems analysts/programmers from employing practices known to be bad.

3. <u>Encourage good practices</u> - When a data processing organization has proved through experience that specific maintenance practices reduce maintenance, good standards and procedures should encourage systems analysts/programmers to use practices known to be effective.

Organizations should eliminate maintenance standards and procedures that cannot be justified according to one of the above three criteria. This eliminates those standards which fall into the following categories:

o   I think it's a good idea, so people should do it this way.

o   I like to do it this way, so other people should do it this way.

o   We have to find some way to do it, so here's a way.

o   Organization X does it this way, and so should we.

The underlying theme of this concept is that standards and policies should be developed based on practice, not speculation. Normally, policies and standards that can be justified are readily accepted, while those standards and policies that are unproved encourage people to think of alternatives which undermine the standard or procedure.

Standards encouraging good practices or discouraging bad practices can easily become out of date. When this happens, what was once a good practice may, in fact, now be an ineffective way of performing a task because other changes have occurred. For example, a maintenance practice which was effective when assembler-type programming languages were used may be an ineffective method when COBOL is introduced.

The systems maintenance cycle, as illustrated in Figure 2-3, outlines a systems maintenance methodology. This methodology describes how to develop the maintenance process. The maintenance process includes the standards, policies, and procedures that systems analysts/programmers must follow in making changes to application systems.

In order to develop an effective maintenance policy, management should take four steps:

o   <u>Review and modify maintenance policy</u> - The policies and procedures established for maintenance should be built upon the previously discussed maintenance criteria.

o   <u>Gather feedback on the maintenance process</u> - The maintenance process should generate feedback which is information generated by feedback mechanisms. Feedback mechanisms are mini report writers that collect, assemble, and present information about the execution of the maintenance process. For example, feedback information can provide data on how many changes were made, the length of time taken to install the change, problems encountered in making the change, etc.

o   <u>Analyze feedback</u> - Feedback data that is not analyzed is worthless. For example, it would be of no value to know how many cars are backing up at traffic lights if no one intended to look at that information. Without analysis, the money and effort expended to gather feedback is wasted, quickly leading to a breakdown of the entire feedback system.

o   <u>Recommended changes</u> - Based on the analysis, effective practices should be formalized through the adoption of new standards and procedures, while ineffective practices should be prohibited through the adoption of new maintenance standards and procedures.

You need to consider other factors when you analyze feedback. The types of external factors that influence the analysis include:

o   Laws and regulations governing application systems

o   General organization policies and procedures

o   Unusual conditions reflected in the maintenance function, such as changing zip codes from five to ten positions in length

FIGURE 2-3

BUILDING AN EFFECTIVE SYSTEMS MAINTENANCE POLICY

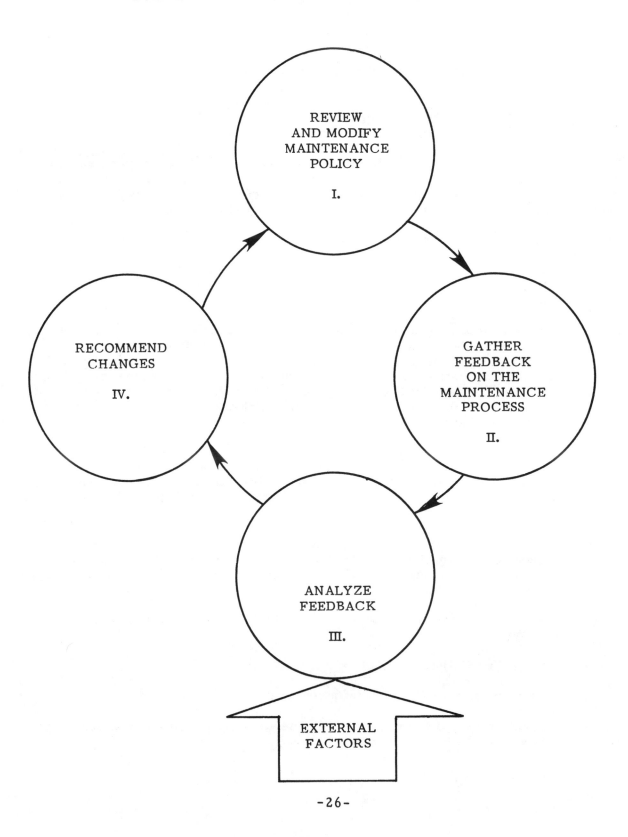

o   Turnover of personnel

o   Utilization of new hardware/software

o   User demands for "crash" installation of changes

POLICY CRITERIA

If management has no agreed upon methods for systems maintenance, they cannot establish a systems maintenance policy. Management also communicates its uncertainty with
the personnel in the department who then become equally confused.

The criteria that management needs to consider in developing a systems maintenance
policy include:

o   Approving a systems development approach that will result in easy-to-maintain
     applications

o   Developing data processing standards and procedures that are supportive of the
     systems maintenance function

o   Developing stringent policy on approval of changes to application systems

o   Creating methods of communication and training that reduce the incidence of
     common error among multiple application systems

o   Enforcing stringent testing procedures

o   Requiring documentation standards that provide the information needed to
     maintain application systems

o   Developing policies and procedures that encourage a close working relationship
     with users

o   Obtaining strong management support that encourages and enforces departmen-
     tal standards

o   Encouraging active management participation in the systems maintenance
     function

o   Presenting systems maintenance jobs as requiring at least as much skill as
     developing new applications

o   Developing a salary structure that rewards systems maintenance analysts/pro-
     grammers as much as or more than systems analysts/programmers who develop
     new applications.

A proposed EDP department maintenance policy is presented as Figure 2-4. This policy
first states the authority for establishing the systems maintenance policy; second, outlines the duties and responsibilities of the systems analysts/programmers assigned to
maintenance projects; and third, indicates management's support of this policy. The
policy must by nature be general. However, there must also be substantial supporting

data explaining how one complies with the policy. This is achieved in the proposed policy by continual reference to departmental standards. An actual policy may reference a specific manual or specific standards.

A policy lacking enforcement procedures has minimal value. The systems analysts/programmers will understand the intent, but the methods of achieving that policy may be so varied as to undermine the intent. This should not discourage data processing departments from issuing the policy because it is better to have the policy and then follow up with the methods of compliance.

SUMMARY

A good systems maintenance policy is the key to effective maintenance. Organizations should periodically assess the effectiveness of their maintenance effort. This chapter has provided a self-assessment tool and a methodology for building an effective systems maintenance policy. A sample policy is included.

The rest of the book supports the implementation, administration, and monitoring of the policy.

FIGURE 2-4

PROPOSED EDP DEPARTMENT SYSTEMS MAINTENANCE POLICY

The data processing department is responsible for maintaining the applications systems of the XYZ Corporation in satisfactory working condition. In fulfilling this responsibility, the systems analysts/programmers assigned to applications systems are charged with performing the following duties:

1. Design new systems which facilitate maintenance and which comply with department system development standards

2. Only install changes that have been approved in accordance with departmental change standards

3. Notify data processing management promptly of any problem uncovered that might affect another application

4. Test all system changes in accordance with departmental system test standards

5. Update all system and program documentation prior to or immediately following the installation of a change

6. Coordinate all maintenance efforts with the system users in order to ensure user satisfaction

Data processing management will actively encourage and support this systems maintenance policy. Performance evaluations of systems analysts and programmers will be largely based on adherence to this policy.

Chapter 3
Analyzing Systems Maintenance Efforts

CHAPTER OVERVIEW

Systems maintenance is a quicksand that can absorb all uncontrolled and undermanaged data processing resources. No organization can afford to build "ideal" computer systems. Systems in operation can always be improved; thus, maintenance dollars can always be expended.

Too many organizations are attempting to monitor their systems maintenance functions without having sufficient information. An informed management can normally make better decisions than an uninformed management. However, many organizations have not established an adequate feedback mechanism for gathering systems maintenance information. The objective of this chapter is to demonstrate how to perform a one-time analysis of the maintenance function.

Organizations that have effective feedback mechanisms to monitor their maintenance function may not need to perform this one-time anaysis. However, those organizations lacking sufficient maintenance information should find this exercise very beneficial. Such organizations should establish a feedback mechanism which then can be used after performing the analysis. The mechanism should be a means of continually gathering the type of information outlined in this chapter.

ONE-TIME VERSUS THE CONTINUOUS GATHERING OF INFORMATION

Continuously-generated information on maintenance is normally more accurate than statically (one-time) generated feedback. Dynamically-generated information is collected continuously over a period of time. When people record data as events occur, that information is normally more accurate than information recalled after an extended period of time has elapsed. However, if systems and programming personnel keep accurate records of their maintenance efforts, then the statically-generated maintenance information becomes as accurate as dynamically-generated data.

Organizations with no information on their maintenance function will find it difficult to evaluate systems maintenance. If information is not already available, the collection of static information on the system maintenance process:

o   Informs systems analysts/programmers that data processing management is interested in the maintenance function

o   Identifies the factors that have an impact on the maintenance function

o   Focuses management attention on the scope of systems maintenance in their organization

o   Notifies top management that data processing management is concerned about data processing costs

GATHERING DATA ON THE SYSTEMS MAINTENANCE FUNCTION

The large percentage of data processing resources expended on systems maintenance justifies a comprehensive study of the function. Many data processing managers have expressed concern over the volume of changes requested by their users. When asked what was the single most important type of support that senior management could provide him, the DP manager of a very large shop responded, "Require my users to cut down on the number of requests for change they send me each month." This implies that users have not adequately developed and planned systems maintenance. The purposes of this study can be twofold: first, to gather information to encourage users to make fewer change requests; and second, to gather information in order to build a more effective, efficient, and economical systems maintenance function.

To convince users or senior management that data processing should not satisfy all user needs takes well-supported arguments. In addition, most data processing organizations pride themselves on being a service group. Thus, it is inconsistent with the philosophy of most data processing departments to encourage users to make fewer requests for change.

The objective of a good maintenance policy is to satisfy user needs with fewer resources and problems. Therefore, the information-gathering objectives also should be to provide a basis for improving systems maintenance performance. This should be the major objective.

SYSTEMS MAINTENANCE ANALYSIS PROCESS

Valuable information can be gathered about the maintenance function with minimal effort. The information does not need to be 100% accurate or complete but, rather, only needs to be representative of the systems maintenance environment in the organization. The information gathered will include the opinions of the project leader about the type of maintenance being performed. This needs to be collected but should be evaluated with caution.

A data processing organization can collect the necessary information by following the following five analysis steps:

- o   Step 1 - Develop analysis strategy

- o   Step 2 - Inform systems analysts/programmers

- o   Step 3 - Collect systems maintenance data

- o   Step 4 - Analyze the data

- o   Step 5 - Management action

STEP 1 - DEVELOP ANALYSIS STRATEGY

Systems maintenance has not received the same attention as new systems development. The methods of developing computerized applications has improved considerably since the early 1960's. The introduction of the systems development life cycle, top-down design, hierarchical input/process/output, and structured design have improved the quality of systems and lowered the cost of developing systems.

Improved systems design has led to improved maintenance. However, many of the improved maintenance procedures have been caused by the use of improved systems design as opposed to the development of a true systems maintenance methodology similar to the systems development life cycle approach. More research is needed in the development of systems maintenance procedures.

Data processing managers report that the older computerized applications cause more maintenance problems. The reasons cited include:

- o Inadequate documentation

- o Use of assembler languages

- o Fewer programming standards

- o Fewer systems standards

- o Patches using machine language

- o Systems analysts/programmers unfamiliar with the systems design structure

- o Systems analysts/programmers unfamiliar with the technology used to design the application

- o Systems analysts/programmers unfamiliar with the programming languages used to code the application

The analysis should concentrate on the systems maintenance process as opposed to specific applications being maintained. The recommended analysis strategy is to concentrate in the following areas:

1. Statistics describing the systems maintenance environment

2. Weaknesses uncovered while conducting the self-assessment questionnaire

The systems maintenance environment relates to the type and quantity of maintenance being performed. This establishes the effort to be expended on the systems maintenance process. The remainder of this chapter will provide the forms and procedures necessary to collect statistics on the systems maintenance environment.

The weaknesses uncovered in conducting the self-assessment questionnaire should be analyzed in more depth. These weaknesses normally pertain to the organization as a whole. It is difficult to prepare generalized approaches to analyzing specific problems. However, the following chapters in this book deal with the areas covered by the self-assessment questionnaire, and the discussions should provide data processing management with areas for further exploration during this analysis.

STEP 2 - INFORM SYSTEMS ANALYSTS/PROGRAMMERS

Getting good information on the maintenance function may be dependent upon obtaining the cooperation of the department systems analysts/programmers. While the information does not have to be 100% accurate and reliable, using poor information results in poor decisions. The data processing staff needs to be apprised of these considerations.

Regular staff meetings provide an excellent forum for the purposes and methods used in discussing management's analysis of the maintenance function. If the staff does not meet regularly, it may be advisable to schedule departmental meetings for at least the key systems analysts/programmers. Relying on written correspondence and not personal interaction with data processing management probably will not obtain the desired cooperation from the staff.

The points that should be made by data processing management during the discussion with the systems analysts/programmers are:

o   The department expends the majority of its resources performing systems maintenance.

o   Improperly performed systems maintenance wastes a lot of the systems analysts/programmers' time.

o   The department management recognizes the pressure put on projects by systems users seeking extensive and rapid changes.

o   The department recognizes that tools, techniques, and practices for the effective implementation of system changes are inadequate.

o   The department management is conducting the study in an effort to find better ways to perform systems maintenance.

o   The department management solicits and welcomes suggestions from the staff on how to reduce the effort going into systems maintenance without reducing service to the system users.

o   The department needs information about systems maintenance in order to evaluate the problems and improve maintenance methods.

o   Only the systems analysts/programmers can provide the needed data.

o   Management needs the help of each individual in the department in order to get accurate and reliable information.

o   Management does not want an extensive amount of time spent on this exercise.

o   The information collected will be used exclusively for improving the systems maintenance function; it will not be the basis of evaluating the individuals' performance.

At the completion of the discussion, management should consider questions posed by the systems analysts/programmers. At the conclusion of the question and answer period, management should explain, and possibly distribute, the data collection forms to the systems analysts/programmers. (These forms will be explained in Step 3.) However, management may first want to seek input from the senior departmental staff prior to making the data collection process final.

STEP 3 - COLLECT SYSTEMS MAINTENANCE DATA

The information collected on systems maintenance should consider maintenance in the past and in the future. Historical maintenance is that which has already occurred, while future maintenance involves changes which are awaiting installation.

Two problems will occur in this categorization of systems maintenance. First are those changes that are in the process of being installed, and second are those changes which may never be installed because of staffing. Changes should be categorized as complete if they are in the testing phase, while those not yet ready for testing should be categorized as future changes. Any future change that has been identified by the data processing department -- regardless of implementation priority -- should be included as a future change. The decision concerning whether or not it will actually be installed may change as time passes, depending on the priorities of users and the availability of people.

The necessary information on the systems maintenance environment can be collected on two forms:

o   Installed changes form (see Figure 3-1)

o   Change backlog form (see Figure 3-2)

The forms are basically the same with the exception of installation dates and effort to install. In the case of changes already installed, all dates are known, while in the case of uninstalled changes, planned dates are included. The same perspective applies to hours of effort.

Installed Changes Form

One copy of the installed changes form should be completed for each application system involving maintenance. The form should be given to the project leader for completion. One line on the form will be completed for each change made to the application system. A tested change is to be considered an installed change.

DP management should determine the length of time for which they desire to collect statistics. The previous twelve months is probably a reasonable time span to collect data on installed systems maintenance. A year's period would provide a good comparison with an annual data processing budget. Ideally, the period for which statistics are collected would exactly coincide with the EDP department's budget.

The instructions on how to complete the Installed Changes Form are contained on the form's completion instructions sheet.

Change Backlog Form

The Change Backlog Form (see Figure 3-2) is designed to document changes requested but not made. The procedures for completing the Change Backlog Form are similar to those for completing the Installed Changes Form. For most changes, the data included on both forms are identical. The only differences between the forms are shown on the form's completion instructions sheet.

FIGURE 3-1

INSTALLED CHANGES FORM

APPLICATION SYSTEM										
Change Number	T Y P E	Change Name Description	R E C E I V E D	Dates		Maintenance Category	Hours of Effort		Origination Code	Importance Code
				Requested	Installed		Budget	Actual		

COMMENTS

PREPARED BY	DATE

FORM COMPLETION INSTRUCTIONS

Figure 3-1 - Installed Changes Form

FIELD	INSTRUCTIONS FOR ENTERING DATA
o Change number	The change number should be the number assigned by the application system to the change. If changes are not assigned unique numbers, then the project leader can use a sequential numbering system for the changes: "1" through "N"; "N" is the last change made.
o Type	Changes fall within the following three categories of types: - errors (code = B for bug) - new requirements (code = R for new requirements) - enhancements (code = E for enhancements) If a change encompasses two or more of the types, it should be categorized according to which is the dominant type. For example, if a change was made that incorporated a new requirement and the change also enhanced performance, the project leader should determine which type of change used more maintenance effort. If the project expended more effort on making changes than on installing the new requirement, then the type should be "new requirement."
o Change/name description	The name given to the change should be listed in this column. If the change is not given a standard name, then enter a succinct description of the change. The description should be precise enough to enable the project leader to recognize the change.
o Maintenance category	The maintenance activity can be divided into seven categories, depending upon the urgency for installing change. The categories range from maintenance which must be handled immediately, to maintenance for which more than three months' notice must be given. Codes 1-7 can be used to describe the following seven maintenance categories: - Code 1: Critical maintenance -- less than 48 hours: This category would normally cover hang-ups, or problems that prevent the application from being successfully completed. These are the types of changes that may be made in the middle of the night, or on the spot, and which might utilize such techniques as SUPER ZAP, or equivalent routines, that can quickly insert object code to correct a problem.

FORM COMPLETION INSTRUCTIONS

Figure 3-1 - Installed Changes Form

FIELD	INSTRUCTIONS FOR ENTERING DATA
o Maintenance category (continued)	- Code 2: Critical maintenance -- over 48 hours: This category of maintenance normally must be made before a computer run can be successfully completed. Within this category the change would normally be made in source code, and then the program would be recompiled and tested prior to being implemented. - Code 3: Normal maintenance -- problem system can live with: Some problems occur in the computer application which require fixing, but which are not serious enough to prevent the successful completion of an application run. The problem may be such that it is undesirable to use the system as is, but the results are still understandable in the manner presented. An example might be the failure to zero suppress to the left significant digits in the dollar-amount field. - Code 4: Normal maintenance -- one-time impact: Many events occur in an organization that, once performed, need not be repeated again. A simple example would be a system in which dates are programmed for the 1970's. When the year changes from 1979 to 1980, a one-time change has to be made to orient the system to the decade of the 1980's. Also, changes to hardware and software can require similar one-time changes in the application. - Code 5: Normal maintenance -- minor (within 3 months): Regularly scheduled, planned maintenance falls into several categories. The first is minor changes that need to be completed within a three-month period. The definition of minor and major would vary with the size of the organization. As a rule of thumb, assume that a minor change can be completed within one week or less of programmer time. - Code 6: Normal maintenance -- major (within 3 months) A normally scheduled change to a computer application which requires more than one week of programmer effort to complete and which must be implemented within three months would fall into this category. - Code 7: Normal maintenance -- over 3 months' notice: These would be normally scheduled changes to applications which are known more than three months in advance. For example, if an organization had a special Christmas promotion, it would be planned and coordinated through the sales department many months before Christmas. In this type of maintenance, the data processing systems analyst could be involved as the promotion develops in order to plan their systems maintenance program accordingly.

FORM COMPLETION INSTRUCTIONS

Figure 3-1 - Installed Changes Form

FIELD	INSTRUCTIONS FOR ENTERING DATA
o Date - Received	This is the date that the data processing department received the change request. If the data processing department was the originator of the request, this is the date of origination.
o Date - Requested	This is the date on which the user requested that the change be installed. Where no date was given or the requested date was as soon as possible (ASAP), the project leaders should be given instructions to use 15 or 30 days or whatever appears reasonable for the normal change. It may be possible to categorize some of them by intent, such as: - as quickly as possible (15 days) - within a reasonable period of time (30 days) - if time is available (90 days)
o Date - Installed	The date when the change went into a production status or was available for production, whichever is more meaningful.
o Hours of Effort - Budget	The number of hours budgeted to install the change. If it was an unbudgeted change, then use zero. If your organization does not budget individually, then develop your budget using time reporting standards which coincide with the practices of your organization (e.g., use whole days or half days).
o Hours of Effort - Actual	The number of hours of effort taken to design, install, test, and implement the change.
o Origination code	Changes originate from many sources. Understanding who is originating the change provides insight into controlling the systems maintenance process. The typical source for a change and the code used on the form to indicate who caused the change includes: - Code A: Senior management Changes originated by senior management and not necessarily requiring a cost/benefit analysis (e.g., a new benefit plan for employees). Senior management institutes most changes through the establishment of new policies and procedures. - Code B: Legal requirement Changes initiated by a law or a regulatory agency. For example, if the federal withholding tax table changes, the social security percent changes, or the controller of the currency issues a new banking regulation, these changes may necessitate making changes in the computerized application.

FORM COMPLETION INSTRUCTIONS

Figure 3-1 – Installed Changes Form

FIELD	INSTRUCTIONS FOR ENTERING DATA
	- Code C: User Change originated by the individual or organizational entity responsible for the computerized application. This is the group from which most of the changes should originate. - Code D: Data processing applications system project personnel Changes that originate from within the data processing personnel assigned to the project. These changes can be made to correct errors that are known to exist within the system or to make operational enhancements to improve the flow, effectiveness, or efficiency of the application system. - Code E: Data processing operations personnel Changes originating from the group operating the application system. Many of the changes originating in computer operations will involve changes associated with the installation of new hardware or software. - Code F: Data processing standards Changes that are necessary because of the adoption of new data processing standards. This category of changes can involve such things as naming conventions, interface with operating software, and programming standards. - Code G through Z: Other Codes G-Z can be used to further subdivide the above groups or to list new groups which can initiate changes to computerized applications.
o Importance code	Some changes are more significant to the organization than other changes. The data processing personnel may or may not be informed of the importance of a change when it is requested. Many organizations have adopted a system for establishing priorities for the implementation of changes. The priority system can be as elaborate or as simple as is necessary to satisfy the needs of the organization. If your organization does not have a change priority code, you can use the following categories: - Code 1: Essential Essential changes are those required by law, regulatory agencies, or the policies and procedures of senior management. Most essential changes are associated with an installation date.

Figure 3-1 - Installed Changes Form

FIELD	INSTRUCTIONS FOR ENTERING DATA
	- Code 2: Very important High-priority changes are usually associated with the organization's business policies and procedures or with the user's methods of operation. Also included in this category might be errors which stand in the way of the successful use of the application system. - Code 3: Important These are important priority changes for the application system. These types of changes normally are not associated with a specific date, but they are necessary for the successful operation of the application system. You should implement both high and important priority changes (i.e., very important and important changes). - Code 4: Desirable Desirable changes affect the appearance of reports and the image projected by the application system. Examples of desirable changes include new analyses, better control systems, improved system manuals, and computer system documentation. - Code 5: Operational Operational changes improve the performance of the application. Performance can be improved by the shifting of functions from manual to computer, or through rearrangement of work flow and restructuring of file formats. - Code 6: Questionable Frequently the originator will ask whether this type of change is worthwhile. Normally, no installation date is given for changes in this category. If there is no priority system for changes, the project manager should code the importance of the change. After working in an application system over a period of time, most project leaders gain insight into the value of requested changes.
o Prepared by	The person who completed the form is the one to whom questions should be directed about the information on the form.
o Date	The date on which the form was completed. All information on the form should be current as of this date.
o Comments	The preparer of the form should use this section for comments relating to the accuracy and reliability of data contained on the form.

FIGURE 3-2

CHANGE BACKLOG FORM

CHANGE NUMBER	TYPE	CHANGE NAME/ DESCRIPTION	DATES		MAINTENANCE CATEGORY	HOURS OF EFFORT		ORIGINATION CODE	IMPORTANCE CODE
			RECEIVED	REQUESTED		BDGT'D	PLANNED		

APPLICATION SYSTEM

COMMENTS

PREPARED BY

DATE

FORM COMPLETION INSTRUCTIONS

Figure 3-2 – Change Backlog Form

FIELD	INSTRUCTIONS FOR ENTERING DATA
Same as Figure 3-1 – Installed Changes Form – except for the following fields:	
o Hours of effort – planned	The planned hours of effort can only be determined after the change request has been analyzed. These are the hours that the project manager believes will be required to design, test, and implement the change. If the project manager has not performed this analysis, then the planned hours of effort should be considered the same as the budgeted hours of effort. If there are no budgeted hours, then the project manager should enter a rough estimate of the hours that will be required to make the change.
o Date – installed	This column is not included on the Change Backlog Form because the change has not yet been installed.

Time Span to Complete the Form

Data processing management should not allow project personnel more than two weeks to complete the form, as people will wait almost until the due date before starting on the form. In addition, a few people will spend as much time completing the project as is allotted to them. A two-week period provides most project leaders with an opportunity to fit the work into their schedule.

A rule of thumb for completing the form is that for a reasonably good-size project, such as one with two to four full-time maintenance people, it should take no more than four hours to complete both forms. The better the project records, the less time needed to complete the form.

STEP 4 - ANALYZE THE DATA

The data collected on the Installed Changes Form and the Change Backlog Form can provide the basis for an understanding of the maintenance function. At the end of this process, the data processing organization will have gathered extensive data on each application maintained. In addition, they will have gathered data on changes awaiting installation.

Organizations that have conducted similar studies have frequently been surprised by the results. They expect maintenance work to proceed according to plan. In reality, the disparity between planned and actual maintenance is often so great that quick management action is necessary.

Data can be analyzed in many different ways. Some of the more common types of analysis include:

- o   A maintenance analysis of each application

- o   Analysis of maintenance by category

- o   Analysis of maintenance by size of task

- o   Analysis of maintenance by type (i.e., errors, new requirements, and enhancements)

- o   Analysis of maintenance by origin of change

- o   Analysis of maintenance by importance of change

- o   Size of change correlated with importance of change

- o   New requirements ranked by size of change

- o   Enhancements ranked by size of change

- o   Trend analysis of number of change

- o   Trend analysis of size of change

o   Comparison of number of changes among application systems

o   Comparison of size of change among application systems

o   Comparison of maintenance category and change among application systems

Some of the more common analyses are presented and discussed individually.

Application System Maintenance Profile

Prepare maintenance profiles for each application system for which you have data. One profile is for implemented errors and the other profile is for changes awaiting implementation. In these profiles, consolidate all the information prepared by the project manager. These profiles show both the number of changes and the total maintenance effort to install those changes. In this profile, continue to break the information down. Data processing management should determine when this more detailed information is needed.

An Application System Maintenance Profile Form is presented as Figure 3-3. The instructions on how to complete the form are contained on the form's completion instructions sheet.

FIGURE 3-3

APPLICATION SYSTEM MAINTENANCE PROFILE

NAME OF APPLICATION			
PERIOD COVERED	FROM		TO
TOTAL HOURS OF MAINTENANCE			
ALLOCATION OF MAINTENANCE EFFORT			

CATEGORY	# JOBS	HOURS

TYPE:
– Errors
– New Requirements
– Enhancements
 	
MAINTENANCE CATEGORY
– Critical Maintenance - within 48 hours
– Critical Maintenance - over 48 hours
– Normal Maintenance - problem system can live with
– Normal Maintenance - one-time impact
– Normal Maintenance - minor (within 3 months)
– Normal Maintenance - major (within 3 months)
– Normal Maintenance - over 3 months notice
 	
ORIGINATION OF CHANGE
– Senior Management
– Legal Requirement
– User
– DP - Systems
– DP - Operations
– DP - Standards
– Other   a)
            b)
            c)
 	
IMPORTANCE OF CHANGE
– Essential
– Very Important
– Important
– Desirable
– Operational
– Questionable
 	
SIZE OF CHANGE (IN HOURS)
– 0-20 hours
– 21-40 hours
– 41-80 hours
– 81-120 hours
– 121-200 hours
– 200 + hours		

COMMENTS/EVALUATION		

FORM COMPLETION INSTRUCTIONS

Figure 3-3 - Application System Maintenance Profile

FIELD	INSTRUCTIONS FOR ENTERING DATA
o Name of application	The name by which the application is known in the data processing department.
o Period covered	The maintenance period which the consolidated data represents.
o Total hours of maintenance	The total maintenance hours expended or planned by the application system.
o Allocation of maintenance effort	This section provides for a breakdown of the number of jobs and the number of hours which the five categories of maintenance require.
o Type of maintenance analysis	This section provides for an analysis of both the number of jobs and hours of effort for errors, new requirements and enhancements.
o Maintenance category	This section provides for an analysis of the total number of jobs and hours of effort for those jobs for the seven categories of maintenance.
o Origination of change	This section presents the number of jobs and hours of effort for the seven common originators of change, plus any additional areas designated by the organization.
o Importance of change	This section presents the number of jobs and hours of effort for those jobs in the six important categories of change.
o Size of change	This section presents the number of jobs and hours expended for those jobs for the six sizes of change. Organizations may wish to vary these strata to show a more detailed breakdown of size of change.

Allocation of Computer Personnel

Few data processing organizations have statistics on the deployment of personnel by maintenance category. They can obtain this information by combining into one report the number of maintenance jobs and the hours of effort allocated to those jobs. This information is most valuable if it is converted into percentages.

One large data processing organization performed this analysis for their maintenance function. The results are presented in Figure 3-4. Note that this organization also included the effort expended on new systems development so that they could consider maintenance in terms of the total systems effort. This organization allocated 75% of all their personnel resources for maintenance.

This information can be used for identifying where time and effort should or should not be expended to improve the maintenance function. For example, 20% of the total resources of this organization are expended on maintenance having a one-time impact. On the other hand, major maintenance efforts (efforts completed within three months) are an insignificant part of the maintenance function. Thus, to improve the maintenance function it might be valuable to develop procedures for improving the performance of maintenance with a one-time impact as opposed to major maintenance that must be completed within a three-month time span.

Planned Versus Actual Use of Computer Personnel

Many data processing organizations plan the use of the data processing personnel by job task. Unfortunately, few of these organizations make a detailed comparison between planned versus actual hours, but not by size of task.

Figure 3-5 illustrates the difference between planned and actual use of computer personnel in one organization. This is the same organization which collected information on categories of maintenance effort. The results of the analysis were surprising to them.

The organization assumed that 90% of their effort would go into tasks that took 200 hours or longer. In actual practice, they found that the smaller tasks consumed 70% of their computer personnel's time. Their investigation showed that their staff requested and made a large number of small changes. The net result was that the planned changes did not occur. The installation of some new maintenance procedures corrected the situation.

This type of analysis is only effective in organizations that have budgeted for maintenance. The comparison presented provides an overview of potential problems, but does not include enough information to suggest solutions. However, organizations can obtain more detailed information by performing the same analysis at the application system level.

Maintenance as a Percent of Development Effort

A series of measurements can be made to allow organizations to analyze the quality of the maintenance effort. These types of analyses use metrics, which are measurements showing the relationship between two variables. Appendix B covers the uses of metrics in evaluating the effectiveness of the maintenance function. The following example

Figure 3-4

One Organization's Computer Personnel Allocation

Category of Use	Allocation As a Percent of Jobs	Allocation As a Percent of Hours
Critical Maintenance – within 48 hours	2%	1%
Critical Maintenance – over 48 hours	9	13
Normal Maintenance – problem system can live with	14	6
Normal Maintenance – one-time impact	14	20
Normal Maintenance – minor (within 3 months)	4	7
Normal Maintenance – major (within 3 months)	2	1
Normal Maintenance – over 3 months notice	27	27
New System Development	28	25
Total	100%	100%

Figure 3-5

Planned Versus Actual Use of Computer Personnel in One Organization

Size of Task in Hours	Allocation Percent Actual	Allocation Percent Planned
0-20	4%	1%
21-40	12	2
41-80	21	2
81-120	5	1
121-200	28	4
200+	30	90
Total	100%	100%

provides an overview of the concept.

One of the metrics that an organization may find useful is the relationship between maintenance and development effort. This relationship can be expressed as a percentage of maintenance to development effort.

Figure 3-6 plots the maintenance to development metric. The constant in the metric is the development effort. At the conclusion of the project, the team can document the total hours or days of effort documented. They should then annualize the amount of maintenance in any given period. For example, if three people are working full time on maintenance, you can assume that at the current rate the project will expend three man years of effort on maintenance. Then you can compare this with effort required to develop the metric. For example, if it took six man years of effort to develop the project, then the metric would be 3/6 or 50% of the development effort. Since the result is a reduction in effort, it would be presented on the graph as a minus 50%.

The example presented from the XYZ Company shows that immediately after implementation the annualized maintenance exceeded the developmental cost. This might have been because a large number of user requests for critical maintenance required more staff effort. The figure then shows maintenance dropping so that at the six-month point it is approximately 50% of the developmental effort. In this example, the amount of maintenance slowly increases over time.

Metrics are most valuable when they have some standard of comparison. For example, if organizations experience maintenance in the range of 50% of the developmental effort, then they can analyze existing projects against this standard metric. The concept is also useful for comparing different application systems. If one system shows extremely low or high maintenance metrics, then someone should investigate the cause. Low maintenance metrics might identify the use of good standards, while high maintenance metrics could identify poor maintenance practices.

Application System Maintenance Comparisons

One effective method for identifying both good and bad maintenance practices is to compare the performance of different application systems. Good systems require little maintenance effort; poor systems require extensive effort.

Many variables affect the amount of effort required for maintenance. Furthermore, project personnel may have no control over those variables. For example, an application system developed fifteen years ago with poor coding and documentation practices may require considerable effort. The objective of this comparison is not to identify good or bad systems analysts/programmers but, rather, to identify good and bad maintenance practices.

A comparison of systems showing the number of days required to make a change is illustrated in Figure 3-7. This figure compares six different application systems named A through F. In this illustration, application system D requires the most maintenance effort. Applications A, B, E and F require approximately the same number of days to make a change, while application C requires substantially fewer days than the other applications.

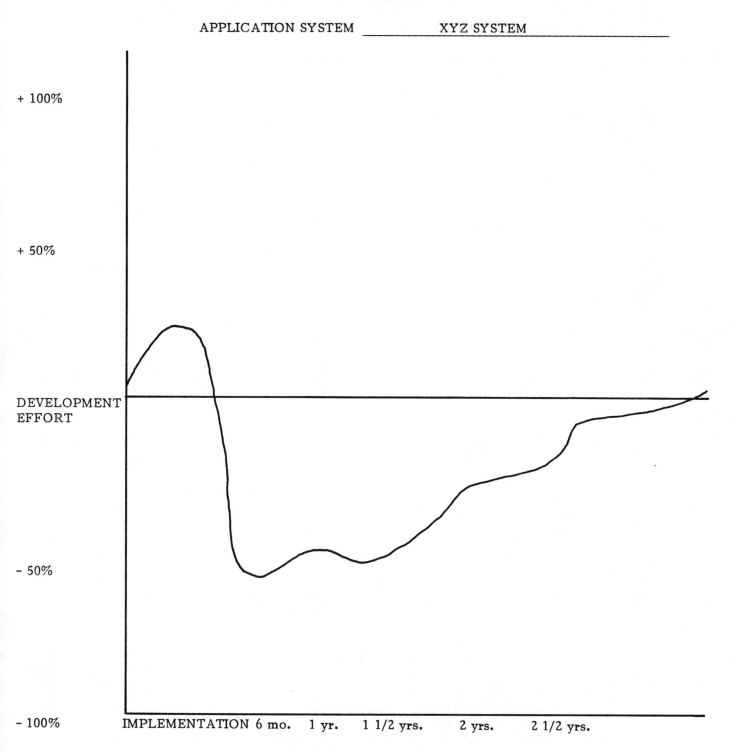

Figure 3-6

ANNUALIZED MAINTENANCE AS A PERCENT OF DEVELOPMENT EFFORT

APPLICATION SYSTEM _____ XYZ SYSTEM _____

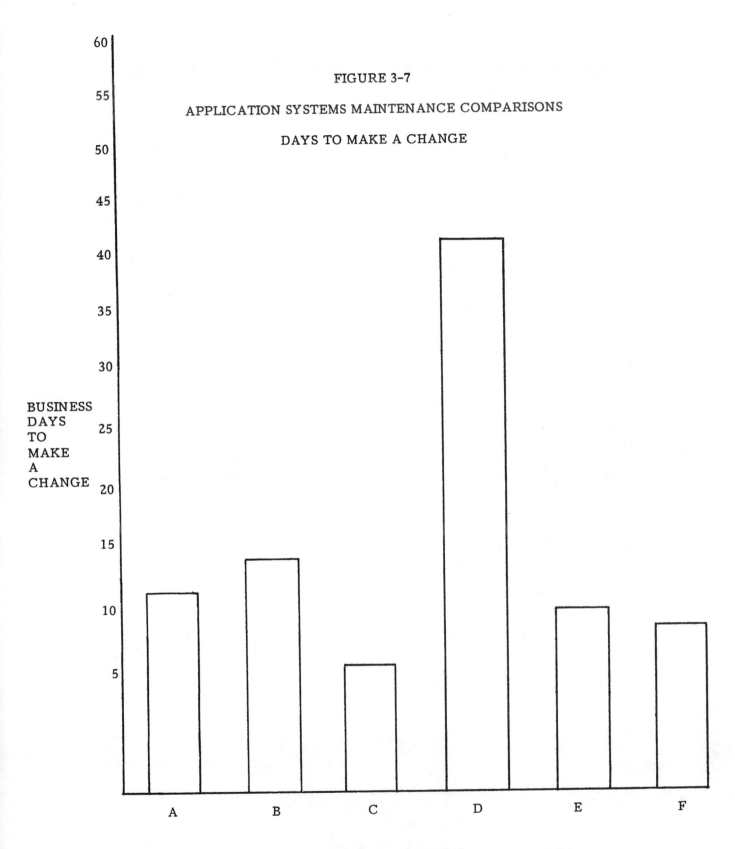

FIGURE 3-7

APPLICATION SYSTEMS MAINTENANCE COMPARISONS

DAYS TO MAKE A CHANGE

BUSINESS DAYS TO MAKE A CHANGE

APPLICATION SYSTEMS

The result of this comparison might be that data processing management would investigate application D to identify why it took so long to make changes. This may identify some systems criteria or practices which need changing. On the other hand, data processing management might want to investigate application C to determine why they are so successful in installing changes in a short period of time. This comparison might identify practices which could be utilized in all application systems, resulting in an across-the-board reduction in the number of days to install changes.

STEP 5 - MANAGEMENT ACTION

Management should use the analysis of the collected systems maintenance data as a basis for taking action to improve the maintenance function. The three actions available to management after the analysis are:

1. Do nothing - Management can decide either that the maintenance function is performing satisfactorily or that at this time they do not wish to spend any additional time or effort to improve the function.

2. Conduct additional investigations - Often the approach recommended in this manual leads to the gathering of information which points out problems. However, the information may not be sufficient to identify solutions. Management may wish to establish a task force to conduct further studies.

5. Take action - If action is clearly warranted, management should take that action. This static analysis of maintenance may provide enough data to identify areas where good practices can be initiated or poor practices stopped.

SUMMARY

The effective management of the systems maintenance function requires informed data processing management. An important part of the maintenance function is the collection of statistics about maintenance activities. This involves obtaining information about both changes installed to application systems and analyzing the backlog of changes awaiting implementation.

Information about the maintenance process can be gathered either continuously or on a one-time basis. To continually collect data is the preferred method as it is an ongoing process which can be incorporated into the department's normal data collection procedures. However, for organizations wanting a quick analysis of maintenance efforts, a one-time procedure can prove valuable.

This chapter has recommended a process for gathering information about the maintenance process. The chapter has provided forms to be completed by the systems analysts-/programmers to gather the data. In addition, methods have been suggested for analyzing and presenting the collected data.

Chapter 4
Administering the Systems Maintenance Function

CHAPTER OVERVIEW

In the future, data processing will be synonymous with systems maintenance. The majority of data processing professionals will spend their time maintaining application systems. This maintenance will enable the application systems to be synchronized with the operations of the organization.

One should not underestimate the technical complexities and challenges of the maintenance process. When maintenance is broadly viewed as including new requirements and enhancements, it poses all of the challenges of new systems development coupled with the challenges of meshing these requirements with an existing system.

Many believe that performing the systems maintenance function requires more skills than developing new systems. The systems maintenance analyst/programmer must be knowledgeable in both old and new technologies. In addition, these individuals must be able to understand the complexities of the operation, be able to troubleshoot, be able to understand other people's computer logic, and be able to convert an application from an older technology to a new one.

This chapter provides data processing management with guidelines on administering the systems maintenance function. It is a how-to-do-it chapter, beginning with guidance on implementing a systems maintenance policy for a data processing organization.

The chapter proposes a systems maintenance life cycle which provides the basis for a systems maintenance methodology. Interwoven into this life cycle are systems maintenance methods and approaches. The chapter also covers the skills needed for systems maintenance versus the skills required for developing new systems. Lastly, the concept of an error tracking analyst is introduced as an important element in administering the systems maintenance function.

IMPLEMENTING THE SYSTEMS MAINTENANCE POLICY

One organization had a "programmers' pledge." The pledge stated that all programmers would devote their efforts to developing programs that conformed with the specifications, were developed in accordance with the standards and procedures of the data processing department, and were written in a manner that would make them easy to maintain. This apple pie pledge was continually discussed and derided by the programmers. However, the message of the programmers' pledge came across.

In retrospect, this programmers' pledge was a plea by data processing management for programmers to perform their function properly. Management not only wrote the pledge but also enforced it. The pledge was incorporated into job descriptions as specific functions to be performed. During performance appraisal periods, management would evaluate programmers on how well they performed the functions included within the pledge. That organization had surprisingly few programming problems.

The concept of developing and implementing a departmental policy on systems maintenance has a similar rationale. Such policy states unequivocally what management wants in the area of systems maintenance. It is surprising how often personnel are uncertain of management's intentions. When a policy is enforced, the employees know what management wants, and normally they will comply with those policies.

Implementing a data processing policy on systems maintenance involves performing the following three steps:

o   Step 1 - Management establishes a systems maintenance policy

o   Step 2 - Management publicizes the systems maintenance policy

o   Step 3 - Management enforces the systems maintenance policy

Step 1 - Management Establishes the Policy

This step was covered in Chapter 2.

Step 2 - Management Publicizes the Policy

The systems maintenance policy is not developed for the benefit of management. It is developed to provide guidance and direction for the systems analysts/programmers when they perform systems maintenance. These are the same people who must be made aware of the policy.

Data processing organizations have used different approaches to publicize their policies to departmental personnel. Among the more effective methods are:

o   Hold a staff meeting to announce and explain all new policies.

o   Hold annual or semiannual staff meetings to reiterate and explain the major departmental policies. The frequency is dependent upon the turnover of personnel.

o   Create a handbook which includes policies, procedures, and standards pertaining to each systems analyst/programmer in the department.

o   Display the major departmental policies on a policy bulletin board.

o   Explain the policies in orientation material for new employees in the department.

o   Include the policy in the systems analyst/programmer training courses.

In addition, some organizations ask their people to sign an annual statement indicating that they have read and understood systems maintenance and other pertinent policies. While signing such a statement has no legal implications, it does ethically obligate the individual to comply with the policies. Also, if management truly evaluates performance according to compliance with these policies, it is a formal method for signifying management's desire to have their people comply with these policies.

Step 3 - Management Enforces the Policy

A large aerospace corporation has the following computer room access policy prominently displayed inside the only door to the computer room: "If unescorted visitors are permitted access to the computer room, all operators will be fired on the spot." Now let's examine two scenarios in which no one challenges an unescorted visitor. In the first scenario an unescorted visitor roams the computer room when a member of management enters the room and challenges the visitor. The manager reminds the operator of the policy, tells the operator to remove the unescorted visitor and warns him that if it happens again he will be fired. In the second scenario the same unchallenged, unescorted visitor roams the computer room when a member of management enters. However, in this scenario all the operators in the room are fired immediately. The question is: "In which instance will management policies be more readily followed in the future?" The answer is obvious.

An unenforced policy is no policy. If management does not intend to enforce the policy, they should either not issue the policy or they should rescind it. Not only is a bad policy ineffective, but also it impedes enforcement of other policies. How can management have ten policies and selectively enforce three and not the remaining seven? Selective enforcement is very confusing to employees.

In developing and issuing policy, management must answer the following questions:

1. Is this the type of policy that we will devote our time and effort to enforcing?

2. If someone fails to follow this policy, what actions will we as management take?

3. How will we communicate this policy to subordinates so that they understand both the policy and our intention of enforcing the policy?

4. Will we as management personally enforce the policy, or will we delegate the enforcement to lower levels of management?

5. If the enforcement of the policy is delegated, to whom will we delegate it?

6. Are we prepared to back the enforcement of the policy by lower level management, and are we prepared to take action when lower level management brings it to our attention that the policy is not being enforced?

7. If enforcement of the policy inhibits the implementation of maintenance, will we allow a deviation from the standard?

8. If we allow deviation from the standard, will we require that project to conform with the standard within X days?

In their answers to these questions, department managers will indicate whether they really intend to enforce the policy. If management is uncertain of the value of the policy, it is best not to issue such a policy until management studies it further, particularly since subordinates delegated the task of enforcing the policy expect management to back them.

SYSTEMS MAINTENANCE LIFE CYCLE (SMLC)

The life cycle concept has proved to be a very effective way for improving the development of new application systems. The same concept is also effective for improving systems maintenance.

The main advantages of the life cycle concept are that the process is subdivided into identifiable and measurable parts. Prior to the development of the life cycle concept, systems maintenance frequently flowed unchecked. There were no clear checkpoints; thus, it was difficult to measure the progress. The only true checkpoint was the date of implementation, and management frequently did not know prior to that date whether or not the applications system could be placed into production on time. In addition, many of the systems analysts/programmers were equally uncertain about the status of the project.

The systems maintenance process can be divided into five phases. These phases provide checkpoints that can be used by management and systems analysts/programmers to measure the progress of installing system changes.

The major difference between developing a new system and installing a change is in the size of the project. New systems are large and thus warrant administrative time and effort to oversee the development and implementation process. A major argument against using the life cycle concept in systems maintenance is that the size of the change may not warrant the administrative effort.

Organizations which think their systems maintenance efforts are too small to warrant using the systems maintenance life cycle should ask the following question: "Should an organization spend time and effort to administer a process which consumes 80% of its total resources?" If the question is asked this way, the answer is obvious.

The real question the data processing management must face is how to administer system changes without consuming more time and effort than are saved by the proper administration of the process. However, let's review the systems maintenance life cycle first, and then consider how to use it for smaller changes.

Five SMLC Phases

The systems maintenance life cycle is a mechanism for dividing the systems maintenance process into the following five phases (see Figure 4-1):

o   Phase 1 - Record and assign

     Record the necessary systems changes and assign who is responsible for analyzing each change. Complete this phase for all changes regardless of why they are needed and whether or not they are implemented. The recording process serves to document the type of change needed. In the case of an error, record the problem or the condition that the change should eliminate. Once you have recorded the change, you can then assign someone to analyze the change. Among the people who might be assigned to the analysis process are the application project group, the operations group, the vendor, the user, or an error tracking analyst.

FIGURE 4-1

SYSTEMS MAINTENANCE LIFE CYCLE

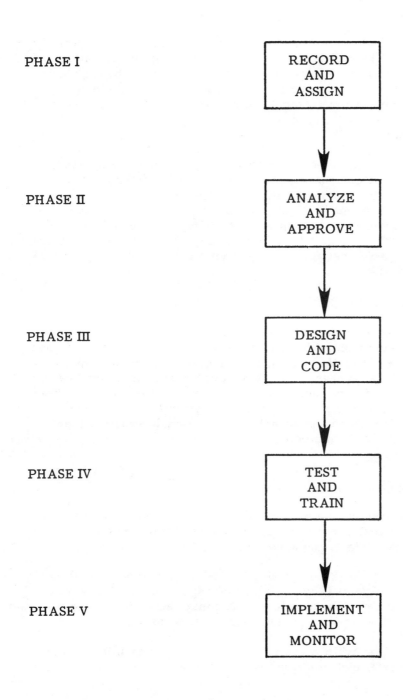

o   Phase 2 - Analyze and approve

Performing the analysis process is equivalent to making the feasibility study in
a new system. In many instances, this only takes a few moments, while in other
situations it may take several days or longer. The analysis process identifies
the solution and estimates the time and effort required to implement that
solution. At that point management must decide whether or not to implement
the proposed solution.

o   Phase 3 - Design and code

This phase of the SMLC is equivalent to the similar phases in the systems
development life cycle. The difference, as stated before, is the magnitude of
effort that may go into this phase. For example, some needs can be satisfied if
you add or change one line of computer code. Again, this may take only a few
minutes, or this phase may take many months of effort.

o   Phase 4 - Test and train

Traditionally, management has been concerned about testing during systems
maintenance. The dilemma confronting project personnel is making a tradeoff
between testing in ideal circumstances and not testing at all. Too frequently,
individual programmers have made testing decisions without referring to department policy. As important as testing is the training of the people using the
application systems. If the change will affect the reports applications personnel receive or the procedures they must follow, they should receive appropriate
training or training materials.

o   Phase 5 - Implement and monitor

Implementation of a change subjects an organization to some new risks. The
first risk is that the change will not be implemented correctly and thus will not
produce the necessary results; the second risk is that once implemented the
change will also impact the unchanged segment of this or another application
system, resulting in unanticipated new problems. One of the solutions to these
dilemmas is to closely monitor the output immediately following a change. The
monitoring process provides management with one additional assurance that the
change has been correctly implemented.

Management Checkpoints During SMLC

Management involvement in the systems maintenance life cycle is essential. The concept of a life cycle is to assure management that the systems and programming process
will be installed on time, within the budget, and according to specifications.

Management gains the needed assurance through a series of major and minor checkpoints
during the life cycle. A major checkpoint is one at which management will decide either
to stop the process or to permit the process to proceed. A minor checkpoint is one more
concerned with administering the process than to managing the process.

During the systems maintenance life cycle there are four major checkpoints and three
minor checkpoints. The steps performed at these checkpoints should be in accordance

with the size of the change and they should be implemented by management.

The four major checkpoints during the SMLC are (see Figure 4-2):

o Major management checkpoint #1 - stop processing

Immediately following the recording of the new need, management must decide whether or not they should stop processing until the system is modified. For example, management may want to stop the system when an error produces illogical results, or perhaps when management approves a new policy or regulation.

o Major management checkpoint #2 - approval to implement

At the completion of the cost/benefit process, management must decide whether or not to implement the change. If management approves the change, the remaining phases continue. However, if management decides not to approve the change, then either all work terminates or analysis begins again so that alternative solutions can be found.

o Major management checkpoint #3 - approval to install

Upon completion of the testing of the change and the training of the appropriate personnel, management must decide whether or not to implement the change. This decision is based upon the results of testing and input from involved parties. If management disapproves implementation, then all effort may be stopped, or the life cycle restarted during any one of the previous phases.

o Major management checkpoint #4 - revert to previous version of system

Postimplementation monitoring usually provides management with hard documentation about the correctness of the change. If problems are identified or suspected, management must decide whether or not to continue with the new version, or whether to revert to performing all processing on previous versions of the system.

The following minor checkpoints occur during the systems maintenance life cycle (see Figure 4-2):

o Minor management checkpoint #1 - impact of change

During the first and second phases of the SMLC, management must make a decision regarding the impact of the error, enhancement, or new requirement on other applications. If the change affects multiple applications, management must take the appropriate steps to involve all related parties in the change process.

o Minor management checkpoint #2 - access to programs

Programmers should not have unlimited access to source and object programs. This access should be controlled by management. Therefore, when a change is not in process, programmers should not have access to the programs, even though they involve approved changes.

FIGURE 4-2

MANAGEMENT CHECKPOINTS DURING SMLC

PHASE #	LIFE CYCLE PHASE	MAJOR CHECKPOINT	MINOR CHECKPOINT
1	Record and Assign	Stop processing (until system is modified)	
2	Analyze and Approve	Approval to implement (change)	Impact of change (to other systems)
3	Design and Code		1 (Authority to) access programs 2 Prioritize change
4	Test and Train	Approval to install	
5	Implement and Monitor	Revert to previous version of system	

o   Minor management checkpoint #3 - prioritize changes

Each approved change has a potential impact on the implementation of all other approved changes. Therefore, as each change is approved, management must reprioritize all of the currently approved changes.

Administering the SMLC

The obvious question is: "What types of changes should use the systems maintenance life cycle concept?" The recommended answer to that question is: "All systems changes." However, allowances should be made for emergency maintenance; for example, program hangups or emergency corrections that must be put in within minutes. However, when these emergency changes are made permanent, then the SMLC process should be followed.

The next obvious question is: "If an entire change can be made with a few hours of effort, should the process still be followed?" The answer is: "Yes, but the process may have to be altered according to the size of the change." The real question management must answer concerning these smaller changes is which, if any, of their management prerogatives are they willing to give up to make smaller changes.

Management should not be willing to give up any of the major prerogatives (major checkpoints) cited earlier even if the change requires only one hour of effort. Obviously management is not going to expend ten hours of effort to administer one hour of change, but that should not be necessary. On the other hand, spending time to administer the one-hour change may eliminate making many additional one-hour changes. Many organizations have learned that if they do not adminster systems changes they waste a great deal of time making unnecessary or unimportant changes.

The steps and procedures outlined in this book will deal with shortcuts that substantially reduce the amount of time and effort required by data processing management when they administer small changes. Much is gained from the approval process even if the approval is perfunctory. For example, how many systems analysts would present unjustified changes to the department manager for approval?

Administering systems maintenance can be aided by:

1.   Establishing a systems maintenance oversight committee

2.   Developing a supportive systems maintenance environment

3.   Adequately staffing systems maintenance

4.   Developing effective systems maintenance procedures

Each of these processes will be discussed individually.

ESTABLISHING A SYSTEMS MAINTENANCE OVERSIGHT COMMITTEE

The purpose of a systems maintenance oversight committee is to provide direction and guidance to the data processing manager. The oversight committee studies systems maintenance procedures and then makes recommendations. Data processing management then asks the committee to perform those studies which they themselves do not have the time to perform.

The oversight committee should consist of senior members of the data processing department, together with other interested parties. A maintenance oversight committee might consist of the following people:

o   One member of senior data processing management (this individual would probably chair the committee)

o   Systems analysts/programmers (the number assigned would depend upon the size of the data processing department)

o   One representative from each of the major user areas

o   One member of senior management

o   One individual concerned with control (this person could be from quality assurance, computer operations control group, or internal audit)

o   One representative of computer operations

o   An outside consultant with an understanding of the problem (this is optional, depending upon the need for improvement in the systems maintenance function)

The committee should be a study group without line authority. If the group is given authority, the involvement with project personnel will become more formal. Project personnel will quickly perceive the task force as a management function within data processing, and they may stop cooperating with the investigators.

The charter of the systems maintenance oversight committee should be to:

1.   Request systems maintenance statistics from project personnel

2.   Analyze statistics in order to identify problems and trends (see Chapter 12 on monitoring)

3.   Review systems maintenance standards and procedures in terms of their ability to facilitate systems maintenance

4.   Review the type of documentation maintained by project personnel and the usefulness of that documentation

5.   Collect information about systems problems to determine if systems maintenance documentation is adequate to resolve the problems

6.   Recommend to department management systems maintenance standards and procedures

7.   Recommend the deletion (or modification) of ineffective standards and procedures

8.   Recommend new or improved procedures for interfacing with user personnel

regarding the systems maintenance function

The oversight committee should meet approximately once per month for a period not exceeding four hours. However, individual members of the committee may have interim assignments, such as gathering or analyzing systems maintenance statistics. While this should be a high-level policy recommending committee, it should not be a time-consuming committee. It should draw upon the experiences and skills of the oversight committee members to propose to management improvements to the systems maintenance process.

DEVELOPING A SUPPORTIVE SYSTEMS MAINTENANCE ENVIRONMENT

Traditionally, maintenance has had negative connotations. Many data processing personnel perceive maintenance to be synonymous with correcting errors and omissions. The image that management must project for maintenance is one of incorporating enhancements and new requirements into operational computer applications.

The mood of the data processing department towards maintenance reflects management's attitude towards this function, as demonstrated by management's actions rather than statements. For example, the following types of actions demean maintenance:

o   Making assignments to a new application system is a reward for hard work

o   Providing larger pay increases and promotions for people on new projects than for people on systems maintenance

o   Giving most management attention to new projects

o   Understaffing systems maintenance

o   Providing systems maintenance project personnel with training in the new technologies

On the other hand, management actions can speak loudly regarding the importance of systems maintenance in their department. The following positive actions by data processing management convey to the members of the department the importance of this systems maintenance function:

o   Establishing a career path in the systems maintenance area

o   Developing systems maintenance job descriptions that have a pay grade as high or higher than the equivalent function on a new application system

o   Establishing a systems maintenance oversight committee

o   Maintaining the proficiency of systems maintenance analysts/programmers in current data processing skills. For example, sending a maintenance programmer to data base school, even though the project being maintained does not use data base. This readies maintenance personnel for upgrading technology when it is appropriate

o   Devoting departmental research time and effort to improving the methods, tools, and techniques of systems maintenance

The above steps can help either to create or to undermine positive attitudes toward systems maintenance. Concurrent with the building of a positive maintenance environment through strong management support should be the developing of programs that aid systems maintenance by:

o   Developing maintenance standards

o   Utilizing structured design

o   Accounting for maintenance

o   Developing maintenance tools and techniques

Some of the steps that can be taken in each of these areas are discussed below:

Developing Maintenance Standards

One of the major objectives of setting departmental standards should be to facilitate the systems maintenance process. This means encouraging those practices that make maintenance easier and discouraging the practices that make maintenance harder. It also implies that standards are continually reviewed.

The type of standards that are effective in improving systems maintenance include:

o   Developing documentation standards

o   Developing numbering conventions

o   Developing structured programming methods

o   Eliminating complex programming methods

o   Designing data with expansion capabilities, such as fields one character longer than anticipated

Of all of the above standards, documentation is the most important. Good documentation facilitates maintenance, while poor documentation makes systems analysts and programmers struggle to modify an application.

In the development of standards, the following questions should be asked:

1.   Will this standard help or hinder the systems maintenance process?

2.   Does this standard adversely affect older technologies, making it difficult for older systems to conform with this standard?

3.   Does this standard encourage straightforward easy-to-understand systems design and programming?

Utilizing Structured Design

Much has been written about the advantages and disadvantages of structured design. Some reports provide glowing statistics citing significant reductions in design and maintenance costs ensuing from the use of structured design principles. Other conflicting reports state that the advantages of structured design and programming have been grossly overestimated.

The key to structured design is structuring the system so that the data relationships are understood for maintenance purposes. Data relationships are the relationships between data as it flows from an event entering a computerized application until it is outputted to meet the needs of a specific user.

The relationship between data flow and maintenance is illustrated in Figure 4-3. The figure pictorially represents a structured approach to data. Organizations utilizing this approach can significantly reduce maintenance.

The structured data flow figure covers both data and the processing rules applied to that data. The figure can be used to show the structure from an event to the output, or from the output back to the event that generated the output. Thus, if either the event or the output changes, the structured relationship through the system can be readily understood.

Let's examine this structure with the event: An employee puts in four hours of overtime. That event, the four hours overtime, must be inputted into the computerized application according to the input and authorization rules. This covers how the data is recorded, authorized, and entered into the computerized application. As it is entered, it becomes a transaction.

The transaction is then processed as part of the payroll application. The processing rules convert the event, the four hours of overtime, into pay for an employee.

The results of processing are computerized data. This data is entered into the data base, or computer files, using update rules. For example, the employee's pay would be entered into the data base for purposes of preparing paychecks, updating the year-to-date figures, and preparing different payroll reports.

The data in the data base is then processed according to the reporting requirement rules. This results in output, which may be a paycheck, a report, or a year-end W-2 statement.

When it becomes necessary to perform maintenance, the requirements are usually expressed in terms of output or results from the computerized application. The individual doing the maintenance must then find where that data comes from in the data base. If it is only a report format change, then changing the reporting requirements rules completes the maintenance. However, if the needed data is not in the data base, or if it is not in the data base in the proper format, then the maintenance personnel must identify the application or program that entered the data in the data base. If the needed data can be entered, then maintenance is complete. However, if the computerized data is not available, then the systems personnel must go further back into the structure.

If the data is available in the computerized application, then the processing rules can be modified to act upon the transactions to create new computerized data. However, if the data is not available, then the maintenance people must go back and generate that data through the occurrence of some type of event.

FIGURE 4-3

DATA FLOW RELATIONSHIPS

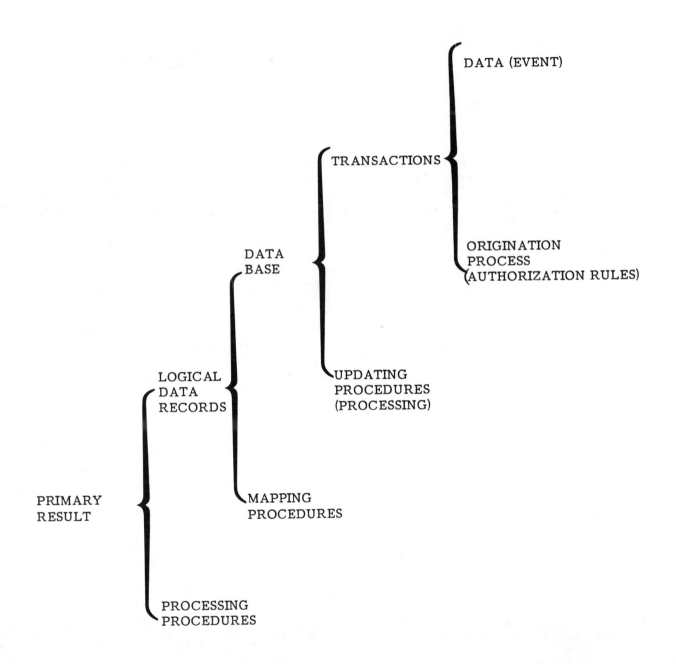

Accounting for Maintenance

Effective management tools for controlling maintenance are the budgetary accounting processes. The stronger these processes, the more control data processing management has of the maintenance function. The weaker the budgetary and accounting process, the less control data processing management has over the maintenance function.

Organizations should use zero-based budgeting for maintenance efforts. Thus, each year each project must refustify its maintenance budget. Maintenance will not be automatically continued at the same level as the previous year.

Project managers may find it very difficult to document all the specific changes that will occur during a year. Many of the larger changes can be identified, but the smaller ones that reflect changes in business conditions may not be known until the time they are requested. However, we know from experience these smaller changes often make up the majority of the maintenance expenses.

The suggested steps in building a budget to solve this dilemma are:

o   Step 1 - Categorize maintenance expenses using the seven categories recommended for this purpose.

o   Step 2 - Estimate the number of changes that will fall in each category during the ensuing year.

o   Step 3 - Estimate the average number of hours per change in each category.

o   Step 4 - Develop the budget based on the frequency and hours of changes in each of the seven categories.

o   Step 5 - Determine if users actually want their maintenance dollars expended in that way. If not, make the appropriate changes.

o   Step 6 - Monitor the actual number of hours required. This encourages adherence to the budget and at the same time enables data processing personnel to improve the budget estimating process.

Developing Maintenance Tools and Techniques

More effort needs to be expended on improving tools and techniques for the systems maintenance analyst/programmer. To reduce the cost of each change, either simplify the changes or improve the tools and techniques used to make the change. Since the data processing department may have little control over the complexity of the changes, they should concentrate their initial efforts on the tools and techniques.

The areas of concern in systems maintenance include:

o   Documenting the need for the change

o   Identifying where in the system the change should be installed

o   Creating new versions of source programs, object programs, and test libraries needed to implement and test the change

o   Ensuring that the installation of a change does not negatively impact unchanged segments of the application system

o   Updating the systems and programming documentation

o   Installing the change on the proper date

The types of tools and techniques that would be beneficial to systems maintenance analysts/programmers include:

o   Forms and procedures to document problems and changes

o   Systems and programming structures that permit the quick identification of where the changes should be installed

o   Documentation that is both easy to follow and easy to update

o   Source code and object program libraries software that facilitates the creation and identification of new versions of source and object programs

o   An audit trail of changes to application programs

o   Operating systems that automatically call the appropriate version of a program based on dates

Organizations should use the results of the self-assessment questionnaire and the recommendations of a systems maintenance oversight committee to improve systems maintenance tools and techniques. However, this must be a continuing effort, and as organizations encounter problems or inefficiencies, they should seek out or develop new tools and techniques.

ADEQUATELY STAFFING SYSTEMS MAINTENANCE

The increased emphasis on systems maintenance has led to the creation of two new functions within the data processing department. These are the systems maintenance analyst/programmer and the error tracking analyst. While both of these functions have been considered part of the existing systems analysts' and programmers' job descriptions, they are really developing into full-time functions within the data processing department.

Systems maintenance analysts have two constraints which systems analysts don't have: first, the operating environment must run the application correctly; second, any change must be implemented within a preestablished structure. If a problem is encountered in a new system, the structure can be changed to complement the new requirement. In an existing system, the cost and effort may make such a solution prohibitive.

Factors that affect the success of the systems maintenance function include:

o   <u>Familiarity with old and new technology</u> - Existing systems frequently use older technology, but maintenance people must continually upgrade them using new technology. This requires the individuals to be familiar with both old and new technology.

o Operation deadline - New systems development has no operational deadline pressures except the pressure to complete the application on a specified date. However, with existing systems the highest priority is always keeping the system operating.

o Error tracking - The maintenance team spends a large percentage of their time tracking errors, many of which are not directly associated with the application system (e.g., operating system problems).

o Integration into user operation - The systems maintenance group has a much closer involvement with the day-to-day operations of the user area than does the new system team. This is because the operational system is an integral part of the user operation, while the user area does not yet feel the impact of the new system.

o Communications - The systems maintenance analyst must be a better communicator because of the closer day-to-day relationship with the user. Also, in operational systems more people are involved in the operation than on the developmental team where only one or two representatives of the user area may be in contact with the project.

o Less data processing direction - Data processing management tends to provide less direction and tends to interface less with operational systems than with systems under development. This is because operational systems are more closely involved with the user operations and data processing management is less familiar with these operations.

o Work with others' system logic - The team developing a new system develops it using their own logic and criteria. Since the developmental team is making the decisions, they understand why and how things happen. This is not necessarily so in an operational system. The people performing the maintenance may not have developed the project and, therefore, may not understand why a certain processing logic was used. In addition, the people involved in making those system logic decisions may not be available in either the data processing or the user department to explain the reasons and the purpose for implementing that logic.

The systems maintenance analyst/programmer combines the function of both the systems analyst and programmer in the maintenance area. Because of the large number of small changes, the same individual may need to do both the analysis work and the coding. Thus, these functions require different types of skills than those possessed by either a full-time systems analyst or a full-time programmer. A sample job description is provided in Figure 4-4.

The error-tracking analyst is an individual who can pinpoint the origin of problems. This individual works exclusively with problems as opposed to enhancements or new requirements. Because problems can originate in operating systems, in communication systems, in hardware, in data preparation, in application systems and with computer operators, it is not always advantageous to have the project team in question attempt to identify the problem. For example, a project team may spend many hours trying to identify and correct a problem which has been caused by the operating system. The error tracking analyst, on the other hand, can interface with all the support groups. A sample

FIGURE 4-4

JOB DESCRIPTION

SYSTEMS MAINTENANCE ANALYST

REPORTS TO - MANAGER OF SYSTEMS AND PROGRAMMING

FUNCTION

The systems maintenance analyst function is to maintain an application system in an operational status. The function receives requests for maintenance in the areas of errors, new requirements and enhancements. Working within a budget and priority system, the systems maintenance analyst designs, implements, tests, documents, and places the changes into a production status in accordance with the needs and requirements of the user. In addition, the systems maintenance analyst is the prime contact point between the data processing department and the user department responsible for the application system.

RESPONSIBILITIES AND DUTIES

The systems maintenance analyst has primary responsibility for maintaining an application system in an operational status. The individual works with both user personnel and data processing personnel to accomplish the function. User management provides the individual with day-to-day direction regarding priorities in work, schedules and budgets. Within these constraints the individual is resonsible for properly implementing user needs and at the same time optimizing the use of computer technology. The individual must maintain the application so that it operates using the current computer hardware and software in an efficient, effective and economical manner. In the performance of the function, the systems maintenance analyst designs modifications to an application system that must fit within the existing application system structure. This may involve supervising less skilled data processing personnel or personally performing feasibility studies, economic analysis, systems design, programming, testing, conversion, and implementation of systems modifications.

QUALIFICATIONS

The systems maintenance analyst must be a skilled systems analyst with the ability to design and implement changes within an existing systems structure. The individual must be capable of understanding and working with systems developed by other people. The individual must implement many of the required changes within a short time span thus putting the individual under continual pressure to perform. The individual must possess all the skills of the systems analyst but with an emphasis on communication skills. Much of the systems maintenance analyst's time will be spent in communication and arbitration with user personnel and data processing personnel. The communication involves negotiating a series of compromises because maintenance must be performed utilizing the existing application systems structure and because maintenance may need to be implemented using older technologies which may cause some deviations from normal standards and procedures. The systems maintenance analyst may also be competing with other analysts for computer time to satisfy user needs.

FIGURE 4-5

JOB DESCRIPTION

ERROR TRACKING ANALYST

REPORTS TO - MANAGER COMPUTER OPERATIONS (SOME QUALITY ASSURANCE ANALYSTS REPORT TO THE MANAGER OF EDP QUALITY ASSURANCE)

FUNCTION

The error tracking analyst function identifies, records, and assigns maintenance needs to the appropriate individual. The error tracking analyst function concentrates on maintenance needs associated with computer hangups, and errors and omissions associated with problems in applications or operating systems. The function tracks the errors from inception, assigns them for implementation, and then reviews the implementation process in order to communicate common errors and good solutions to other parties within the data processing function.

RESPONSIBILITIES AND DUTIES

The error tracking analyst has the responsibility of being the first individual involved when problems occur. The individual has the responsibility for documenting the facts and conditions surrounding the problem. This normally involves some type of investigation and analysis so that the error tracking analyst can isolate the cause of the problem in specific application and/or operating software. The error tracking analyst will then assign the responsibility to correct the problem to the individual responsible for the system apparently causing the problem. If the error tracking analyst makes a wrong assignment, then additional investigation and analysis must occur to determine the cause of the problem, and again to assign it to an individual to correct. The results of this identification and analysis are reported to management, at least in summarized format. Thus, the error tracking analyst has the responsibility of informing data processing management of the emergency systems maintenance occurring in the department. The error tracking analyst also monitors the implementation of the fix in order to first determine that it has been fixed, and second to identify the true cause of the problem and the implemented solution. If the cause may impact many systems the error tracking analyst has the additional responsibility of recommending general solutions for the entire department. The error tracking analyst should also differentiate bad from good practices in order to develop standards which encourage good practices and discourage bad practices.

QUALIFICATIONS

The error tracking analyst should have a minimum of five years systems and programming experience. At least three of the five years should be involved in systems maintenance in which the individual had responsibility for maintaining an application system in an operational status. The individual should possess skills in computer programming, job control language, systems design and structured systems, and programming concepts. The individual normally would be a better than average systems analyst. In addition, experience in both computer operations and system generation and maintenance of operating software would be helpful but not essential.

error tracking analyst's job description is presented in Figure 4-5.

DEVELOPING EFFECTIVE SYSTEMS MAINTENANCE PROCEDURES

Included within the systems maintenance life cycle are procedures, approaches, and methods for performing maintenance. These options are available to data processing departments using the life cycle concept. These procedures incorporate the methodology used in implementing specific changes.

The three factors management should use to make decisions are:

o   Maintenance approach - Who performs the maintenance

o   Methods to install changes - Which changes are installed individually and which by groups

o   Use of override procedures - The controls established on the maintenance utilities, privileged instructions, and features

Maintenance Approach

One of the first questions to be answered about systems maintenance is who should perform the maintenance. Organizations have taken different approaches in assigning maintenance responsibility. The four most common approaches are:

o   The development team maintains the application system

o   A new team maintains the application system

o   A maintenance pool maintains the application system

o   A combination of permanent people and individuals from a maintenance pool is responsible for the application system

The advantages and disadvantages of each approach are summarized in Figure 4-6 and discussed below.

Maintenance by Development Team

The original approach to maintenance, and the one followed by most organizations, is to make the development team responsible for maintenance of the application system. This may involve only part of the development team. Some of the individuals assigned to the development process may not be needed for the maintenance process.

Assigning the maintenance to the development team has the advantage of putting the most skilled people on the project. There is no better way to understand an application system than to develop that system. In addition, it encourages the developmental team to do a good developmental effort. If the people developing the project know that they will have to maintain it, they probably will invest the extra time and effort necessary to create an easy-to-maintain application.

FIGURE 4-6

MAINTENANCE APPROACH

APPROACH	ADVANTAGES	DISADVANTAGES
Development team maintains the application system.	o assigns maintenance to people most familiar with the project o encourages development team to do a good development effort	o development team may not be experienced in maintenance methods o development team may not document extensively because they know the system
New team assigned to maintain the application system.	o brings new perspective to project o forces good documentation o forces implementation of the specified requirement	o team not familiar with project o developmental team may not be concerned with building an easy to maintain application
A maintenance pool maintains the application system.	o optimizes department maintenance capability o helps improve maintenance methods o forces good documentation	o team may not be familiar with project o developmental team may not be concerned with building an easy to maintain application
Combination of permanent maintenance people supplemented by a maintenance pool maintain the application system.	o optimizes department maintenance capability o minimizes maintenance project staff	o maintenance pool staff may not be available when needed o lack of continuity of maintenance personnel

Two disadvantages are associated with assigning the development team maintenance responsibilities. The first is that the project personnel may not be experienced in maintenance methods. One needs to recognize that there are different skills required for maintenance than for new development. However, the major disadvantage may be that the development team will not document the application sufficiently because they know the system. Therefore, they do not perceive the same need for documentation as those who are assigned maintenance later.

The maintenance team, as with any other data processing team, is subject to turnover. This should not be unexpected, but through continual training the developmental team maintains the skills of its people. Prior to leaving, these people can teach the newly assigned members the system logic as well as the reasons for building the system in its current format.

Maintenance by New Team

Another approach to systems maintenance is to assign one team to develop the system and then turn it over to another team for maintenance. The developmental team must complete the system according to the specifications. When it has been agreed that the applications have been met, a maintenance team takes over the project. However, the developmental team must stay with the project until the specifications have been achieved.

This approach to maintenance is similar to that of having a consultant or software house develop a computer system for a customer. The consultant builds the system according to the specifications, but when it is complete it belongs to the customer. It then becomes the customer's responsibility to maintain the system. With this approach, the maintenance team consists of different people than the development team.

This approach has two major advantages. First, it brings a new systems perspective to the project. The systems maintenance team does not have the same perspective as the development team; thus it can often recommend new improvements and enhancements. Second, this approach forces the project to develop good documentation; and third, it forces the project to implement the requirements. Until the project has met the developmental requirements, the systems maintenance team normally refuses to accept the project for maintenance purposes.

The disadvantages of assigning a new team are twofold. First, the systems maintenance team is less experienced than the development team. (The maintenance team must expend effort to gain this expertise.) Second, the development team may not be concerned with building easy-to-maintain applications. Their primary concern may be achieving specifications which may lead to some shortcuts in systems development, programming, and documentation in order to meet dates and budgets.

Maintenance by a Maintenance Pool

Many organizations have formed a maintenance pool for all applications. The objective of the maintenance pool is to have one group responsible for maintenance of all application systems. In such instances, maintenance is usually defined more narrowly than in this book. Large changes, for example those requiring more than two months of effort, are not performed by the maintenance pool.

Many organizations that adopted the maintenance pool concept several years ago have abandoned the concept. The major drawback of the maintenance pool is that it means centralized maintenance over systems which are not designed for maintenance. Concepts such as structured design, structured programming, standardized documentation, and standardized approaches to systems analysis and programming may make the maintenance pool concept feasible.

The main advantage of the maintenance pool approach is that it optimizes department maintenance capabilities. People assigned to an application full time for maintenance will find work to fill their time. However, having a maintenance pool permits the assignment of people to tasks that are most in need of implementation. Other advantages include helping improve maintenance methods and forcing the writing of good documentation. People that spend full time working as part of a maintenance pool need to develop good maintenance methods.

There are two major disadvantages to the maintenance pool concept. First, it may take the people in the pool time to become familiar with projects they have to maintain. In addition, the developmental team may not be concerned with building an easily maintained application if they know that maintenance will be turned over to a maintenance pool.

Combination of Developmental Team and Maintenance Pool

A combination approach is currently being tried by several organizations. A minimum cadre of permanent maintenance people is assigned to each application. These are usually people who have been on the developmental project or who have been trained by development people. This cadre should be understaffed and when it is necessary the cadre should be augmented with people from a maintenance pool.

The permanent cadre of maintenance people assures the continuity of experience. In addition, it offers continuity to the users. For small applications and low-maintenance applications, one permanent maintenance systems analyst/programmer may be assigned to several applications. Then, as work develops, people from a maintenance pool can be assigned to the project to complete that specific task.

This approach offers economy and efficiency of operation. The maintenance capabilities of the data processing department are optimized. In addition, the number of people assigned to a project for maintenance is minimized. The probability that people will look for work with this approach is minimal.

The disadvantages of the combination approach are twofold. The full-time cadre may not be able to get assistance from the maintenance pool because other requests have higher priority. Under this approach, priorities are based on the needs of the entire organization and not the needs of a specific application system. The second disadvantage is the lack of continuity in maintenance personnel. The project may not get the same person twice from the maintenance pool, and thus will need to continually train people.

METHOD TO INSTALL CHANGES

Changes to application systems can be installed individually or by groups. Most organizations leave this decision to the discretion of the project manager. However, maintenance is facilitated when there are guidelines.

The four most common methods for installing changes to application systems are (See Figure 4-7):

o   Install each change as it is completed

o   Periodically install a batch of completed changes

o   Install changes in homogeneous groups

o   Install changes according to a predetermined schedule

The advantages and disadvantages of these methods are listed in Figure 4-7 and explained below.

Install Each Change Individually

Change requests are usually given to the project manager individually. They can be estimated individually, designed individually, implemented and tested individually, and installed individually. This approach is followed by many project leaders.

The advantage of installing each change individually is that it gets installed quickly. It also isolates the source of problems should they occur. For example, if a problem occurs immediately following a single change, the project manager can be relatively certain that the change caused the problem.

The disadvantage of installing changes individually is that it may be a costly method of installing changes. The same steps are repeated again and again rather than being combined. Also, subsequent changes may be delayed, i.e., difficulties occur during the installation of a current change.

Installing Changes in Batches

It is normally cheaper to process similar items in a batch than to process them individually. Each change follows similar procedures. The batch installation minimizes the maintenance steps and at the same time permits more extensive testing. While it may not be economical to test a single change extensively, it is economical to test a batch of changes extensively.

One disadvantage of batch installation of changes is that it may delay a needed change. In addition, it may be more difficult to isolate problems associated with a group of installed changes.

Installing Changes in Homogeneous Groups

The disadvantage of batched installation of changes may be overcome by installing changes in batches of homogeneous groups. The two most common categories of homogeneous groups are those:

o   Grouped by data processing function - These groups would be processing,

FIGURE 4-7

METHODS TO INSTALL CHANGES

METHOD	ADVANTAGE	DISADVANTAGE
Install each change individually	o Gets changes in quickly o Minimizes source of problems if they occur	o May be a costly method of installing changes
Periodically install a batch of completed changes	o Minimizes maintenance steps o Should permit more extensive testing	o May delay needed changes o May increase difficulty of finding problem associated with an installed change
Install changes in homogeneous groups	o Minimizes maintenance steps o Concentrates changes simplifying monitoring	o May delay needed changes o May increase difficulty of finding problem associated with an installed change
Install changes on a schedule of predetermined dates	o Minimizes maintenance steps o Identifies date(s) on which all changes will be installed	o May delay needed changes o May increase difficulty of finding problem associated with an installed change

updating, report writing, storage, communications, audits, and edits.

o   Grouped by system function - All changes in a system such as a payroll system are grouped by function such as processing overtime, deducting federal taxes, recording absences, and preparing paychecks.

o   Grouped by program - All changes to a single program are installed at the same time.

The advantages of installing changes in homogeneous groups include minimizing the maintenance steps and concentrating changes in one area. This concentration aids in monitoring problems. The disadvantages are that it may delay needed changes and it may make it harder to find problems associated with an installed change.

Installing Changes on Predetermined Dates

A method of concentrating changes and problems is to select dates upon which changes can be made. Some organzations only permit installing changes on one day per month. This can be spread among as many applications as there are days per month. Thus, people monitoring the system know what system might cause problems that day.

The advantages of installing changes on a predetermined date is that it minimizes maintenance steps. The installation date can be a predetermined calendar date or can be scheduled every X days. An additional advantage is that users and management know on what date particular changes are installed. The disadvantages are the same as with installing changes in a homogeneous group.

Installations cannot ensure that every change will conform to this schedule; however, having a schedule minimizes the deviations. Also, setting specific dates requires special management approval for making changes in the schedule. This may have the positive effect of discouraging the installation of low priority changes.

MAINTENANCE ADMINISTRATION CHECKLIST

A maintenance administration checklist is included as Figure 4-8. The purpose of this checklist is to permit data processing management to periodically assess the adequacy of their maintenance administration duties. The checklist is designed to identify potential administration weaknesses in the systems maintenance. These are identified by either qualified "Yes" answers or "No" answers. The "Not Applicable" (N/A) answers relate to questions governing procedures or methods not utilized by the organization conducting the review.

The checklist should be used by members of data processing management. It, too, is a self-assessment questionnaire. Room is provided on the questionnaire for comments which may become the basis of studies or the initiation of new standards and procedures. Potential administration weaknesses identified by the checklist can be given to the systems maintenance oversight committee for study so that they can recommend solutions.

FIGURE 4-8

MAINTENANCE ADMINISTRATION CHECKLIST

NUMBER	MANAGEMENT QUESTION	RESPONSE			COMMENTS
		YES	NO	N/A	
1.	Has a departmental systems maintenance policy been established?				
2.	Does the systems maintenance policy outline the duties that must be followed in fulfilling the maintenance responsibilities?				
3.	Does the policy strongly state management's support for the systems maintenance function?				
4.	Does data processing senior management enforce the systems maintenance policy both verbally and by their actions?				
5.	Has a systems maintenance oversight committee been established?				
6.	Are all concerned groups represented on the oversight committee?				
7.	Are sufficient time and effort allocated to the oversight committee to assure its success?				
8.	Does the department give maintenance high priority when it considers new or modified standards?				
9.	Does the department utilize a structured approach to systems that facilitates maintenance?				
10.	Does the department budget maintenance expenses by maintenance category?				
11.	Does departmental management monitor the maintenance budget to assure that exceptions are approved?				

FIGURE 4-8

MAINTENANCE ADMINISTRATION CHECKLIST (Cont'd)

NUMBER	MANAGEMENT QUESTION	RESPONSE			COMMENTS
		YES	NO	N/A	
12.	Are departmental resources expended to develop or improve systems maintenance tools and techniques?				
13.	Does the department use a systems maintenance life cycle?				
14.	Does the life cycle include sufficient checkpoints to assure that management is in charge of systems maintenance?				
15.	Are the checkpoints utilized by departmental management?				
16.	Are procedures established to ensure that there are no deviations (except those approved by management) from the systems maintenance life cycle?				
17.	When emergency changes are made, must the permanent version of that change be implemented using the systems maintenance life cycle?				
18.	Does departmental management, or their representative, review how changes affect other application systems?				
19.	Does departmental management control access to programs?				
20.	Are priorities reevaluated each time a new change is approved?				
21.	Has the department established a job description for a systems maintenance analyst/programmer?				
22.	Has the department recognized the error tracking analyst function?				

FIGURE 4-8

MAINTENANCE ADMINISTRATION CHECKLIST

NUMBER	MANAGEMENT QUESTION	RESPONSE			COMMENTS
		YES	NO	N/A	
23.	Are systems maintenance analysts/ programmers rewarded as well as or better than developmental analysts and programmers?				
24.	Has the department established an approach to maintaining application systems?				
25.	Has the department developed a standardized method for installing changes?				
26.	Does departmental management control the use of systems maintenance privileged instructions, utilities, and features?				
27.	Does data processing management periodically assess the effectiveness of the administration of the systems maintenance function?				

SUMMARY

Careful administering of the systems maintenance function should make it a more effective and more economical function. The amount of time allocated to administration of
systems maintenance should be approximately equal to the amount of data processing
resources consumed by systems maintenance. The cornerstone of this management
effort is the development of a systems maintenance policy.

This chapter has suggested that systems maintenance be incorporated into a systems
maintenance life cycle. This life cycle with its major and minor checkpoints is designed
to put management in charge of the systems maintenance in their organization. The
establishment of a systems maintenance oversight committee can help management in
the fulfillment of this responsibility.

The administration of systems maintenance involves both staffing and setting policy.
Management must address the issues of developing maintenance standards, designing
systems which facilitate the performance of maintenance, as well as using special privileged features for system software for maintenance purposes. This chapter includes a
checklist to help management identify potential weaknesses in their systems maintenance administration function.

Chapter 5
Emergency Maintenance

CHAPTER OVERVIEW

The systems maintenance policy may break down when the need for emergency maintenance occurs. When a serious problem occurs, extensive pressure may be placed upon systems analysts and programmers to correct that problem. Given the option of satisfying an angry user or complying to a departmental policy, it may be difficult for a programmer not to act in favor of the angry user.

Emergency maintenance involves fixing problems as quickly as possible in a matter of minutes. For example, in an on-line banking system many of the normal banking operations can't take place when the computer system goes down. This is no time to be completing forms but, rather, this is a time for action.

Data processing departments should plan for two categories of maintenance. These are planned maintenance or maintenance which can follow normal procedures and emergency maintenance or maintenance when there is no time for attempting to comply with normal maintenance procedures.

This chapter explains the emergency policies and procedures needed when emergency circumstances occur. The process allows for temporary fixes to applications. However, when the change is made permanent, it should be done using normal procedures.

EMERGENCY MAINTENANCE DEFINED

Emergency maintenance normally bypasses the established system of maintenance controls. This type of maintenance may need to be performed without proper management or user approvals. It may not produce an audit trail showing the type and location of changes made. Furthermore, it may require the use of very powerful utilities which can change any part of the processing environment. Thus, special precautions must be taken to assure that this critical type of maintenance is not abused.

Organizations should define what types of maintenance fall into the emergency category. All other types of maintenances must then comply with the normal systems maintenance policies and procedures. However, even emergency maintenance should be subject to a minimal level of control.

Emergency maintenance is normally a type of change or correction that must be made in twenty-four hours or less. In many instances, this maintenance must be performed within a matter of minutes. The problem usually occurs without warning. When the problem occurs, the full effort of the maintenance team is often consumed until they have corrected the problem.

The two common categories of unplanned uncritical maintenance are:

1. __Hang-up__

A computer hang-up is a situation in which an application system stops running. Maintenance personnel must take immediate action if the application system is to return to operational status.

2. Underline: System errors

A system error might be severe enough to prevent the use or dissemination of processing results. An example is if all the payroll checks were issued for the same amount of money, regardless of pay grade or hours worked.

When either of these two types of conditions occurs, the maintenance team must take immediate action. The challenge facing data processing management is effectively controlling emergency maintenance without inhibiting the process. This chapter is designed to help data processing management establish the policies and procedures for emergency maintenance.

ESTABLISHING AN EMERGENCY MAINTENANCE POLICY

The risks associated with emergency maintenance warrant the time and effort required to control this function. It is a time in which systems analysts and programmers are subject to extensive pressure so that they may make poor decisions simply because there are no policies and procedures to determine what action they should take.

Data processing management's initial step should be to establish a departmental emergency maintenance policy. Once the policy has been established, they can develop standards and procedures to support that policy. However, without a policy, inconsistent or ineffective procedures may be developed.

Data processing management should be responsive to emergency problems. The options available when critical problems occur are to:

o   Rerun the application and hope the rerun is successful.

o   Identify which data caused the problems, eliminate those data, and rerun the application.

o   Delay processing until the problem can be corrected through the normal systems maintenance procedures.

o   Change the operating environment so that the application system can become operational again.

In different situations, management may select any one of the above options. What is needed is an analysis of the problem including an assessment of the risks involved. Having the factual information about the problem assists management in selecting the proper option.

Considerations for an Emergency Maintenance Policy

Prior to writing an emergency maintenance policy, data processing management should determine the criteria that they need to consider in performing the maintenance.

Whichever maintenance methods they pick should be followed consistently by all members of the data processing department.

Many data processing managers draw upon the experiences of their senior personnel when they develop emergency maintenance policies. However, the final policy must be decided upon by data processing management. The people who should be consulted in developing this policy include:

o   Computer operations manager

o   Quality assurance manager

o   Key senior systems analysts

o   Key lead programmers

o   Manager standards group

o   Senior software programmer

As data processing management considers the criteria to be included in the policy, they must also consider the standards and procedures necessary to support that policy. It is the procedures that make the policy work.

The major factors that management needs to consider in developing an emergency maintenance policy include:

o   Documenting problems

o   Use of privileged facilities

o   Approval of fix

o   Enforcement of policy

o   Permanent correction of quick fix

o   Rerun priorities

Each of these factors is discussed individually.

Problem Documentation

The tendancy in solving critical problems is to fix first and document second. The arguments for this approach are convincing: Time is of the essence, and it may be possible to fix a problem before it can be completely documented.

The counter arguments are equally persuasive. If an organization fixes without going through the analysis required by documentation, they may make erroneous corrections. Documentation proponents argue that the proper way is the quick way.

Documenting problems requires that someone formally records the characteristics of the problem and other pertinent information prior to attempting to fix the problem. It also assumes that there will be some type of supervisory review and approval prior to fixing. Therefore, the type of questions that management must consider in determining whether they want critical problems documented prior to fixing include:

1. How much documentation should be required before the maintenance team fixes the problem?

2. Is supervisory review required before they fix the problem?

3. What uses will be made of the documentation?

Use of Privileged Facilities

Computer vendors provide special capabilities to handle unusual problems. It's been recognized over the years that "what can go wrong will go wrong." To compensate for the phenomenon Murphy described, vendors have added special privileged facilities to operating systems and other operating environment software.

Examples of these special facilities include:

o DEBE (Does Everything But Eat) - This IBM utility is a multipurpose utility for bypassing many of the operating systems and library controls.

o SUPER ZAP - Another IBM utility designed to insert machine language patches into object programs.

o Privileged instructions - A set of very powerful instructions that control the facilities that affect the environment. Examples are the special privileged instructions that enable key people to change the passwords in the password library. Because passwords control access to facilities, any instruction that can change those passwords can also control access to the facilities.

o User exits - Most major software packages include exits which allow the insertion of special routines. Normally these user exit routines can bypass most of the system controls. For example, some of these routines can modify data in the data buffer areas.

Management's dilemma is how to permit the use of privileged facilities for good purposes, but prohibit their use for improper activities. The questions that management must consider in the use of these privileged facilities include:

1. What privileged facilities should be made available for maintenance purposes?

2. Who should have access to those privileged facilities?

3. How will unauthorized people be prevented from using those privileged facilities?

4. What type of approval will be required prior to using the privileged facilities?

5. What type of records will be maintained to document who used the privileged facilities and for what purposes?

Approval of Fix

Obviously management does not want unapproved fixes installed; the question is: "Should the fix be approved prior to installation?" As with other aspects of critical maintenance, both the pros and cons are convincing.

The arguments for not requiring approval are considerations related to time. Approval to install the fix should be obtained from the individual or organization responsible for the application system. In many instances it may be too difficult and too time consuming to obtain prior approval. Thus, waiting to gain approval may negatively impact operations.

The arguments favoring prior approval are arguments related to control issues. If the user is responsible for the application, then the user must also be responsible for all types of maintenance. A fix installed by the data processing department without the approval of the user may be a fix not desired by the user.

Another consideration pertaining to approval is what is meant by approval. Approval could be given in any of the following ways:

o   Signing a document

o   Approving by telephone

o   Approving specific types of maintenance in advance

The decision by users and data processing management to require approval prior to implementing emergency maintenance depends upon how much authority they want to retain or delegate. The questions they should ask themselves are:

1.   Does data processing have the authority to change processing rules without the approval of user management?

2.   Do the approval considerations vary based on the time of day and day of the week?

3.   If the user is unavailable, who can approve a critical change?

4.   If approval is given other than in writing, should a written approval be sought after the fact?

Enforcement of Emergency Maintenance Policy

Whenever data processing management issues a policy, they should consider the question of enforcement. They should develop procedures and standards to support the policy. If data processing personnel violate these standards, management must determine what action should be taken. If no action will be taken, then they should eliminate the policy, procedure, or standard.

A major complaint by data processing quality assurance groups is that management doesn't support the enforcement of standards. What these quality assurance analysts have concluded is that most of management's standards and policies are, in fact, merely guidelines. The systems analysts and programmers can follow or not follow policies and standards at their discretion.

The questions data processing management must ask themselves regarding enforcement of their emergency maintenance policy include:

1. Does management really intend to enforce the policy?

2. If the policy is not followed, what action will be taken by management?

3. If an exception is needed to the policy or standards, who will grant that exception?

Permanent Correction of a Quick Fix

Many quick fixes are installed using privileged facilities. For example, a necessary change can be installed in a matter of minutes using a utility like SUPER ZAP. However, this fix is temporary and should be incorporated into the source code of the application system.

If management doesn't take positive steps, the quick fix may not become a permanent change. For example, a new version of the object program could be put into production that does not include the critical change. When a positive action must be taken for each critical change, the probability of a change being lost is substantially reduced.

The questions that management should ask themselves regarding converting a quick fix into a permanent change include:

1. What procedures would ensure that an installed quick fix is saved?

2. Should a time limit be established for making a quick fix permanent?

3. What type of feedback would verify that the quick fix has been permanently installed?

Rerun Priorities

The quick fix is often installed to overcome an operating problem severe enough to invalidate the results of processing. Thus, the application system must be rerun.

When reruns are required, operating priorities must be changed. This may mean that the application awaiting rerun may be delayed, or other applications may be delayed. Management should predetermine how these rerun priorities will be established.

The questions management must ask themselves about rerun priorities include:

1. Should a rerun priority policy be established for critical problems?

2. Who should have the authority to change the priority for running applications?

Recommended Emergency Maintenance Policy

The policy for emergency maintenance is described in Figure 5-1. This policy is intended to help data processing management establish their own policy. The recommended policy is divided into three parts. The first part defines the authority and states the reason for the policy. The second part outlines the specifics of the policy. The third part of the policy states management's intent to enforce the policy. Any policy adopted by a data processing department should include all three parts.

ROLE AND RESPONSIBILITY FOR EMERGENCY MAINTENANCE

Responsibilities must be established for implementing the unplanned critical maintenance policy. It is important that these responsibilities be identified and that the individuals involved understand and accept the responsibilities. When critical problems occur there normally is not enough time to develop effective working procedures.

Many parties are involved in emergency maintenance. Each of the following may be involved in the fixing of a critical problem:

o   Data processing management

o   Computer operator

o   Computer room supervisor

o   Control group coordinator

o   Application system project manager

o   User

o   Vendor

Not all of the above will be involved in every problem. The role of the error tracking analyst is to determine who should be involved in each problem. The role and responsibility of each of the above parties is discussed individually and summarized in Figure 5-2.

Data Processing Management Responsibility

The data processing manager has the ultimate responsibility for the correction of emergencies. While the user is responsible for the application system, the data processing manager is responsible that the systems are maintained in a successful operating status. The discharge of this responsibility involves:

o   Establish policy - Develop and implement an emergency maintenance policy for the data processing department

o   Implement policy - Ensure that the standards and procedures are established, implemented, and enforced for emergency maintenance

FIGURE 5-1

RECOMMENDED EMERGENCY MAINTENANCE POLICY

It is the policy of the data processing department to incorporate all changes to application systems through use of the normal systems maintenance process. However, it is recognized that in the course of production, processing events will occur which require taking unusual steps to keep the application functioning. When the normal systems maintenance process cannot satisfy user requirements, the following policies apply:

1. All problems are to be documented before any action occurs.

2. Computer operations supervisors must approve the use of any privileged facility required for the fix.

3. User management must approve the installation of the fix.

4. The temporary fix procedures and standards should be strictly followed throughout the temporary fix process.

5. Steps are to be taken as soon as possible to make a permanent correction of the problem.

6. Reruns are to be performed in accordance with rerun standards.

Data processing management will actively encourage and support this emergency maintenance policy. Performance evaluations of systems analysts and programmers will be based on adherence to this policy.

FIGURE 5-2

RECOMMENDED QUICK FIX RESPONSIBILITIES

POSITION FUNCTION	RESPONSIBILITY
DATA PROCESSING MANAGEMENT	o Establish policy o Implement policy o Control use of quick fix methods
COMPUTER OPERATOR	o Identify problem o Document problem o Save needed data
COMPUTER ROOM SUPERVISOR	o Call appropriate people o Assure that needed data is saved o Approve use of privileged instructions o Assist in installing fix
CONTROL GROUP COORDINATOR	o Identify problem o Monitor "fixed" application data
APPLICATION SYSTEM PROJECT MANAGER	o Identify problem o Recommend quick fix solution o Document permanent fix request o Install fix
USER	o Identify problem o Approve or disapprove installing quick fix
VENDOR	o Identify vendor product problems and impact o Provide fix for vendor-caused problems o Install fix for vendor-caused problems

o   Control use of quick-fix methods - The tools and techniques used to implement quick fixes are high-risk tools and techniques. Therefore, they need to be controlled by data processing management.

Computer Operator Responsibility

The computer operator is the individual responsible for running the application. In batch type systems, the computer operator reports to the data processing manager. However, in on-line applications, the operator may be an employee of the user department. Regardless, this individual is the one who normally identifies the problem.

Responsibilities of the individual who identifies the problem include:

o   Identify problem - Recognize a problem has occurred.

o   Document problem - Record the event and its characteristics to help determine the cause of the problem.

o   Save needed data - The operator should reserve all of the evidence produced as a result of the problem. This evidence includes such things as computer files, operator messages, and action taken by the operator.

Computer Room Supervisor

Normally, the computer operator's responsibilities are minimal. The computer room supervisor has the responsibility for initiating action to have the problem fixed. These responsibilities include:

o   Call appropriate people - Inform the individual responsible for making a correction that a problem has occurred. In organizations that have error tracking analysts, the responsibility of the computer room supervisor may be to call the error tracking analyst.

o   Assure that needed data is saved - The supervisor is responsible for determining that the computer operator has performed the job of saving the needed data correctly. Some computer room supervisors use a checklist for this purpose.

o   Approve use of privileged instructions - If privileged instructions or facilities are required to install the fix, the computer room supervisor is the individual who should be controlling access and use of those privileged facilities.

o   Assist in installing fix - Where appropriate the computer room supervisor, and the operator, should help the team install the fix.

Control Group Coordinator Responsibility

The control group controls the accuracy and completeness of processing within the computer center. In many organizations, the group receives input, initiates computer operations, and then reviews the output for reasonableness prior to submitting the output to the user. In some organizations, the control group also has responsibility for correcting some data errors.

The control group may uncover severe problems in reviewing computer output. Thus, they may be the group that identifies and initiates emergency maintenance. The control group has two basic responsibilities:

o   Identify problems - In the fulfillment of their control responsibility, they should be looking for problems in the systems they control.

o   Monitor "fixed" application data - After the problem has been corrected, the control group should put extra emphasis on monitoring the results. (The monitoring function is discussed in more detail in Chapter 12.)

Application System Project Manager

The application system project manager should make sure that the application is operational. Normally, when problems occur the application system project manager is heavily involved in the correction of the problem. If the problem is the result of errors or omissions in the application system, then the project manager has the responsibility for correcting those problems.

Primary responsibilities of the application system project manager include:

o   Identify problem - Continued involvement in the project may cause the project manager to uncover critical problems.

o   Recommend quick fix - If the problem is associated with the application project, the manager must determine and recommend the fix needed to correct the problem.

o   Document permanent fix request - The project manager should initiate action to permanently correct the critical problem.

o   Install fix - If the problem is associated with the application system, the project manager is responsible for making the correction.

User

The user is responsible for the accuracy and completeness of data processed by the application. Thus, any critical problem is a user problem. The two main responsibilities of the user are:

o   Identify problem - The user receives the system output and, thus, is logically in a position to identify problems which have not caused the system to hang up.

o   Approve or disapprove installing its quick fix - The users responsible for the application are also responsible for the type of changes made to the application.

Vendor

Vendors are responsible for the hardware and software supplied to their customers. Thus, if the problem stems from vendor-supplied hardware or software, the vendor should be responsible for making the correction. The responsibilities that the vendor should be given include:

o   Identify the product problems and impact - If the vendor knows of problems through routine analysis from the reports of another customer, the vendor should notify all of their customers of these problems.

o   Provide fix for vendor-caused problems - If the vendor's hardware or software caused the problem, they should be responsible for correcting those problems.

o   Install fix for vendor-caused problem - Not only should the vendor be responsible for developing a fix, but also they should be charged with the responsibility for installing the fix.

ADMINISTRATION OF THE EMERGENCY MAINTENANCE POLICY

The success of the emergency maintenance policy is dependent upon good administrative procedures. Some organizations make one individual responsible for emergency maintenance to ensure the consistency and effectiveness of the procedures. This approach appears to work better than when the policy is administered by many individuals.

The administrative procedures involve the development of forms and manuals to govern emergency maintenance. This is normally a one-time procedure needing few modifications after the procedures have proven effective. Thus, sometimes the procedures are established through a task force specially formed for this purpose.

The administrative procedures for emergency maintenance should be incorporated into a manual which should be disseminated to everyone responsible for maintenance. New systems analysts and programmers should be instructed on these procedures as part of their orientation to the data processing department.

At a minimum, the emergency maintenance administrative procedures should include:

o   Call in list - Who is to be called for critical maintenance and when should they be called.

o   Inventory of privileged instructions - A detailed listing of what are the privileged instructions and how does one gain access to those facilities.

o   Computer room procedures - What happens in a computer room when a hang-up occurs.

o   Data to be saved - What information should be documented and saved when a critical problem occurs.

o   Critical problem report - A form designed to record the pertinent information at the time the problem is identified.

o   Approval - A form providing the information needed by management in order to make a decision on whether or not to approve a quick fix.

o   Control - The methods that management uses to assure that emergency maintenance has been performed properly.

o   Converting temporary to permanent changes - A procedure designed to ensure that temporary changes are preserved.

o   Emergency checklist - A procedure for management to conduct a periodic self-assessment on the adequacy of their critical maintenance program.

Each of these administrative procedures will be discussed individually, and where appropriate, forms will be presented which facilitate the performance of administrative procedures.

CALL IN LIST

Each application system should have a call in list. The objective of the call in list is to identify who should be called and under what circumstances.

The call in list should normally be kept in the computer room or by the error tracking analyst if there is one. When problems occur in an application system, the call in list establishes whether immediate action should be taken. Thus, the call in list defines when people must be called immediately and when the problem can wait until normal working hours for resolution.

The user responsible for the application system is also responsible for preparation of the call in list. However, this is normally prepared in conjunction with the application system project manager. The list should be approved and dated and stay effective until it has been superseded by the new call in list.

A sample call in list form is included as Figure 5-3. The instructions on how to complete the Call In List form are contained on the form's completion instructions sheet.

FIGURE 5-3

CALL IN LIST

APPLICATION SYSTEM NAME		NUMBER	
CALL IN CONDITIONS			
PEOPLE TO CALL			
WHO	ORDER OF CALLING	NAME	TELEPHONE
APPLICATION PERSONNEL	1 2 3 4		
USER PERSONNEL	1 2 3 4		
VENDOR PERSONNEL	1 2 3 4		
APPROVED BY:		DATE	

FORM COMPLETION INSTRUCTIONS

Figure 5-3 - Call In List

FIELD	INSTRUCTIONS FOR ENTERING DATA
o Application system name	The name the application is known by in the data processing department.
o Number	The number that identifies the application system for billing purposes.
o Call in conditions	The specific conditions that result in calling a particular individual. This section should be as specific as possible. At a minimum, it should indicate whether people should be called outside of normal working hours. The conditions also should indicate who should be called when there is a particular problem and what to do if the situation does not fit any other problem condition.
o People to call	The various groups having responsibility for application system problems. Figure 5-3 lists application personnel, user personnel, and vendor personnel. If other groups are involved, they should be listed.
o Order of calling	The sequence in which people should be called. If the first person called does not answer or is unavailable, the second person should be called.
o Name	The name of the individual to be called.
o Telephone	The telephone number of the individual to be called, or other means of reaching the individual.
o Approved by	Normally the supervisor in the user department.
o Date	The date on which the call in list is effective.

INVENTORY OF PRIVILEGED CAPABILITIES

Before an organization can control the use of privileged instructions, it must inventory the instructions and facilities requiring control. Many organizations are uncertain as to the number of capabilities that should be subject to control. Thus, the process may be a two-step process. The first step is to identify the types of facilities that should be controlled, and the second is to list or inventory those capabilities.

Initially, data processing organizations must state what they believe to be high-risk facilities. Among the types that might be included are the instructions or facilities that:

- o   Can directly change machine language

- o   Avoid traditional audit trail

- o   Can change controls such as passwords

- o   Can start up or shut down the operating environment

- o   Are problem diagnosing utilities, can restart or recover operation

- o   Establish file organization structure and reorganize files

Most of these criteria should be self-explanatory to data processing personnel, but some clarification may be desirable for the control modification features. Many data processing people may consider these normal operating facilities; thus, they may not perceive the control implications. However, following a brief orientation to the objectives of the categorization exercise, most data processing personnel should comprehend what is meant by control modification.

Figure 5-4 is a form for inventorying privileged maintenance capabilities. This form both inventories the privileged maintenance facilities and identifies who has access to use these capabilities. The instructions on how to complete the Inventory of Privileged Maintenance Capability form are contained on the form's completion instructions sheet.

COMPUTER ROOM PROCEDURES

The computer room personnel should perform a predetermined series of steps when critical problems occur. These steps should be known to operations personnel and should be practiced routinely when a critical problem occurs. A description of the steps which are part of a hang-up checklist (see Figure 5-5) is contained on the form's completion instructions sheet.

Normally it is easy to record the necessary information about a hang-up at the time it occurs. If additional information is later required, it may not be available, or it may be almost impossible to reconstruct. Some extra time and effort taken at the time the problem occurs usually pays dividends during the analysis phase.

A checklist like that presented in Figure 5-5 should be readily available at the time of a hang-up. The checklist might be supported by the procedures to be followed to accomplish the items on the checklist. For example, if all the parts of core storage are to be dumped, the procedures should explain the utility program to be used and the

FIGURE 5-4

INVENTORY OF PRIVILEGED MAINTENANCE CAPABILITY

IDENTIFICATION NUMBER	NAME OF CAPABILITY	PRIVILEGED CAPABILITY	LOCATION OF CAPABILITY	WHO HAS ACCESS	HOW ACCESS IS RECORDED	HOW ACCESS IS CONTROLLED	COMMENTS

FORM COMPLETION INSTRUCTIONS

Figure 5-4 – Inventory of Privileged Maintenance Capability

FIELD	INSTRUCTIONS FOR ENTERING DATA
o Identification number	The number by which the privileged capability is identified or the facility in which the privileged instruction resides.
o Name of capability	The name by which the privileged program, or feature or instruction, is identified should be used as the name of the facility. If it is an instruction in a security or operation system, both the instruction and the program or system to which that instruction is a part should be identified. The name should be the common name by which it is referred to in the data processing department.
o Privileged capability description	The privileged capability should be described. This section should describe the technical capability and then provide some insight into the data manipulation or other damage that could be caused by the improper use of the privileged maintenance capability. For example, IBM's SUPER ZAP has the capability of inserting machine language instructions into an object program. This could result in a system hang-up if the procedure were improperly performed. Furthermore, it could permit the entry of instructions which permit proper manipulation of data but which fail to leave an audit trail.
o Location of capability	Where the capability program or instruction is physically stored. For example, is it part of the operating system or is it in the program library which must be called prior to use?
o Who has access	The names of the individuals and/or programs that can utilize the privileged capability.
o How access is recorded	The audit trail record of who has access to privileged capability and for what purpose.
o How access is controlled	The procedures that an individual and/or program must follow in order to gain access to the privileged capability.
o Comments	Special concerns about use of the capability, or insight into the type of controls protecting the capability.

FIGURE 5-5

HANG-UP CHECKLIST

APPLICATION SYSTEM _____

- ☐ recorded console registers

- ☐ recorded hang-up message/indication

- ☐ job control language saved

- ☐ special program changes saved

- ☐ version of the problem program saved

- ☐ application tapes/disks saved

- ☐ printed output saved

- ☐ core storage dumped

- ☐ data base segments involved in problem dumped

- ☐ unusual conditions documented

- ☐ program version documented

- ☐ program queues saved

- ☐ on-line terminal status saved

Checklist performed by _____ Date _____

FORM COMPLETION INSTRUCTIONS

Figure 5-5 - Hang-Up Checklist

FIELD	INSTRUCTIONS FOR ENTERING DATA
o Record console registers	Document the status of registers. This information may be valuable for tracing either hardware or software problems.
o Record hang-up message/indication	Document what message or event signified that a hang-up condition had occurred.
o Job control language saved	Save the instructions given to the operating system for the execution of the program or programs.
o Special program changes saved	Save any special program instructions which the operator installed for this run.
o Version of problem programs saved	Save the version of the program which was involved in a hang-up.
o Application tapes/ disks saved	Retain and analyze all the input/output records.
o Printed output saved	Save any output produced by the run prior to the occurrence of the problem.
o Core storage dumped	Dump and analyze the core storage or the part of the core storage containing the program with the problem.
o Data base segments involved in problem dumped	Dump and analyze the data base records utilized by the application system. If they are too extensive, copy the entire data base for analysis purposes.
o Unusual conditions documented	If the computer operator noticed a different processing rhythm or some event that might help with the analysis of the problems, it should be recorded.
o Program version documented	Document all information regarding the number and version of the program operating at the time the problem occurs.
o Program queues saved	In data processing environments, save the input and output queues, and if there is pertinent data at remote sites, save that, too.
o On-line terminal status saved	Document the number of terminals operating and their relationship to the problem.

process to be followed in using the facility. Upon the completion of the procedures, the computer room supervisor should review the performance of the steps to determine if they have have been performed adequately.

If the operating environment is a distributed environment, the process should be coordinated between two or more sites. Those installations that designate a lead site should assign the responsibility to the lead site for ensuring what the procedures are and that they are followed in case of problems.

CRITICAL PROBLEM REPORTING

The critical maintenance approach outlined in this chapter calls for the documentation of a problem prior to the fixing of the problem. Regardless of the ease of the fix or the complexity of the problem, the documentation of the problem should be the first step. This may or may not occur at the point of a hang-up, but should occur shortly thereafter. For example, computer operations personnel may have to pull the bad application to restart computer operations prior to the formal documentation process. However, critical data should be recorded immediately.

The error tracking analyst should be the documentor of critical problems. This individual may do part or all of the problem documentation. It will become apparent that the error tracking analyst may need the assistance of the application project team.

The documentation of an emergency is a two-part process. The first part consists of documenting the problem characteristics and conditions, together with the need to fix that problem. The second part explains how the problem could be fixed and solicits authorization to make that fix.

Emergency Problem Report

The objective of documenting the problem is to provide management with an overview of the seriousness of the problem. It is as easy to panic over an unimportant problem as it is to complacently accept a serious problem. Both of these situations can be avoided through an analysis of the problem. However, this analysis does not go into detail on how to fix the problem.

The critical problem report prepared by the error tracking analyst includes information management can use to evaluate the business risks associated with a problem. (See Figure 5-6.) The information to be collected on the Emergency Problem Report is contained on the form's completion instructions sheet.

AUTHORIZATION OF QUICK FIX

The result of the critical problem report is a decision by management whether or not to proceed with making the fix. Management may wish a second checkpoint after more analysis has been performed on specifically how the fix will be made. The gathering of this information requires more analysis of the problem and the recommendation of a solution.

FIGURE 5-6

| EMERGENCY PROBLEM REPORT | PROBLEM NUMBER | |

| APPLICATION SYSTEM NAME | | NUMBER | |

| PROBLEM DATE | | PROBLEM TIME | |

DESCRIPTION OF PROBLEM:

IMPACT OF PROBLEM

    IF NOT FIXED WITHIN 1 HOUR:

    IF NOT FIXED WITHIN 1 DAY:

    IF NOT FIXED WITHIN 1 WEEK:

ESTIMATE OF QUICK FIX EFFORT AND TIME:

RISK OF QUICK FIX:

RECOMMENDATION:

PREPARED BY:

FORM COMPLETION INSTRUCTIONS

Figure 5-6 - Emergency Problem Report

FIELD	INSTRUCTIONS FOR ENTERING DATA
o Problem number	A sequential number used to identify and keep track of critical problems.
o Application system name	The name by which the application is known.
o Number	The number used to identify the application during operations.
o Problem date	The date on which the problem occurred.
o Problem time	The time of day or shift on which the problem occurred.
o Description of problem	The description would normally consist of a summary of the information provided by computer operations personnel. However, where the problem is encountered in other than computer operations, such as the user area or control group, the information may have to be gathered through interview.
o Impact of problem	Management is vitally concerned with the impact the problem has on the organization. For some applications this is known in advance. For example, when an on-line airline reservation system goes down the airline virtually shuts down. In many applications the severity of the risk will vary based on the time of the day or day of the week in which the problem occurs. For example, payroll processing hang-ups occurring three days before the payroll is due would not cause a severe problem; however, if the system running the checks were to hang up three hours before the checks need to be distributed, then the severity of the problem would be much greater.

Management would like two pieces of information about the business risk. First is a quantification of the risk. Expressions like "very serious" mean different things to different people and have limited value in explaining the severity of a problem. On the other hand, telling management 208 employees will be idled until the system is fixed is providing very explicit and meaningful information. Second, management wants to know how this risk changes over time. What may not be serious this hour, or today, may become very serious tomorrow or in a week.

The time spans during which risks should be analyzed will vary from industry to industry. Some suggestions which are used on the critical problem report form are:
- If not fixed within one hour
- If not fixed within one day
- If not fixed within one week |

FORM COMPLETION INSTRUCTIONS

Figure 5-6 - Emergency Problem Report

FIELD	INSTRUCTION FOR ENTERING DATA
o Estimate of quick fix	Management needs two pieces of information to make any business decision. The first is the benefits -- in the case of a problem the benefits are the avoidance of the risk -- and second is the cost to implement the fix. This cost/benefit analysis provides management with a business evaluation of making the fix. Many data processing personnel, including error tracking analysts, find it difficult to make this estimate on minimal information. However, they must recognize that they are in a better position than data processing management to make the estimate, plus the fact that management recognizes that it is a rough estimate.
o Risk of quick fix	There is a risk of both not fixing a problem and fixing it incorrectly. Management should be apprised of the degree of risk involved in making the fix. This is dependent upon both the method that would be used to fix the problem as well as the skill of the people involved in making quick fixes.
o Recommendation	The error tracking analyst should make a recommendation to management as to the best course of action. Again, many error tracking analysts are reluctant to make these recommendations because of the probability of being wrong. However, the recommendations are useful, and management should be given the benefit of the analysts' experience.
o Prepared by	The name of the error tracking analyst or other individual preparing the form.

The information needed to fix the problem probably requires the assistance of the application project team for application-related problems. Based on personal experience, the error tracking analyst can probably estimate the amount of effort using guidelines derived by analyzing simlar problems. The study by the systems analyst would either confirm or reject the preliminary estimates. The systems analyst may also wish to comment about the severity of the risk. For this reason the project manager should be asked to comment on the critical problem report.

The objective of documenting the authorization process is to present management with a detailed analysis of how the fix will occur. At this point, someone will have considered the risks of fixing or not fixing the problem. Management's second checkpoint is designed to ensure that the fix will be installed on time, within the estimated dollar amount, and with minimal problems.

A suggested form for authorization entitled "Quick Fix Authorization Form" is included as Figure 5-7. The information to be contained on this form is listed on the form's completion instructions sheet.

CONTROLLING EMERGENCY MAINTENANCE

Data processing management has two problems in controlling emergency maintenance. The first problem is that identified and approved changes may not be installed. The second, and perhaps more difficult, problem is that undocumented and unapproved changes may be installed into the application system.

The responsibility to maintain a controlled operating environment resides with data processing management. They are responsible for establishing a system of controls in the critical maintenance area which will ensure adherence to policies and procedures. Management should also take steps to ascertain that those procedures are followed.

Implementing Approved Changes

The most effective way to assure that approved changes are implemented is to uniquely identify each approved change and then determine that the required action is taken. This is a simple three-step process as follows:

o   Step 1 - Establish a sequential numbering system on the forms used to document and approve changes

o   Step 2 - Appoint one individual to be in charge of issuing the sequential numbers

o   Step 3 - Monitor each issued number during the implementation process

The development of a numbering system need not be complex. A logical person to control the process is the error tracking analyst, or if there is none, someone from the data processing control group or the computer operations manager. If prenumbered forms are to be used, the responsible individual can maintain those forms. If numbers are to be issued, the individual can have a sheet of paper with, for example, the numbers 1-100 written on them. As the individual issues the number, he/she merely notes to whom

FIGURE 5-7

QUICK FIX AUTHORIZATION FORM

AUTHORIZATION #

CRITICAL PROBLEM NUMBER		DATE
APPLICATION NAME		NUMBER
FORM PREPARED BY:		
FIX TO BE PERFORMED		
ESTIMATED FIX DATE		ESTIMATED COST
INDIVIDUAL RESPONSIBLE FOR FIX		
METHOD OF INSTALLING FIX		
ABNORMAL INSTALLATION PROCEDURES APPROVED BY:		DATE
TESTING TO BE PERFORMED		
PRECAUTIONS TO PREVENT FIX FROM CAUSING ADDITIONAL PROBLEMS		
PLAN TO MAKE PERMANENT FIX		
ESTIMATED DATE OF PERMANENT FIX		
APPROVED BY:		DATE

FORM COMPLETION INSTRUCTIONS

Figure 5-7 - Quick Fix Authorization Form

FIELD	INSTRUCTIONS FOR ENTERING DATA
o Authorization number	Sequential number used to control the authorization.
o Critical problem number	The number of the critical problem report form.
o Date	Date on which the authorization form is prepared.
o Application number	Name by which the application is known.
o Number	Number to identify the application/program during operation on the computer.
o Form prepared by	The individual developing information included on the form.
o Fix to be performed	A detailed description of what changes will be made in order to achieve the fix. This may differ from the recommendation on the report form since additional systems analysis may have taken place. If processing results will appear in a new format, that should be discussed under this section.
o Estimated fix date	The date or time the fix is to be installed.
o Estimated cost	The amount of dollars or effort required to complete the fix. This may be different from the cost reported on the report form.
o Individual responsible for fix	The name of the systems analyst/programmer who is in charge of installing the fix.
o Method of installing fix	The procedure which the systems analyst/programmer will follow in correcting the problem. For example, a programmer might use SUPER ZAP to place a machine language patch in the program, or the correction may be made by recompiling the program using new source code.
o Abnormal installation procedure approved by	If the method of installing the fix requires the use of a controlled privileged feature, then the use of that feature should be approved.
o Date	The date on which the use of the abnormal installation procedure was approved.

Figure 5-7 - Quick Fix Authorization Form (Cont'd)

FIELD	INSTRUCTIONS FOR ENTERING DATA
o Testing to be performed	A description of the steps the systems analyst/programmer will take to ensure the installed correction will perform as expected. If the programmer is not going through normal testing procedures, then alternative steps for monitoring or examining output should be covered if appropriate.
o Precautions to prevent fix from causing additional problems	The previous segment covering testing assures that the fix will be performed as expected. This regression testing is designed to show that the fix would not inadvertently affect unchanged portions of the application system.
o Plans to make permanent fix	If the installed correction to the problem is temporary in nature, then the systems analyst/programmer should indicate what steps will be taken to permanently install the change.
o Estimated date of permanent fix	The date on which it is expected that the fix will be made permanent.
o Approved by	A member of management responsible for the area in which the problem occurred.
o Date	The date on which the manager authorized the installation of the fix.

the number was issued. Some organizations restart the cycle with 1 after they reach 100. Other organizations use prenumbered change forms. Number sequences should be maintained on both the error reporting form and the error authorization form.

Monitoring changes can be accomplished using a control sheet. The objective of this control sheet is to indicate what steps have been accomplished during the correction process, and when. If the individual in charge of the oversight procedure finds a correction is not progressing at a reasonable rate, the individual should initiate action to determine the status of the correction.

A sample emergency problem control form is illustrated in Figure 5-8. This or a similar form can be used to control the approved change process. This form uses the critical problem number as the method of control. The instructions on how to complete the Emergency Problem Number Control Form are contained on the form's completion instructions sheet.

Controlling Unapproved Changes

Individuals make unapproved changes because they:

o   Are unfamiliar with the control procedure

o   Consider the change too unimportant to warrant following the control procedure

o   Piggyback the change on an approved change

o   Intend to circumvent the control policy

Management can initiate three procedures that have effectively reduced the installation of unapproved changes. These procedures are:

o   Procedure 1 - Publish management policy

If management feels strongly about the approval process for changes, it is very effective if it makes that sentiment known to the employees of the data processing department. An important part of this process is quick and fair punishment for policy violators.

o   Procedure 2 - Monitor the environment

The computer operating environment provides records on most of the events that occur in that environment. Management should monitor the events to determine that only unauthorized changes occur. Management should become aware of most unauthorized attempts through analysis of operating system logs.

o   Procedure 3 - Violation audit

Members of the data processing department and/or the organization's audit department should periodically conduct an investigation to determine if violations have occurred.

FIGURE 5-8

EMERGENCY PROBLEM NUMBER CONTROL FORM

Emergency Problem Number	Application System Affected	Problem Dates and Action Taken				
		Documented	App'd	Approval Number	Disapproved	Installed

FORM COMPLETION INSTRUCTIONS

Figure 5-8 - Emergency Problem Number Control Form

FIELD	INSTRUCTIONS FOR ENTERING DATA
o Emergency problem number	The number issued is a sequential control number issued for use on the critical problem identification form.
o Application system affected	The name and/or number of the application as recorded on the critical problem report form.
o Problem dates and action taken	The dates during which the correction process occurred. This is divided into the following dates: - Documented date - the date in which the critical problem report on form was completed. - Approval date - the date on which the quick fix authorization was approved for implementation. - Approval number - the number assigned to the quick fix approval form. - Disapproved date - the date on which the reported problem was disapproved for change. - Installed date - the date on which the fix was placed into production.

FORMALIZING INSTALLED CRITICAL MAINTENANCE

The emergency maintenance process is not complete until the needed change has been permanently installed in the application system. Many times the emergency maintenance process results in the installation of a patch which must then be converted into a permanent change. This may involve incorporating the patch into the source code or it may involve additional analysis resulting in an improved solution.

The process of permanently correcting a quick fix should follow normal maintenance procedures. The process should be formalized according to procedures outlined in Chapters 6-10. The process commences when someone initiates a request for a permanent fix. This is the last step of the emergency maintenance process.

An example of the form that can be used to request a permanent installation of the temporary fix is illustrated in Figure 5-9. The information on the form consists of information needed to make the temporary patch permanent and is contained on the form's completion instructions sheet.

MONITORING EMERGENCY MAINTENANCE

Periodically management should assess the effectiveness of the emergency maintenance procedures. This process is designed to uncover weaknesses in the current procedures and to make recommendations for improved emergency procedures. The Emergency Maintenance Checklist (Figure 5-10) should be used by data processing management for analysis purposes.

SUMMARY

Unplanned problems will continue to plague data processing operations. While improved systems development and maintenance procedures should continue to reduce the number of these unplanned problems, they will not eliminate them. Therefore, data processing management must develop policies and procedures on how to handle these unplanned critical problems when they occur.

The successful resolution of emergency problems is simplified if organizations have an effective strategy for providing quick and effective fixes to the problem. This strategy should include a thorough documentation and analysis of the problem prior to the implementation of a temporary or permanent fix. Armed with the proper information, management can select the best solution among the available alternatives. Without having the necessary information, management cannot address a critical problem from a business perspective.

The roles and responsibilities of parties involved in critical maintenance should be established. The user should have the authority for determining whether or not to make a temporary fix to the problem. Again, when adequate information is available, the solution normally becomes obvious.

This chapter has recommended the use of the error tracking analyst in the documentation and preliminary analysis of critical problems. Included within the chapter have been the policies, procedures, and forms that can be used to achieve those goals.

The error tracking analyst can also monitor the implementation of the temporary change so that problems are not lost only to recur later.

Management should implement procedures which prevent (or detect) the making of unauthorized changes. They should publicize and then enforce this policy by punishing violators.

FIGURE 5-9

REQUEST TO FORMALIZE INSTALLED QUICK FIX

MAINTENANCE REQUEST NUMBER	EMERGENCY PROBLEM NUMBER		
APPLICATION NAME		NUMBER	

DESCRIPTION OF INSTALLED FIX

PROGRAM AFFECTED

DATA AFFECTED

SUGGESTED ACTION TO MAKE FIX PERMANENT

CONSTRAINTS IMPOSED BY QUICK FIX

TEMPORARY FIX PERFORMED BY		DATE
PERMANENT CHANGE APPROVED BY		DATE
COMMENTS		PERMANENT CHANGE NUMBER

FORM COMPLETION INSTRUCTIONS

Figure 5-9 - Request to Formalize Installed Quick Fix

FIELD	INSTRUCTIONS FOR ENTERING DATA
o Maintenance request number	A sequential number used to control the installation of permanent maintenance requests.
o Emergency problem number	The number assigned to the emergency problem used to cross-reference information gathered during the identification and correction of the critical maintenance.
o Application name	The name by which the application is known in the data processing department.
o Number	The number used to identify the application and/or programs by the operating system.
o Description of installed fix	A brief description summarizing the correction(s) made. More information can be obtained by referring to the quick fix authorization form and the supporting material to that form.
o Program affected	The program or programs in which patches have been installed.
o Data affected	Any effect made on data that may impact the permanent correction process. For example, information which needs to be modified or removed may have been inserted in records.
o Suggested action to make fix permanent	Recommendations by the group installing the temporary fix as to what is needed to install the fix permanently. In some situations, necessary source code may be attached.
o Constraints imposed by quick fix	Any processing constraints, or data use constraints, imposed during the installation of a temporary fix.
o Temporary fix performed by	The name of the individual who made the temporary fix. This is given for reference purposes in case questions need to be answered.

Figure 5-9 - Request to Formalize Installed Quick Fix (Cont'd)

FIELD	INSTRUCTIONS FOR ENTERING DATA
o Date	The date on which the temporary fix was installed.
o Permanent change approved by	The name of user management approving the permanent fix.
o Date	The date on which approval to install the permanent fix was given.
o Comments	Comments regarding the permanent fix by either the group requesting the change or by user management approving the change.
o Permanent change number	A cross-reference to the normal change control procedure forms and methods of controlling the installation of normal change.

FIGURE 5-10

EMERGENCY MAINTENANCE CHECKLIST

NUMBER	MANAGEMENT QUESTION	RESPONSE			COMMENTS
		YES	NO	N/A	
1.	Has the department issued an emergency maintenance policy?				
2.	Must problems be documented before any corrective action can be taken?				
3.	Is approval required for the use of privileged facilities?				
4.	Must user management approve any change to an application system before that change is installed?				
5.	Does data processing management ensure that the temporary fix procedures and standards are followed during the temporary fix process?				
6.	Have procedures been established to initiate a permanent change for each temporary fix?				
7.	Has a rerun priority been established in the event an application system does not successfully complete the processing?				
8.	Has the role of all individuals involved in the temporary fix process been established?				
9.	Has responsibility of the vendors of both hardware and software been established, explained and accepted by the vendors?				
10.	Has a call in list been established in the event emergencies occur?				
11.	Does the call in list include all involved parties?				
12.	Does the call in list provide alternates in case the desired individual cannot be reached?				

FIGURE 5-10

EMERGENCY MAINTENANCE CHECKLIST (Cont'd)

NUMBER	MANAGEMENT QUESTION	RESPONSE			COMMENTS
		YES	NO	N/A	
13.	Are privileged maintenance facilities inventoried?				
14.	Does the inventory identify where the facility is located?				
15.	Does the inventory indicate who can use the privileged maintenance facility?				
16.	Has a procedure been established in computer operations regarding the steps to be taken in the event of a hang-up?				
17.	Has a procedure been established on how to document critical maintenance problems?				
18.	Does the documentation of problems include the impact of the problem on the organization?				
19.	Does the problem documentation include an estimate of the time and effort required to fix the problem?				
20.	Is a procedure established to document the authorization to install a temporary fix?				
21.	Is the project leader required to identify how a temporary fix will be tested?				
22.	Is one individual appointed to be responsible for overseeing temporary fixes?				
23.	Are procedures established to monitor the installation of temporary fixes so that a change cannot be lost?				
24.	Does management establish procedures to prevent and detect the installation of unapproved temporary changes?				

FIGURE 5-10

EMERGENCY MAINTENANCE CHECKLIST

NUMBER	MANAGEMENT QUESTION	RESPONSE			COMMENTS
		YES	NO	N/A	
25.	Is a numbering system established to control temporary fixes?				

Chapter 6
Phase 1—Record and Assign Phase

CHAPTER OVERVIEW

The record and assign phase commences with the identification of a need and concludes with the assignment of the responsibility for the implementation of that need to a specific individual. The two parts of the phase are to record the attributes of the need and then through analysis to assign the implementation to the group best qualified to satisfy the need. The assignment can be to the user, the application system personnel, the operating environment, or to the vendor. The documentation of a system maintenance need performed during this phase establishes the parameters for the change. If a user wants X, and it is documented as Y, then Y will be installed. The attention to detail in this first phase of maintenance is essential.

This chapter provides forms and checklists to help in the recording of problems and the assigning of resonsibilities for implementation. This chapter also includes the duties and responsibilities of an error tracking analyst.

PHASE 1 CONTROL CONCERNS

If all steps of the maintenance process were performed correctly, there would be no need for controls. Management establishes controls in order to reduce the number of errors and omissions. Management must anticipate problems before it can assess controls. Until the control concerns are identified, there is no logical basis for the design, implementation, and monitoring of controls.

The control concerns that need to be addressed in the record and assign phase include:

   o   Will problems/enhancements/new requirements be identified early enough to minimize the probable loss?

Problems and needs can be identified by:

   -   Operators detecting a change in processing rhythm

   -   Data entry people questioning the reasonableness of input

   -   Control personnel questioning the reasonableness of output

   -   Customers complaining about the system

   -   Programmers identifying programming and system problems

   -   Vendors noting problems in their own software

   o   Was the wrong problem/requirement/enhancement identified?

People frequently speak in terms of symptoms as oppposed to causes. If the symptom is treated rather than the cause, the solution may be inappropriate. For example, a patient reports symptoms to a doctor. The patient might tell the doctor that he/she has a severe pain in his/her left arm. If the doctor only treated the symptom by putting the arm in a sling, the real cause, which might be heart disease, could go undetected for some period of time. The longer the cause of a problem remains undetected, the greater the probability of serious problems.

    o   <u>Will the analysis identify the cause?</u>

Symptoms may be associated with multiple causes. During the analysis process, determine the most likely cause in order to satisfy the need. If the analysis process is cut short, you may miss the actual cause. As a result, during the rest of the maintenance process you might deal with the symptom, not the cause.

    o   <u>Will the wrong individual be given maintenance responsibility?</u>

At the conclusion of the record and assign phase of maintenance, a specific individual is assigned to implement the need. Before this assignment can occur, someone must document and analyze the facts to determine which individual or group is best qualified to satisfy that need. This normally is a process which assigns responsibilities to manual systems, application systems, and operating systems. If the wrong group is given responsibility — for example, the application system people when the problem is really in the operating system — then time and effort will be wasted.

This chapter addresses these control concerns. The checklists, forms, and procedures included in the chapter are controls that can be implemented by management to lessen the probability of loss. The individuals responsible for developing the procedures for this phase of the maintenance life cycle should continually keep in mind these control concerns and address them through incorporating the methods and procedures into the maintenance process.

If problems can be anticipated and caught before they can become serious, or caught before they become problems, the ideal maintenance solution will have been achieved.

ANTICIPATING APPLICATION SYSTEM NEEDS

If people know the major types of errors, new requirements and enhancements, they will have more insight into application system maintenance needs. Good system design anticipates as many of these needs as possible. Among the effective methods for anticipating maintenance needs are the following:

    o   Anticipatory audit/edits - Designing routines either to verify that the input is correct or to anticipate and modify incorrect input.

    o   Warning messages - Asking people to verify the correctness of processing when predetermined logic indicates that the processing may not be correct.

    o   Simple accounting proofs - Verifying that the old balance, plus additions, minus deletions, equals the new balance.

    o   Control totals - Verifying processing against predetermined totals.

The development of controls which anticipate problems is possible if systems development or systems maintenance project teams identify potential problems. Many of the types of potential problems and unspecified needs discussed are common to all systems, although some will be unique to specific applications. The systems maintenance project leader should attempt to identify as many unspecified maintenance needs as possible. This list then becomes the basis for developing procedures and controls to anticipate these needs and attempt to satisfy them quickly. These unspecified needs can be thought of as <u>symptoms</u> of problems whose cause has yet to be determined.

The type of symptoms that need to be identified include:

- o   Internal table limitations

- o   File limitations

- o   Processing turnaround times

- o   Field size limits

- o   Cost per unit of work

- o   Use of features/routines

- o   Customer complaints

- o   Time to install changes

- o   Input error rates

The above symptoms by themselves have little value. For example, how much it costs to process a transaction is a meaningless piece of data until that piece of data can be put into the proper perspective. The systems maintenance project team can anticipate a cost problem and a potential performance improvement change request when processing costs exceed what users expect them to be.

The systems maintenance project leader should attempt to use a checklist to identify as many symptoms of needs as possible. The basic checklist might be standardized for the department and then modified for each application where appropriate. An Anticipated Need Identification Checklist form is illustrated in Figure 6-1. The information to be entered on the form is contained on the form's completion instructions sheet.

STEPS INVOLVED IN RECORD AND ASSIGN PHASE

The objective of this phase is to make the proper person responsible for satisfying an identified need. This phase of the maintenance process should be performed by an error tracking analyst or equivalent. The tendency when application personnel analyze problems is that they first attempt to correct that problem within the application system, and if that can't be accomplished they spend more time looking elsewhere for the source of the problem. The error tracking analyst should be skilled in all areas of the computer environment, including applications.

The record and assign phase is divided into four steps. These steps commence with an event or condition which leads someone to believe there is an unsatisfied need. In actual practice, the error tracking analyst may perform several of the following steps simultaneously:

FIGURE 6-1

ANTICIPATED NEED IDENTIFICATION CHECKLIST

Symptom #	SYMPTOM	REQUIRES INVESTIGATION			COMMENTS
		YES	NO	N/A	

FORM COMPLETION INSTRUCTIONS

Figure 6-1 - Anticipated Need Identification Checklist

FIELD	INSTRUCTIONS FOR ENTERING DATA
o Symptom #	A sequentially increasing number used to identify each need symptom.
o Symptom	A condition or statistic that indicates that needs are not being satisfied in the application system. These needs suggest impending changes.
o Requires investigation	If the checklist uses general applicable systems, then this column would be used. A "yes" indicates that the symptom is applicable in this case; a "no" indicates it is not applicable; and a "not applicable (N/A)" response indicates that the symptom is not relevant in this situation. If the checklist is prepared for a specific application, then the "requires investigation" column is not necessary.
o Comments	A brief description of the symptom and how it might indicate that a need is not being satisfied.

FIGURE 6-2

PHASE 1

RECORD AND ASSIGN

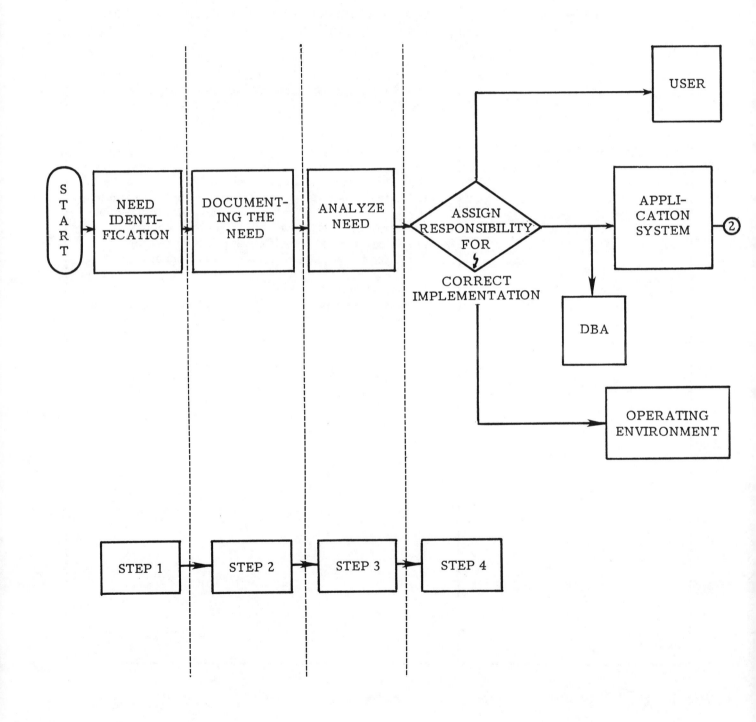

o   Step 1 - Problem identification

o   Step 2 - Documenting the need

o   Step 3 - Analyzing needs

o   Step 4 - Assigning responsibility for implementation

These four steps are illustrated in Figure 6-2. These steps, together with the checklists and forms needed to execute the steps, are discussed individually.

STEP 1 - NEED IDENTIFICATION

A need consists of problems to be corrected, new requirements to be implemented, or enhancements to be installed. All three types of needs occur over a period of time in every application system. Therefore, management should clearly establish procedures and steps for identifying those needs.

There are two general approaches to identifying needs. The first approach is a passive approach in which the project team waits to be notified that a need has occurred. This approach requires minimal time and effort because people just wait for something to happen. The second approach is an active approach in which someone anticipates needs before someone else formally identifies them. With the active approach, concerned people attempt to anticipate and satisfy a need before it becomes a problem.

The active approach is a two-step process. The first step consists of attempting to identify the types of problems that may occur and then periodically checking to determine if they have occurred. Many of these anticipation checks have been automated using the newer technologies. Some general categories of needs are listed in Figure 6-3. This figure discusses types of problems or needs in each of the following four categories:

o   __Error category__

   -    Software interface: Software systems such as operating systems, data base management systems, and communication systems improve the performance of application systems. The power of these software systems is utilized through the passing of parameters or through interfacing with the software systems. Incorrect interfaces can lead to problems.

   -    Data error: Using data values inconsistent with the requirements of application systems can result in incorrect processing or termination of processing. For example, if a field should contain numeric values, but actually contains alphabetics, incorrect processing will result.

   -    Program/system error: The processing rules are implemented through program instructions assembled into application programs. If the program code is inconsistent with computer language requirements, or if it fails to follow specifications, incorrect processing can result. In addition, the processing can terminate.

FIGURE 6-3

```
┌─────────────────────────────────────────────────────────────┐
│                                                             │
│  CATEGORIES OF PROBLEMS/REQUIREMENTS/ENHANCEMENTS           │
│                                                             │
│                                                             │
│                        ERRORS                               │
│                                                             │
│                   Software interface                        │
│                                                             │
│                   Data error                                │
│                                                             │
│                   Program/system error                      │
│                                                             │
│                   Operator error                            │
│                                                             │
│                   Hardware/software                         │
│                                                             │
│                                                             │
│                   NEW REQUIREMENTS                           │
│                                                             │
│                   Input                                     │
│                                                             │
│                   Processing                                │
│                                                             │
│                   Storage                                   │
│                                                             │
│                   Audit trail                               │
│                                                             │
│                   Output                                    │
│                                                             │
│                   Subsystem                                 │
│                                                             │
│                                                             │
│                    ENHANCEMENTS                             │
│                                                             │
│                   Usability                                 │
│                                                             │
│                   System performance                        │
│                                                             │
│                   Environmental performance                 │
│                                                             │
│                   Manual interface                          │
│                                                             │
│                   Deletion of a feature                     │
│                                                             │
│                GOVERNMENT REGULATIONS                        │
│                                                             │
│                   Laws                                      │
│                                                             │
└─────────────────────────────────────────────────────────────┘
```

-   Operator error: Application system operators can either be computer room operators or users stationed at terminals. In either case, these individuals are provided procedures to follow in using the application system. If they don't follow the procedures for the application system in the correct sequence using the correct process, the results may be inaccurate. In addition, they can terminate operations.

-   Hardware/software: If vendor-provided hardware and software malfunction, they can cause application systems problems. Furthermore, insufficient training in the use of vendor hardware/software can result in the faulty generation of software and the misuse of hardware.

o   New requirements category

-   Input: The origination, authorization, and conversion of source data to computer media. The process normally involves customers of the system who have transactions to process, user personnel who review and authorize those transactions, and data entry personnel who convert the information to computer media.

-   Processing: Matching, merging, and updating of computer files; comparing values and the computations performed on the data; verifying that input data meets systems specifications; and reformatting data. This segment of application processing is performed by computer programs using system rules and specifications.

-   Storage: The retention of computer data on media that is machine readable.

-   Audit trail: The logical capability to trace transactions from the source of origination to the organization's financial statements and from the financial statements back to the supporting source documents. Audit trails are required by law (e.g., Internal Revenue Service rulings); they substantiate the values in the financial statements; and they support the validity of processing.

-   Output: Preparing report formats, reformatting computer data, accumulating totals in report formats, and outputting that information on the desired media. Output media includes paper, cathode-ray tubes, microfilm, and graphics.

-   Subsystems: Special procedures or hardware utilized to perform some special technique or process on computer data. Examples include cryptography, reorganization of disk files and data bases, and system modeling.

o   Enhancement category

-   Usability: The value of the application system in the day-to-day operation of the user organization. One measure of the usability of a system is whether additional systems are necessary to support user operations. The more manual processes required, the less value the application system may have for the user.

-   System performance: The efficiency, effectiveness, and economy with which the system performs its tasks. Performance can be measured against a standard or against other systems of like size and complexity.

- Environmental performance: The effectiveness, efficiency, and economy of the structure and procedures by which people must work so that the results of processing will be performed in accordance with the intents of management.

- Manual interface: The mix of work between people and equipment and the interchange of information between the two. Also involved is the effectiveness of the flow of work.

- Deletion of a feature: The elimination of a superfluous hardware, software, or application processing capability.

o Government regulations category

New application system requirements frequently develop out of governmental regulations and/or interpretations of those regulations. In some industries, such as banking and insurance, a significant percent of application system maintenance efforts deal with implementing new and revised governmental regulations.

Some organizations have established government regulation analysts who are responsible for monitoring government regulations. Their responsibility is to interpret regulations for application systems analysts. As such, these government regulation analysts generate, or identify, needs to be implemented in application systems.

The type of government regulation that affects computerized applications include:

- Federal privacy laws

- State privacy laws

- Federal Wage and Hour Act

- Manufacturing Practices Act

- Equal Opportunity Employment Act

- Occupational Health and Safety Act

- Foreign Corrupt Practices Act

- Pension regulations

A form for government regulation analysts or their equivalents to complete is illustrated in Figure 6-4. The information contained in this form is contained on the form's completion instructions sheet.

This section has dealt with governmental regulations, but it would be equally applicable to other requirements imposed by outside sources on an organization's application systems. Other regulatory groups imposing requirements on organizations are:

- American Institute of Certified Public Accountants through their Statement on Auditing Standards

FIGURE 6-4

GOVERNMENT REGULATION REQUIREMENT

GOVERNMENT REGULATION

REQUIREMENT IMPOSED

APPLICATIONS AFFECTED

PENALTIES FOR NONCOMPLIANCE

DATE REQUIRED _____

CONTACT FOR
INFORMATION_____ DEPT_____ PHONE #_____

PREPARED BY_____ DATE _____

FORM COMPLETION INSTRUCTIONS

Figure 6-4 - Government Regulation Requirement

FIELD	INSTRUCTIONS FOR ENTERING DATA
o Government regulation	The name, date, and other pertinent information needed to identify the specific piece of regulation. Sometimes it may be useful to attach the regulation to the form. Frequently it is best for the government regulation analyst to interpret the regulation for the application systems analyst.
o Requirement imposed	State the imposed requirement as a positive system need. Because noncompliance with governmental requirements normally incurs penalties, state specifications for implementing the regulations clearly enough that the application systems analyst cannot misinterpret them.
o Applications affected	Specify all the applications in which the requirement must be implemented or monitored. In a later step, all of these applications will become responsible for implementing the new or revised regulations.
o Penalties for noncompliance	Outline the penalties for noncompliance. Knowing the penalties will help the systems analyst determine the priority for implementation. Further, it will explain to the analyst why the regulations must be followed exactly.
o Date required	Either the date on which the organization wants the need implemented or the date on which the regulation becomes effective.
o Contact for information	The name of the individual, department, or function whom the application systems analyst should contact or get more information about the government regulation. The more common contacts are the government regulation analyst, the corporate legal department, other corporate lawyers, the auditing department, the organization's independent auditors, or the federal agency responsible for the regulation.
o Department	Location of the contact.
o Phone number	Telephone number of the contact.
o Prepared by	The name of the individual preparing the information on this form.
o Date	The date the form was completed.

- Financial Accounting Standards Board through accounting procedures and requirements

- Cost Accounting Standards Board through cost accounting procedures

- Industry associations through the development of industry practices and standards

STEP 2 - DOCUMENTING THE NEED

Once the organization has identified the need, it is imperative that it record precisely what is needed to avoid misunderstandings. Many project leaders shortcut the recording phase because they feel they can perform the maintenance without taking the extra time and effort to document the need. This approach works if the project leader understands the need and will not forget about satisfying the need. Project leaders don't want users to have to remind them that maintenance personnel "forgot" to take care of a need.

Specific objectives of the documenting step include:

o   Documenting what conditions caused the need

o   Specifying precisely what is required to satisfy the need

o   Indicating what people and what projects will be affected once the need is satisfied

o   Indicating what data and what programs will be affected by the implementation of the need

A form to document the maintenance need is illustrated in Figure 6-5. Data processing people should complete the form. The information contained on the form is shown on the form's completion instructions sheet.

User Version - Documentation of Maintenance Need

Many application system users wish to request changes on their own. Prepare a form for this purpose. An example of a user need identification form is illustrated as Figure 6-6. The form is designed to collect information needed to make an application system change. However, the form illustrated is a simple version designed for unsophisticated users. As users become more knowledgeable, the complexity of the form should increase. Items that might be added to the form include:

o   Programs affected

o   Data files affected

o   Fields affected

o   Computer processing required

o   Manual support needed

FIGURE 6-5

DATA PROCESSING VERSION

DOCUMENTATION OF MAINTENANCE NEED

APPLICATION
NAME _____ APPLICATION
NUMBER _____ FORM
NUMBER_____

IDENTIFIED/REQUESTED BY _____ DEPARTMENT_____

UNFAVORABLE SYMPTOMS OF CURRENT SYSTEM

DESCRIPTION OF NEED

AFFECTED AREAS

- ☐ OPERATIONS PROCEDURES
- ☐ DATA RETENTION
- ☐ OPERATIONS PERFORMANCE
- ☐ PROGRAMS
- ☐ JOB CONTROL

- ☐ APPLICATION PERFORMANCE
- ☐ ACCURACY OF DATA
- ☐ SECURITY/PRIVACY
- ☐ OPERATING SOFTWARE
- ☐ DOCUMENTATION

PROGRAMS/SYSTEM AFFECTED_____

DATA FILES AFFECTED_____

PREPARED BY _____ DATE _____

FORM COMPLETION INSTRUCTIONS

Figure 6-5 – Documentation of Maintenance Need
Data Processing Version

FIELD	INSTRUCTIONS FOR ENTERING DATA
o Application name	The name by which the application is known.
o Application number	A number that identifies the application and production.
o Form number	The sequential number identifying the form so that no requests will be lost.
o Identified/requested by	The name of the individual who either identified or requested the change.
o Department	The organizational unit in which the individual who identified/requested the change is located.
o Unfavorable symptoms of current system	This section can be used both to describe what needs correcting and to discuss problems indirectly associated with the need.
o Description of need	Explanation of the problem.
o Affected areas	Identification of the areas in which the symptoms reside. Check all applicable areas.
o Programs/systems affected	Indicate all programs and systems which this need impacts. This is a preliminary indication of where to begin the analysis process. In a hang-up situation, this would identify the system and program where the system terminated.
o Data files affected	Indicate all the data files affected by this need. Again, this is used as a starting point in the analysis process.
o Prepared by	The name of the individual who prepared the form.
o Date	The date on which the form was prepared.

o   Alternative implementation solutions

The information contained on the simplified user version of the Documentation of Maintenance Need form is described on the form's completion instructions sheet.

STEP 3 - ANALYZE NEED

The most technically complex step of the record and assign phase is the analysis step. The objectives of this step are twofold:

1.   Identify the cause of the problem or pinpoint where to install a new requirement or enhancement.

2.   Identify the individual or function who should implement the need.

The analysis function should be performed by an individual familiar with analysis techniques, and with the operating environment and application system in which the need appears to reside. This normally falls to the more experienced people in the data processing department.

The maintenance analysis process consists of the following seven parts:

o   Part 1 - Obtain evidence

The first part is to gather as much factual information as possible about the need. For a problem, this may involve detailed listings of errors; descriptions of memory dumps; interviews with concerned parties; and data processing department forms similar to those outlined in Steps 1 and 2 of this phase for new requirements and enhancements to normal system specifications.

o   Part 2 - Organize evidence

Evidence appears as unassembled pieces of a jigsaw puzzle. The analysis process requires assembling the evidence into a logical structure. The type of processes that have proved effective in organizing evidence include:

-    Identifying each piece of evidence by a structured number.

-    Categorizing evidence by area of origination, such as computer programming and storage, interview sheets, output reports, etc.

-    Structuring data by common areas such as data relating to report; data relating to hang-up in program; or data relating to the use of information by customers of the system.

-    Identifying data relationships or indicating what evidence is related to other evidence, such as a relationship between a problem, a computer program, and the customer of the application.

The key to the analysis process is structuring the evidence in a meaningful manner. It may take several iterations before the evidence is placed together in a logical pattern.

o   Part 3 - Compare with known symptoms

The same types of problems and needs tend to repeat over and over again. There may be variations, but they can be traced to a common cause or method of implementation. Although data processing organizations plead that "if you must make a mistake, let it be a new one," we know from experience that some problems recur. Maintenance people should compare known problems, requirements, and enhancements with the evidence they have gathered about this problem.

o   Part 4 - Investigate unknown symptoms

New problems and requirements are more difficult to solve than ones that have been solved previously. Therefore, when a problem or need appears to be unique, additional investigations are necessary. Contrary to popular belief, investigations are not exciting; they frequently involve repetitive and monotonous processes such as extensive paper debugging of application programs. The types of techniques effective for investigating unknown symptoms include:

-     Brainstorming potential causes and solutions

-     Talking with vendors and other concerned individuals

-     Organizing a team to analyze the problem (a single individual is more likely to overlook the problem)

-     Simulating conditions in an attempt to identify the cause

-     Eliminating suspicious data records and rerunning the application

-     Rerunning the application, making no changes in case the problem was associated with a temporary malfunction

-     Paper debugging

-     Rerunning the program using the trace option and/or the dump option

-     Simulating the need independently of the application to determine if there is a flaw in the logic

o   Part 5 - Develop cause/solution hypothesis

After comparing the evidence with known symptoms, the investigator should determine a probable cause. The probable cause is considered to be the hypothesis. A hypothesis is an assumption that needs to be proved before the true cause is established and implementation begun.

In some cases, the hypothesis will be the actual solution or cause. However, in the case of more difficult problems, investigators may have to develop several hypotheses before determining the best solution. Then they use a "what if" scenario in order to identify some of the higher probable causes.

FIGURE 6-6

USER VERSION

DOCUMENTATION OF MAINTENANCE NEED

APPLICATION NAME _____	APPLICATION NUMBER _____	FORM NUMBER ____

UNFAVORABLE SYMPTOMS OF CURRENT SYSTEM

DESCRIPTION OF NEEDS

DATE CHANGE NEEDED_____

PRIORITY OF CHANGE _____

FORM IS AUTHORIZATION TO:

☐ DISCUSS NEED
☐ ESTIMATE COST TO IMPLEMENT
☐ IMPLEMENT CHANGE

COMMENTS

APPROVED BY_____ DEPT_____DATE_____ CHARGE NUMBER_____

FORM COMPLETION INSTRUCTIONS

Figure 6-6 – Documentation of Maintenance Need
User Version

FIELD	INSTRUCTIONS FOR ENTERING DATA
o Application name	The name by which the application is known.
o Application number	The number used to identify the application during processing.
o Form number	The sequential number identifying the form so that no requests will be lost.
o Unfavorable symptoms of current system	This is a section for discussing preliminary and secondary problems in the current system.
o Description of need	Explanation of the problem.
o Date change needed	The date on which the user would like the change implemented.
o Priority of change	The importance of the change.
o Form is authorization to	The action the user desires. The most common options are: - Discuss needs – The user uses the completed form as a basis for discussing the change. - Estimate cost to implement – The user wants to know how much time, effort, or dollars are required to implement the change. Alternative solutions might be provided. - Implement the change – The change must be installed so no discussion or estimates are necessary.
o Comments	Additional information that may be helpful to the data processing people who will have the responsibility for implementing the change.
o Approved by	The individual approving the change.
o Department	The department to which the approver belongs.
o Date	The date on which the change was requested.
o Charge number	The accounting number to which the charges for making the change are to be accumulated.

o   <u>Part 6 - Testing the hypothesis</u>

Unless the investigators can be certain that the hypothesis is the true cause, they should test the hypothesis. The most common testing approaches are:

1.   Install and run a quick change to determine if the need is satisfied. If the problem condition is corrected, then the hypothesis tested is the correct hypothesis.

2.   Simulate the conditions in a test environment to determine if the need is satisfied. If the proper results are produced in a test environment, then the hypothesis tested is the correct hypothesis.

o   <u>Part 7 - Document cause</u>

The end product of the analysis process is the documentation of the cause that when changed will result in a need being satisfied. The analysis of the cause can be presented two ways. The first way is to make a positive statement as to what must be done to satisfy the need. The second method is to negatively present why the cause resulted in the unfavorable condition. Sometimes it is more appropriate to present an uncovered problem in terms of a negative perspective, while it is best to present a new requirement or enhancement from a positive perspective.

STEP 4 - ASSIGN RESPONSIBILITY FOR CORRECT IMPLEMENTATION

The last step of Phase 2 is to assign responsibility for the implementation of the need. Generally, the individuals responsible for implementing a need and their area of responsibility include:

o   <u>User</u> - The individual responsible for the application system. Usually the user is also responsible for implementing manual procedures that either originate, enter, or use application system data.

o   <u>Application system project manager</u> - The person who develops the computerized segment of the application and ensures that the programs within the application system remain operational.

o   <u>Customer</u> - An individual who is normally a third party in the origination or use of application data; for example, the customer of an organization who must work with the computer's order entry application in order to obtain service from the organization. Customer-related problems can be corrected by the customers if they have more education and training.

o   <u>Software programmers</u> - The individuals responsible for the generation and maintenance of most vendor-produced software systems. Correcting problems in software systems such as operating systems, communication systems, utilities, and report writers becomes the responsibility of the systems programmer.

o   <u>Vendor</u> - The organization that sold or leased hardware or software to the organization should correct problems directly attributable to faulty hardware or software.

o   General management - If problems are caused by noncompliance with management policies and procedures, maintenance people can either force the people involved to comply with the policies and procedures, or management can change the policies and procedures to make them comply with the way the tasks are being performed by the application system.

The assignment process involves documenting the needs analysis. A form designed for this purpose is illustrated in Figure 6-7 entitled Needs Analysis and Estimation Request. The objective of this form is to request that a specific individual or function conduct further analysis and cost/benefit estimation in order to satisfy needs. It is assumed that in addition to this form, other pertinent evidence will be submitted to the designated individual. The information contained on the form illustrated in Figure 6-7 is explained on the form's completion instructions sheet.

FEEDBACK ON PHASE 1 ACTIVITIES

One of the important aspects of controlling any process is getting feedback. Feedback provides the information needed to monitor an application. The information is produced by feedback mechanisms which are minireport writers designed to produce data about an operation for use in analyzing the operation.

Applications are activities subject to control. Each application introduces new risks into the organization. These risks are reduced to an acceptable level through the implementation of controls. To be effective, controls need to be continually adjusted.

Management has the responsibility of monitoring the maintenance process. To fulfill this responsibility, management needs feedback mechanisms.

During each phase of the maintenance life cycle, the feedback appropriate to that phase will be discussed. Chapter 12, which discusses monitoring the maintenance process, will explain how that information can be used by management to monitor the maintenance process.

Record and Assign Phase Feedback Information

The type of data valuable for monitoring the record and assign phase is described below, and summarized in Figure 6-8, which lists the feedback data, a suggested source for obtaining that data, and then the purpose for which the data can be used in monitoring the record and assign phase of the maintenance process.

o   Changes made without record and assign process

Conditions occur which cause people to violate normal processing procedures. These can be emergency conditions, inexperienced personnel, or uncooperative staff. Changes to programs should be monitored to determine how frequently unapproved changes are made.

o   Hours to record/hours to assign

Feedback should monitor how much effort is devoted to the record and assign processes. This will point out how effective the procedures are and will help data processing

FIGURE 6-7

NEED ANALYSIS AND ESTIMATION REQUEST

(NOTE: DOCUMENTATION OF NEED FORM SHOULD BE ATTACHED)

SENT TO_____	NEED IDENTIFICATION #_____

RE:
APPLICATION SYSTEM _____ NUMBER _____

ANALYSIS OF NEED

OTHER AREAS AFFECTED

IMPLEMENTATION CONTACTS

ACTION REQUESTED

☐ NO ACTION
☐ VERIFY CAUSE
☐ DEVELOP SOLUTION
☐ ESTIMATE COST OF SOLUTION
☐ PRESENT SOLUTION/COST TO USER FOR APPROVAL
☐ IMPLEMENT SOLUTION

PREPARED BY_____ DATE _____

FORM COMPLETION INSTRUCTIONS

Figure 6-7 – Need Analysis and Estimation Request

FIELD	INSTRUCTIONS FOR ENTERING DATA
o Sent to	The name of the individual assigned to perform the needs analysis or estimation.
o Need identification #	The number that uniquely describes the form on which the need was identified. The form itself would probably be attached.
o Re: Application system	The application system which caused the problem. If the problem occurred in system software, that would be listed in lieu of the application system; likewise, if the problem occurred in a manual segment of an application system that, too, would be identified.
o Number	The number by which the problem application system is known.
o Analysis of need	A narrative description explaining either what needs to be performed, or what are the results of the problem.
o Other areas affected	A description of areas that have been or may be affected by the problem requiring the change. If the problem occurs throughout the data processing department, then all applications may be affected by the implementation of this need. However, normally one application will make the change in order to assess the effect of the change on operations. If the change is successful, other involved applications will then make the same change.
o Implementation contacts	Individuals to contact to obtain further information about the need.
o Action requested	The action to be taken by the individual responsible for implementation. The type of action normally requested includes: - Find cause - Develop solution - Estimate cost of solution - Present solution/cost to user for approval - Implement solution The individual responsible for maintenance may be asked to undertake one or several of these actions. For example, the individual may be asked to verify the cause, develop a solution, estimate the cost of the solution, and then present it to the user for approval.
o Prepared by	The name of the individual who prepared the form.
o Date	The date on which the preparation of the form was completed.

management monitor the use of maintenance resources.

o   Number of change requests assigned by individuals/function

The identification and analysis of problems, new requirements, and enhancements results in action being taken by specific individuals or functions. In an effort to determine the workload of individuals and functions, as well as potential problem areas, management needs to analyze the assignment of tasks. This information is available from the assignment forms; periodically it should be accumulated and presented to management.

o   Government regulations causing changes

Organizations should assess the effect on the organization of complying with government regulations. They should consider whether an excessive amount of time and money are involved. They should also consider what methods are used in the organization to achieve compliance. This information is available from the change request forms.

o   Time to find cause

Organizations should monitor the effectiveness of their analytical procedures. If excessive amounts of time are spent on analyzing the system structure, the analytical techniques are probably inadequate. Management may then have to develop better analysis methods.

o   Data needed not on forms

The maintenance process uses a series of forms designed to collect, disseminate, and retain information necessary for the maintenance process. When these forms are effective, the process is effective. However, if maintenance analysts are not provided with the needed information, they must develop new methods to obtain the desired information. The effectiveness of the maintenance form can be assessed by interviewing maintenance systems analysts.

o   Request by individual/function/system

The source of the problem should be identified. It is important to trace those individuals, functions, or systems that cause the expenditure of maintenance resources. This information is available from the maintenance request form.

o   Action requested by type

Management can authorize various actions. These include making estimates and analyses, implementing the maintenance, and taking no action. Categorizing information in this manner provides data processing management with an assessment of the amount of additional investigation they should require prior to the implementation of maintenance procedures. The information can be helpful in improving the performance of the identification, recording, and analysis phase.

FIGURE 6-8

RECORD AND ASSIGN PHASE FEEDBACK

#	FEEDBACK DATA	SOURCE	PURPOSE
1.	Changes made without "record and assign" process.	Comparing actual number of changes made to the production environment versus the number of changes processed through the record and assign process.	To determine the effectiveness of the process and to reprimand violators.
2.	Hours to record/hours to assign.	Hours reported system.	To quantify maintenance effort by category.
3.	Number of change requests assigned by individual function.	Change request forms.	To assess the extent of the change process by individual assigned the change.
4.	Government regulations causing changes.	Government change request form.	To assess the extent of maintenance effort going into making changes to comply with government regulations.
5.	Time to find cause.	Time reporting system.	To assess the effectiveness of the maintenance need analysis program.
6.	Necessary data not on forms.	Interviews of maintenance analysts.	To determine the effectiveness of the maintenance process forms.
7.	Request by individual/function/system.	Maintenance change request forms.	To determine the extent of requests by individual, function, and system.
8.	Action requested by type.	Need analysis and estimation request form.	To quantify the types of action taken by type.

RECORD AND ASSIGN PHASE CHECKLIST

Data processing management has the responsibility of continually assessing the effectiveness of each phase of the maintenance program. A checklist for the record and assign phase is included to aid management in this function. (See Figure 6-9.)

SUMMARY

The record and assign phase is essential to designing a successful systems maintenance function. The proper recording of the problems and assignment of the solution to the right person solves many of the maintenance process functions. Often, time is misspent in performing maintenance because someone attempts to solve the wrong problem.

This chapter suggests how to get the right information into the hands of the right people to solve the maintenance need. The chapter has presented the steps involved in this process, together with suggested forms to be used in the process. The checklist which follows allows data processing management to periodically review the effectiveness of this maintenance phase.

FIGURE 6-9

RECORD AND ASSIGN PHASE CHECKLIST

#	ITEM	RESPONSE			COMMENTS
		YES	NO	N/A	
1.	Has a process been established to record maintenance needs?				
2.	Has a process been established to assign the implementation of those needs to the proper individual?				
3.	Has maintenance been categorized into different problems/requirements/ enhancements?				
4.	Are these categories used as an aid in maintenance need identification?				
5.	Has one individual or group of individuals been assigned to document maintenance needs?				
6.	Has a formal method been established to document the symptoms associated with a maintenance need?				
7.	Does the maintenance need documentation process record both the description of the need and the unfavorable symptoms occurring in the current system?				
8.	Does the maintenance need documentation include the program/systems affected?				
9.	Does the maintenance need documentation include the data files affected?				
10.	Is there both a data processing version and user version of the procedure for documenting maintenance needs?				
11.	Must the user indicate the priority of the need when the user originates the need?				

FIGURE 6-9

RECORD AND ASSIGN PHASE CHECKLIST (Cont'd)

#	ITEM	YES	NO	N/A	COMMENTS
12.	Are changes required by government regulations identified?				
13.	Are the penalties for noncompliance with government regulations stated?				
14.	Is there a formal procedure for notifying the individual responsible for implementing the maintenance?				
15.	Is the individual responsible for taking initial maintenance action notified of the type of action required?				
16.	Are identified maintenance needs controlled through a prenumbering system?				
17.	Has feedback from the record and assign phase been identified?				
18.	Does management periodically review the effectiveness of record and assign phase?				

Chapter 7
Phase 2—Analyze and Estimate Phase

CHAPTER OVERVIEW

The objective of the analyze and estimate phase is to provide the user with sufficient information for making an implementation decision. Not all identified needs will result in system changes. It is only after the implications of the needs have been analyzed that the user can realistically make a proper business judgment. Of course, some requirements, such as governmental regulations, must be implemented regardless of cost. However, even in those situations the first solution recommended may not be the ideal solution and the user may wish to request additional study and analysis.

This chapter divides this phase into seven steps; in actual practice many of these tasks may be performed simultaneously. The chapter provides forms, checklists, and guidelines for completing the tasks. These are documentation tools for facilitating the maintenance process. In many cases the documentation tools also serve as action documents on which supervisors can indicate if they approve of the recommended action. Managers should use the list of controls and the checklist provided in this chapter to monitor the analyze and estimate phase.

OBJECTIVE OF ANALYZE AND ESTIMATE PHASE

The analyze and estimate phase is the responsibility of the systems maintenance project team, especially the systems maintenance analyst who has the responsibility of developing a solution. The procedures established for systems maintenance determine at what point the systems maintenance analyst becomes involved in the maintenance process. However, in many instances the systems maintenance analyst either detects problems or anticipates problems; thus he initiates the request for systems maintenance.

Then the systems maintenance analyst must perform a systems analysis process in order to develop the maintenance solution. This is a two-part process. The first part is the identification of how the application system should handle the problem until the need is implemented. The second part is determining how to implement a maintenance solution in the application system.

During the analysis, the systems maintenance analyst must perform two additional tasks. The first is to determine whether the maintenance need impacts other application systems. The second task is to develop a cost/benefit estimate for the solution. The analyst then presents the recommended solution to the user for approval.

In the accomplishment of these tasks, the following objectives should be achieved:

o   Develop a satisfactory systems maintenance solution

o   Notify other project teams if their projects are affected by the need

o   Inform the user of the economics of implementing the solution

o   Seek the user's approval and require the user to establish implementation priorities

During this phase, management is responsible for developing and enforcing procedures for analyzing problems and estimating the cost of solutions. Management should follow the suggestions in this chapter. Data processing management should also analyze risks occurring during this phase and develop controls in order to lower these risks to an acceptable level.

The control concerns in the analyze and estimate phase include:

o   <u>Has the maintenance team assessed the impact on other systems?</u>

One of the risks in a data processing environment is allowing errors to cascade. In other words, an error in one application system may result in an error in one or more other application systems. In addition, problems introduced through systems software -- such as operating systems and compilers -- can cause problems in the application systems. Therefore, for each problem identified the maintenance team should determine the potential impact of that problem on other application systems.

o   <u>Has the maintenance team notified other impacted systems of common problems?</u>

Determination that a problem impacts other application systems is not enough. The maintenance team must document and transmit that information to the application systems affected. Data processing management has the additional responsibility of ensuring that those other application systems take appropriate action.

o   <u>Has the maintenance team calculated the cost/benefit of systems maintenance?</u>

Without a cost/benefit analysis, the user cannot make a good business decision on whether to implement the solution. In addition, good cost/benefit analyses may indicate to users that they should explore other solutions. Some of these solutions may be in the manual segment of the application system, while others are alternative solutions to the one presented.

o   <u>Has the maintenance team assured that maintenance changes will not be implemented without user approval?</u>

Since users responsible for applications are also responsible for the maintenance of the application, users should decide which systems maintenance changes to implement. Even though maintenance people may have noble intentions, data processing management should not allow them to implement changes without user consent.

o   <u>Will users have the option of requesting alternative solutions?</u>

The user should be provided the option of requesting alternative solutions, if the solution presented is not cost-effective or, if in the user's opinion, it is not a good solution.

o   <u>Will users establish priorities for the implementation of change?</u>

For most application systems, there is a backlog of maintenance to be performed. Rather than implementing changes on a first-come, first-served basis, the maintenance team should use a priority system, with the user responsible for setting the priorities.

o   <u>Will the phase be performed in an economical, efficient, and effective manner?</u>

Data processing management should be continually concerned about performance of the systems maintenance function. Many factors are involved in the performance of maintenance. These factors should be regularly reviewed by management at a project and departmental level. Data processing management should continually seek maintenance solutions that improve performance.

STEPS INVOLVED IN ANALYZE AND ESTIMATE PHASE

The analyze and estimate phase is illustrated graphically in Figure 7-1 which depicts the following seven steps:

o   Step 1 - Determine maintenance need solution: perform needed analytical steps to develop a solution.

o   Step 2 - Determine impact on this and other systems: evaluate the impact of having this need or error cascade through other application systems, as well as the impact on this application.

o   Step 3 - Common problems: if the maintenance need or problem is common to other applications, notify those applications.

o   Step 4 - Cost/benefit analysis: determine the cost to implement the solution, operate the solution, and the benefits obtained from implementing that solution.

o   Step 5 - Change approval: present the change to the user requesting agreement to implement.

o   Step 6 - Determine alternative solutions: if the user does not approve the recommended solution, develop alternative solutions and then perform a cost/-benefit analysis for those solutions.

o   Step 7 - Set priority: the user should establish the priority for implementing the change.

STEP 1 - DETERMINE THE MAINTENANCE SOLUTION

The record and assign phase should identify the cause of the problem and develop a solution. This phase may or may not be performed by the maintenance systems analyst. If not, the maintenance systems analyst must review the work and make the final determination of the cause of the problem. The steps and procedures to perform this task were outlined in Chapter 6.

Traditionally, determining the solution to the maintenance need is a systems analyst function. However, the system must be kept operational while the maintenance process occurs. Determining the maintenance solution is a four-part process:

o   Part 1 - Determine solution and identify impact on system parts

FIGURE 7-1

ANALYZE AND ESTIMATE

(PHASE 2)

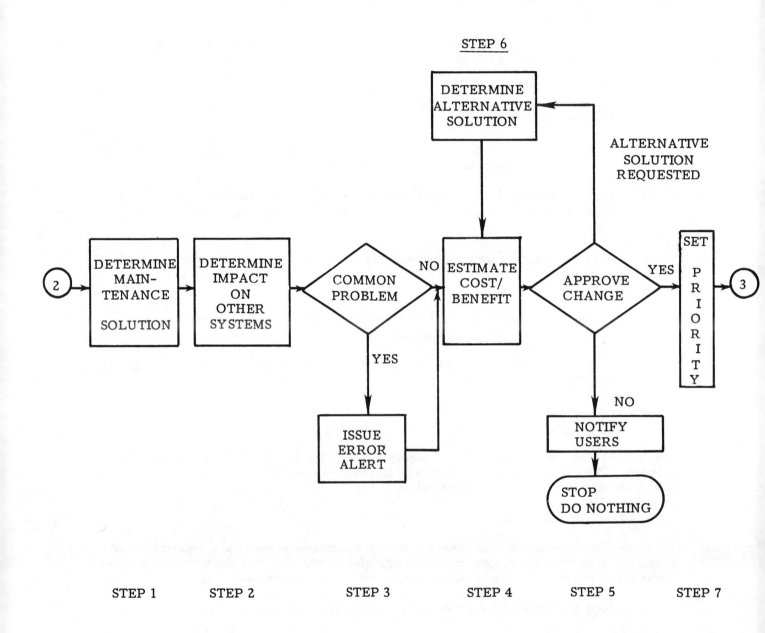

o   Part 2 - Document changes needed on each data element

o   Part 3 - Document changes needed on each program

o   Part 4 - Document other changes needed

Part 1 - Determine Solution and Identify Impact on System Parts

An important aspect of installing a systems maintenance change is identifying what parts of the system will be impacted by that change. The impact can be in any part of the application system, both manual and computerized, as well as the supporting software system. Regardless of whether impacted areas will require changes, at a minimum investigate the extent of the impact.

The types of analytic action helpful in determining the parts impacted include:

o   Review system documentation

o   Review program documentation

o   Review undocumented changes

o   Interview user personnel regarding procedures

o   Interview operations personnel regarding procedures

o   Interview job control coordinator regarding changes

o   Interview systems support personnel if the implementation may require deviations from standards and/or EDP departmental procedures

This is a very important step in the systems maintenance process. The time and effort spent in this step is usually returned in the form of more effective implementation procedures and fewer problems during and after the implementation of the change.

The end product of this step should be developing a solution, the identifying of the areas impacted, and the assigning of responsibility for reviewing that impact and/or making the necessary changes. If the user approves the solution, the results of this step will be a plan of action for implementing the change.

A maintenance need solution control form is presented in Figure 7-2 as a documentation tool for this step. The form is used to record the proposed solution. The information contained on the form is explained on the form's completion instructions sheet.

Part 2 - Document Change Needed on Each Data Element

Changes in processing normally impact only a single program or a small number of interrelated programs. On the other hand, changes to data may impact many applications. Thus, changes that impact data may have a more significant effect on the organization than those that impact processing.

FIGURE 7-2

MAINTENANCE SOLUTION CONTROL FORM

APPLICATION SYSTEM _____ NUMBER _____	MAINT IDENT # _____

MAINTENANCE NEED DESCRIPTION

MAINTENANCE SOLUTION OVERVIEW

CHANGES REQUIRED

ITEM AFFECTED	ITEM IDENTIFICATION	ASSIGNED TO

PREPARED BY _____ DATE _____

FORM COMPLETION INSTRUCTIONS

Figure 7-2 - Maintenance Solution Control Form

FIELD	INSTRUCTIONS FOR ENTERING DATA
o Application system	The name by which the application system is known.
o Number	The identification number of the application system.
o Maintenance ID #	The control number for the change.
o Maintenance need description	A succinct description of the change. If you need more information, reference the appropriate identification form from the previous phase.
o Maintenance needs solution overview	This section should describe the solution and general terms, such as issue a new report, add an input data edit, or utilize a new processing routine. The detailed information will be described in the supporting forms developed in later steps.
o Changes required	This section describes all the areas impacted and provides instructions on the changes that need to be made or the investigations that need to be undertaken regarding the impact of the proposed solution. The type of items that may be affected include: - Data elements - Programs - Job control language - Operations manuals - User training - User manuals For each of the affected items, the following information should be provided: - Item affected: the program, data element, job control or other area affected by the change. - Item identification : the program number of method of identifying the affected item. - Assigned to: the name of the individual/function/department assigned the responsibility of making the change or conducting the investigation (pending user approval of the maintenance solution).
o Prepared by	The name of the individual completing the form.
o Date	The date on which the form was completed.

Maintenance changes can impact data in any of the following ways:

o   Length - The length of the data element can be lengthened or shortened.

o   Value - The value or codes used in a data element can be expanded, modified, or reduced.

o   Consistency - The value contained in the data elements may not be the same in various applications or data bases; thus, it is necessary to improve consistency.

o   Reliability - The accuracy of the data may be changed.

In addition, changes to a data element can require additional documentation. As organizations move into a data base environment, they need to expend additional effort to ensure that they are consistent, reliable, and understandable. Much of this effort is translated into data documentation.

A form recommended for documenting data changes is illustrated in Figure 7-3. This form should be used to provide an overview of the data change. In a data base environment a copy of the data definition form should be attached to the data change form which can be a control vehicle. The information contained on the Data Change Form is explained on the form's completion instructions sheet.

Part 3 - Documenting Changes Needed In Each Program

The implementation of many maintenance needs will require some programming changes. Even a change of data attributes will often necessitate program changes. Some of these are minor in nature, while others can be extremely difficult and time consuming.

The change required for each program should be documented on a separate form. This serves several purposes. First it provides detailed instructions at the individual program level regarding what will be required to change the program. Second, it helps ensure that changes will be made and not lost; it is difficult to overlook a change that is formally requested. Third, and equally important, it provides a detailed audit trail of changes in the event that problems occur.

Figure 7-4 provides a form for documenting program changes. This form should be completed even though completion of the form may require more time than the implementation of the change. The merits of good maintenance documentation have been established again and again.

The information contained on the Program Change Form is listed on the form's completion instructions sheet.

Part 4 - Documenting Other Changes Needed

The implementation of a maintenance need can result in changes to the application system support areas. These changes can be as important as the changes to the data and the processing. Frequently, the major impact of the change is on the support system.

FIGURE 7-3

DATA CHANGE FORM

APPLICATION SYSTEM _____ NUMBER _____	MAINT IDENT # _____
DATA ELEMENT NAME _____	DATA IDENT # _____
RECORD NAME _____	RECORD IDENT # _____
FILE NAME _____	FILE IDENT # _____

ASSIGNED TO_____ DATE REQUIRED_____

DATA CHANGE

    ☐ ADD ELEMENT
    ☐ DELETE ELEMENT
    ☐ MODIFY ELEMENT ATTRIBUTES
    ☐ MODIFY ELEMENT DESCRIPTION

DESCRIPTION OF CHANGE

COMMENTS

PREPARED BY_____ DATE_____

FORM COMPLETION INSTRUCTIONS

Figure 7-3 - Data Change Form

	FIELD	INSTRUCTIONS FOR ENTERING DATA
o	Application system	The name by which the application is known.
o	Number	The number used to identify the application system.
o	Maintenance I.D. #	The sequential number used to identify the maintenance need.
o	Data element name	The name by which the data element is known.
o	Data I.D. number	The identifier used to uniquely identify the data element. In a data dictionary system this should be the data dictionary data element number.
o	Record name	The record or records in which the data element is contained.
o	Record I.D. #	The number that describes the record or records in which the data element is contained.
o	File name	The file or files in which the data element is contained.
o	File I.D. number	The numbers that uniquely describe the file or files in which the data element is contained.
o	Assigned to	The name of the individual/function/department responsible for making the change to the data element and the associated records and files.
o	Date required	The date by which the change should be made (pending user approval).
o	Data change	The type of change to be made on the data element. The options on the form include: - Add data element - Delete data element - Modify data element attributes - Modify a data element description
o	Description	A detailed narrative description (with examples when applicable) explaining the type of change which must be made to the data element. When a data dictionary is used, the data dictionary form should be attached to the data change form.
o	Comments	Information that would be helpful in implementing the data change.
o	Prepared by	The name of the individual who completed the form.
o	Date	The date on which the form was completed.

FIGURE 7-4

PROGRAM CHANGE FORM

APPLICATION SYSTEM _____ NUMBER _____	MAINT IDENT # _____
PROGRAM NAME _____ NUMBER _____ VERSION # _____	
NEW VERSION # _____ DATE REQUIRED _____	ASSIGNED TO _____
DESCRIPTION OF CHANGE	
SOURCE STATEMENT AFFECTED	
COMMENTS	
PREPARED BY _____ DATE _____	

FORM COMPLETION INSTRUCTIONS

Figure 7-4 - Program Change Form

FIELD	INSTRUCTIONS FOR ENTERING DATA
o Application system	The name by which the application to be changed is known.
o Number	The identifier that uniquely describes the application system.
o Maintenance I.D. #	The sequential number used to identify the maintenance need control.
o Program name	The name by which the program to be changed is known.
o Number	The number that uniquely identifies the program.
o Version number	The version number of the program to be changed.
o New version number	The version number that will be assigned to the altered program.
o Date required	The date in which the change is to be implemented, assuming the user approves the changes.
o Assigned to	The name of the individual who will make the change in the program.
o Description of change	A narrative description of the change to be made to this specific program. This narrative should provide examples of programs produced before and after the change.
o Source statements	A description of the source statement or statements that should be changed, together with the change to be made. The change may be described in terms of specifications and not specific source statements.
o Comments	Tips and techniques on how best to install the change in the application system.
o Prepared by	The name of the individual who completed the form.
o Date	The date on which the form was completed.

The types of support systems vary so much that it is difficult to develop a standardized form or approach to changing the support system. However, the same type of information that is needed for changes to data and to processing is also needed for changes in support systems. The type of information that should be documented for changes to a support system includes:

o Description of the application being changed

o Cross-reference to the maintenance need identification number

o Description of the change to be made

o Detailed specifications of what is to be changed and what results should ensue

o The individual responsible for making the change

o The date on which the change is to be made

o The individual who is coordinating the change from an application system perspective

Organizations can develop or may already possess forms for documenting changes in these support areas. If a formal documentation procedure does not exist, then the organization should develop one. The documentation form can be similar to the ones used for documenting changes to data and processing.

These support areas that most frequently require change include:

o Job control language - The statements necessary to support programs in the operating environment. When the program changes, the job control statement supporting those statements may also change.

o Utility program specification - Utility programs may be incorporated into the application system, and sometimes changes can be made through changing utility program parameters.

o Operating instructions/manual - Changes to the program may require new operating procedures in the computer room; these procedures should be documented in the operations manual.

o User procedures/training manuals - Changes in input, output, or use of application data may require new user procedures which should be documented in manuals.

o User training - User personnel should receive instruction on using the new procedures and system capabilities.

o Security procedures - Changes in the security classification and/or security procedures over application data.

STEP 2 - DETERMINE IMPACT ON OTHER SYSTEMS

The application systems analyst has a responsibility for evaluating whether or not a change to an application system will impact other applications. First are those applications that interface with the application being changed. Second are those that are not related to the application being changed.

The types of application that will be most impacted are those that interface with the changed application. The methods by which a change in one application impacts another include:

o   Common processing routines - The method by which a particular result is achieved is repeated in two or more applications. It might be a common module or common processing logic.

o   Data movement - The attributes of data are changed so that other applications using that data have to modify their processing rules accordingly.

o   Master data changes - Master information may contain new categories of information, such as a new product line or new category of customers. Each application that uses the type of master information needs to be changed accordingly.

o   Security classification - A change to security classification of data or processing logic will impact other applications using that same data or processing logic.

o   Timing/consistency/reliability - If general system attributes change and affect the inclusion or exclusion of certain types of data, the timing of preparing input or producing reports, the consistency of data, or the reliability of data, then all applications involved with those attributes must be changed accordingly.

The impact of a change on nonrelated applications are usually not application-related changes. Changes made to nonrelated applications are normally those concerned with vendor-produced hardware and software, as well as good and bad maintenance practices. The type of maintenance changes that should be considered as having an impact on nonrelated applications include:

o   Hardware/software encountered problems - Features or variations in the use of features that cause problems for one application system may also cause problems in nonrelated applications.

o   Effective maintenance practices - Techniques that have proven to be good practices in performing system maintenance.

o   Ineffective maintenance practices - Those techniques which, when practiced, either do not get the job done or do it ineffectively.

o   Programming procedures - Instructions or combinations of instructions which produce erroneous results or which operate ineffectively or inefficiently.

o   Vendor manual documentation errors - Variances between what a vendor

FIGURE 7-5

IMPACT OF SYSTEM MAINTENANCE

APPLICATION SYSTEM _____	NUMBER _____	MAINT IDENT # _____

APPLICATION SYSTEMS IMPACTED

DESCRIPTION OF IMPACT

IMPACT OF INTERFACED APPLICATIONS AND RECOMMENDED SOLUTION

IMPACT ON NONRELATED APPLICATIONS AND RECOMMENDED SOLUTION

ACTIONS REQUIRED

☐ NONE
☐ NOTIFY INTERFACED SYSTEMS
☐ ISSUE ERROR ALERT

PREPARED BY _____ DATE _____

FORM COMPLETION INSTRUCTIONS

Figure 7-5 – Impact of System Maintenance

FIELD	INSTRUCTIONS FOR ENTERING DATA
o Application system	The name of the application system in which the problem was uncovered.
o Number	The unique number identifying the application system.
o Maintenance I.D. #	The maintenance need identification number.
o Application systems impacted	The name and/or number of the application system impacted by the maintenance change. When the change is universal in nature, a category of applications (such as the applications written in COBOL) can be listed in lieu of specific application numbers.
o Description of impact	A narrative overview of the problem and/or impact that has been identified. This should describe the general type of problems such as COBOL compiler error or change to size of data element X.
o Impact on interface applications and recommended solutions	If the applications interfacing with the changed application are affected, the systems maintenance analyst should complete this section. This section should describe in detail the type of change to be made, how it may impact the application, and what must be done to avoid problems in the affected application.
o Impact on nonrelated applications and recommended solutions	The systems maintenance analyst should describe the type of problem encountered together with the impact that problem can have on an application system. A recommended solution should be given if applicable. This is normally the solution implemented in the application in which the problem was first encountered.
o Action required	The action recommended by the maintenance systems analyst who uncovered the problem. The type of actions that can be recommended include: - None (the maintenance systems analyst may believe that the problem is not serious; nevertheless, data processing management should be made aware of it) - Notify interfaced systems (each affected application system should be individually notified of the problem) - Issue error alert (all project leaders in the data processing area should be notified of the problem)
o Prepared by	The name of the individual preparing the form; this should be the individual who is to be contacted for more information.
o Date	The date on which the form was prepared.

manual states their product will accomplish versus what it actually accomplishes in practice.

Figure 7-5 provides a vehicle for recording the impact of systems problems and procedures on other application systems. This form should be completed by the systems maintenance analyst uncovering the problem. The information should then be given to data processing management (or their designated representative), who should determine if, how, and when to disseminate that information to other project analysts.

The information contained on the Impact of Systems Maintenance Form (Figure 7-5) is described on the form's completion instructions sheet.

STEP 3 - COMMON PROBLEMS

When data processing management is alerted that a maintenance problem may impact multiple applications, they should perform a risk analysis to assess the impact of the situation. Management should compare the risk to the organization versus the cost of correcting the problem.

If the potential loss (i.e., the risk) is greater than the cost of making the correction, then the correction should be made to all application systems. On the other hand, if the cost is greater than the risk, then management may decide to live with the risk and correct problem data as necessary. When the risk and cost are approximately equal, management is challenged to determine which course of action is most appropriate.

A potential problem is just that, a potential problem. When a series of conditions causes a problem in one application, there is no need to issue an error alert since that combination of circumstances will not recur. On the other hand, the problem may have already occurred without having been detected in many applications.

Management may take different courses of actions to correct a problem without involving multiple projects in the corrective action. These alternatives include:

o   Retrofit the problem - Change the condition to what the condition should have been. For example, if a particular code was misstated, change the code, keeping in mind the wishes of the project.

o   Vendor correction - If there is a problem in the hardware/software, or in the documentation, the vendor can be requested to make the necessary change to conform with the wishes of the involved people.

o   Sample other applications - Data processing management can assess how frequently the problem occurs by determining if the problem attributes exist in other applications. If they find the problem occurs frequently, they should recommend that department-wide action be taken; however, when the conditions do not appear to be duplicated in other applications, data processing management may decide to live with the risk until the problem recurs.

o   Alert other projects - Make other projects aware of the condition, but do not ask them to make corrections. The objective of the alert is to have the projects look for symptoms of the problem in their applications.

When management deems that action should be taken, they should plan the process to minimize the effort expended by other application systems. At a minimum, the problem and condition should be documented together with the recommended solution. Different application systems should not have to solve the same problems.

Methods by which data processing management can notify impacted projects of the problem and solution are:

- o   Selective notification - Each application system affected would receive an individual notification of the problem and recommended solution for that specific application. This is most effective when the problem is application oriented and only impacts interfaced applications.

- o   Departmental staff meetings - The problem and recommended solution can be explained and discussed at a staff meeting.

- o   General alert notification - Each individual in the department receives a notification and is alerted about the problem, its symptoms, attributes, and the solution or solutions available for correcting the problem. This can be accomplished using an error alert form.

Error Alert Form

Generalized problems should be documented on a departmental form. This form serves the purpose of documenting the attribute and the solution(s) to a problem in a format familiar to those who must deal with the problem. It also can be filed in a notebook for reference purposes. The use of a sequential numbering system assures personnel that they have all of the error alert forms which the department has issued.

The error alert forms should be prepared by a group in the data processing department. When the department has a quality assurance function, that function should be responsible for preparing the form. These forms should be issued on a timely basis. A gap between the time when the problem is encountered and when project personnel are alerted can result in a substantial loss to the organization.

A suggested Error Alert Form is illustrated as Figure 7-6. The information contained on the form is listed on the form's completion instructions sheet.

STEP 4 - ESTIMATE COST/BENEFITS

Changes should not be implemented in application systems unless they are cost-effective. Obviously, there are exceptions to this rule such as to comply with senior management or government regulations. However, if they could, most users would base implementation decisions on cost/benefit evaluations.

Experience has shown that individuals feel comfortable estimating costs to the nearest penny, but when it comes to benefits they are reluctant to estimate much closer than the nearest $1,000.00. However, it is unnecessary to estimate costs with any more precision than benefits.

FIGURE 7-6

ERROR ALERT FORM

CONTACT_____ DATE_____	ERROR ALERT #_____
ERROR DESCRIPTION AND RISKS	
ERROR SYMPTOMS	
SYSTEMS AFFECTED	
RECOMMENDED SOLUTION	
COMMENTS	

FORM COMPLETION INSTRUCTIONS

Figure 7-6 - Error Alert Form

FIELD	INSTRUCTIONS FOR ENTERING DATA
o Contact	The name of the individual to contact if more information is needed about the problem. This individual should be located in the data processing department, ideally in the quality assurance function.
o Date	The date on which the problem was identified.
o Error alert #	A sequential number used to control the issuance of error alert forms.
o Error description	A narrative description that explains the type of problem that may be encountered. This section should also describe the risk associated with the error. The risk should be described in as much detail as possible to include the frequency with which errors might occur and the dollar loss or magnitude of the error.
o Error symptoms	The condition that caused the error or symptoms that will help other application systems identify the error.
o Systems affected	The specific application systems or the type of application systems affected.
o Recommended solution	The solution that can either be incorporated in anticipation of the problem or after the problem has been identified.
o Comments	Any additional information that may prove valuable to application systems personnel in either preventing, detecting, or correcting the problem in their application system. This section should include tips and techniques successfully utilized in other application systems. Note that the same type of form could be used to "alert" systems analysts/programmers to good systems and programming practices.

The key factor in deciding whether or not to implement a change is normally what benefits will be derived from that change. Benefits include cost reduction, cost avoidance, and intangible benefits. Frequently, the intangible benefits are the most difficult to assess, but even calculating cost reductions and cost avoidance causes problems for some maintenance systems analysts. However, often the intangible benefits provide the greatest return associated with a change. A technique valuable for estimating benefits is risk analysis.

Risk Analysis[1]

The risk analysis concept has been used for hundreds of years in the insurance industry. The risk analysis procedure requires the user to estimate both the frequency of occurrence of an event and the value of that event. For example, if an investigation attempts to estimate the additional product orders that might be obtained from improved customer goodwill, it would have to estimate:

1. The average value of extra orders which the customers place because of the increased good will.

2. The frequency, or number of times per year, that the customers would issue those orders.

Knowing these two factors, the investigator can estimate the benefit. In other words, if the average value of an order placed is $100, and a customer places five of those orders per year, then the value per customer because of improved good will is $500. This procedure helps organizations calculate difficult-to-estimate benefits.

Experience has shown that while people can neither estimate a value or exact frequency, they can differentiate between magnitudes of values and occurrences. For example, it would be difficult to estimate exactly how many losses a professional football team would have in a single season. On the other hand, if an individual were asked to distinguish between one, five, or ten losses a year, the estimating procedure would be much easier.

The essential elements of risk analysis are an assessment of the damage which can be caused by an unfavorable event and an estimate of how often such an event may happen in a period of time.

As it will be impossible for the team to know absolutely either the impact or frequency of many events, these must be estimated using a combination of historical data, the team's knowledge of the system, and their own experience and judgment. However, estimates within an order of magnitude are sufficiently accurate for the purpose of risk analysis in most cases. Later, at the time of selecting safeguards, if it becomes important to refine specific items, that can be done, but during the analysis gross statements of impact and frequency are all that are required.

Quantitative means of expressing both potential impact and estimated frequency of occurrence are necessary to performing a risk analysis.

---

[1]The risk assessment methodology is reprinted from FIPS PUB 65, U.S. National Bureau of Standards

To date no better common denominator has been found for quantifying the impact of an adverse circumstance — whether the damage is actual or abstract, the victim a person, a piece of equipment or a function — than monetary value. It is the recompense used by the courts to redress both physical damage and mental anguish. Some methodologies advocate the use of abstract symbols of impact. "$" is, in fact, a symbol, yet one which transfers directly to fiscal usage without any intermediate translation.

Since impact will be expressed monetarily and fiscal matters are organized on an annual basis in federal agencies, a year is the most suitable time period to specify in expressing expected frequency of occurrence of threats. Some threats occur only once in a number of years while others happen many times a day. Such frequencies are not always easy to express in terms of years: "five times a day," for instance, converts to "1825 times a year" and "once every five years" converts to "one-fifth of an occurrence per year."

The time needed for the analysis will be considerably reduced, and its usefulness will not be decreased, if both impact and frequency estimates are rounded to the factors of ten shown in Figure 7-7. There is no significant difference in the overall exposure whether the damage from a certain event is estimated at $110,000 or $145,000. Assigning value to such things as loss of career caused by disclosure of confidential data or suffering caused by undue delay in the delivery of an annuity check is, in fact, more readily done in orders of magnitude than in actual figures. Here again, there will be no difference if the frequency of an event is expected to be twelve times a year or thirty. Using the scales for frequency from Figure 7-7 will avoid the use of unwieldy fractions and maintain the flexibility to work with high probability events in days and low probability events in years.

If the impact of an event, i.e., the precise amount of damage it could cauase, and the frequency of occurrence of that event, i.e., the exact number of times it could happen, could be specified, the product of the two would be a statement of loss, or

$$\text{Loss} = \text{Impact} \times \text{Frequency of Occurrence.}$$

However, because the exact impact and frequency can usually not be specified, it is only possible to approximate the loss with an annual loss exposure (ALE), which is the product of estimated impact in dollars (I) and estimated frequency of occurrence per year (F).

For ease in use, the orders of magnitude for estimated impact and estimated frequency of occurrence can be indexed, as shown in Figure 7-8.

When i and f are indices to possible orders of impact and frequency,

The relationship of i to I is $I = 10^{i}$ and

the relationship of f to F is $F = 10^{(f-3)}/3$

or $\quad F = 10^{f}/3000.$

Thus, the annual loss expectancy can be calculated by the formula

$$\text{ALE} = 10^{i}/3 \times 10^{(f-3)},$$

which reduces to

$$\text{ALE} = 10^{(f+i-3)}/3.$$

FIGURE 7-7

ORDERS OF MAGNITUDE OF ESTIMATED IMPACT AND FREQUENCY

IMPACT:

$10
$100
$1000
$10,000
$100,000
$1,000,000
$10,000,000
$100,000,000

FREQUENCY:

Once in 300 years
Once in 30 years
Once in 3 years (1000 days)
Once in 100 days
Once in 10 days
Once per day
10 times per day
100 times per day

FIGURE 7-8

TABLES FOR SELECTING OF VALUES OF i AND f.

If the estimated cost impact of the event is:

$10, let i = 1
$100, let i = 2
$1000, let i = 3
$10,000, let i = 4
$100,000, let i = 5
$1,000,000, let i = 6
$10,000,000, let i = 7
$100,000,000, let i = 8

If the estimated frequency of occurrence is:

Once in 300 years,	let f = 1
Once in 30 years,	let f = 2
Once in 3 years,	let f = 3
Once in 100 days,	let f = 4
Once in 10 days,	let f = 5
Once per day,	let f = 6
10 times per day,	let f = 7
100 times per day,	let f = 8

Values of F

	1	2	3	4	5	6	7	8
1					$300	$ 3k	$ 30k	$300k
2				$300	3k	30k	300k	3M
3			$300	3k	30k	300k	3M	30M
4		$300	3k	30k	300k	3M	30M	300M
5	$300	3k	30k	300k	3M	30M	300M	
6	3k	30k	300k	3M	30M	300M		
7	30k	300k	3M	30M	300M			

(Values of i — rows)

K = $1,000   M = $1,000,000

VALUES OF ALE

FIGURE 7-9 TABLE FOR DETERMINING VALUES OF ALE.

The tables from Figures 7-8 and 7-9 can be combined as shown in Figure 7-10 for greater convenience.

	f=	1 Once in 300 yrs (100,000 days)	2 Once in 30 yrs (10,000 days)	3 Once in 3 yrs (1,000 days)	4 Once in 100 days	5 Once in 10 days	6 Once per day	7 10 per day	8 100 per day
$10	1					$300	$3,000		$300k
$100	2				300	3,000	30k	300k	3M
$1000	3			300	3,000	30k	300k	3M	30M
$10,000	4		300	3,000	30k	300k	3M	30M	
$100,000	5	300	3,000	30k	300k	3M	30M	300M	
$1,000,000	6	3,000	30k	300k	3M	30M	300M		
$10,000,000	7	30k	300k	3M	30M	300M			
$100,000,000	8	300k	3M	30M	300M				

FIGURE 7-10 COMBINED MATRIX OF i, f and ALE.

Using the table shown in Figure 7-9 will be faster than following the formula for ALE but will produce the same result. Find the appropriate row and column for the i and f selected from Figure 7-8.; the cell where they intersect will contain the ALE.

Cost/Benefit Analysis Form

A recommended cost/benefit analysis form is illustrated in Figure 7-11. The risk analysis process can be used in estimating the value of the benefit.

The form includes two categories of cost and one of benefit. The cost categories are the cost to implement and the cost to operate the change. The cost to implement is the one-time cost, while the cost to operate and the benefits should be continuous.

When you have determined both the cost and benefits, then you must calculate the cost/-benefit. The two most common methods for performing this are:

- o   Cash flow rate of return (CFRR)

- o   Return on investment (ROI)

Many organizations specify which of these methods they prefer. In addition, many organizations have computer programs to perform the calculations. The data documented on Figure 7-11 can be fed into a computer program to produce the cost/benefit calculations. The one additional piece of information is the number of years duing which the benefits will be reduced.

For small changes, a simplified procedure might be preferable. However, even in those instances the cost/benefit analysis form can prove helpful. If someone simply documents the facts, the conclusions are obvious (performing the calculations).

The information included on the Cost/Benefit Analysis Form is outlined in the form's completion instructions sheet.

STEP 5 - APPROVE CHANGE

After all the information regarding the maintenance need has been collected, the user must decide whether or not to implement the change. This is the responsibility of the user, not the maintenance systems analyst. The user should be presented with as much information as possible to aid the user in making the final implementation decision.

The best way to present the necessary information to the user is on an approval form, such as Figure 7-12. The form also provides space for users to indicate the type of action they would like performed, as well as the money they are willing to authorize to make the change and the priority of the change. By providing this type of information, users make certain they remain in charge of the maintenance process.

The information contained on the Maintenance Approval Form is listed on the form's completion instructions sheet.

FIGURE 7-11

COST/BENEFIT ANALYSIS FORM

APPLICATION   MAINT
SYSTEM_____NUMBER_____IDENT #_____.

DESCRIPTION OF CHANGE _____

| | COST OF CHANGE | ESTIMATED | |
AREA		HOURS	DOLLARS
COST TO IMPLEMENT			
Design Specifications			
Programming			
Testing			
Documentation			
Job Control			
Conversion			
Training			
Supplies			
Other			
TOTAL			
COSTS OF OPERATIONS (ANNUAL)			
Computer Time			
EDP Operations Personnel			
User Personnel			
Supplies			
Other			
TOTAL			
BENEFITS (ANNUAL)			
Cost Reductions			
Personnel			
Computer Time			
Supplies			
Overhead			
Other			
Cost Avoidance			
Personnel			
Computer Time			
Supplies			
Overhead			
Other			
Intangible Benefits			
Good will			
Improved Service			
Other			
TOTAL			

PREPARED BY_____, DATE _____

FORM COMPLETION INSTRUCTIONS

Figure 7-11 - Cost/Benefit Analysis Form

FIELD	INSTRUCTIONS FOR ENTERING DATA
o Application system	The name by which the application system is known.
o Number	The unique identifier for the application system.
o Maintenance #	The sequential number identifying and controlling the maintenance change.
o Description of change	A succinct description of the change.
o Cost of change	For each area the number of hours of effort should be included as well as the cost, either on a one-time basis or annual basis.
o Cost to implement	The following criteria should be used in determining the cost to implement: - Design specifications: the effort to design the solution - Programming: the cost to code, compile, and test the program - Testing: the cost to test the change at the system level - Documentation: the cost to document the change for the application system, users, operation, and control area - Job control: the cost to design, prepare, and test job control language - Conversion: the cost to convert files and/or programs from the old version to the new version - Training: the cost to train operations, control, and user personnel - Supplies: the cost to purchase the forms, disk packs, and other items needed to implement the change - Other: any costs not included in the above criteria
o Cost of operation (annual)	The cost to operate the controls on an annual basis. If the change is small and implemented in a single program, the cost may be negligible. The types of operations costs include: - Computer time: additional run costs associated with the changes - EDP operations personnel: extra effort required by operations personnel to perform the new procedures

FORM COMPLETION INSTRUCTIONS

Figure 7-11 - Cost/Benefit Analysis Form

FIELD	INSTRUCTIONS FOR ENTERING DATA (Cont'd)
	- User personnel: extra effort required by the user personnel to operate the new procedures - Supplies: new forms or other supplies used in operation of the change - Other: costs not included in the above

o Benefits (annual)	The benefits should be computed on an annual basis for the following three categories:
	
	- Benefit category 1 - cost reductions
	  - Personnel: reduction in personnel costs
	  - Computer time: reduction in computer time charges
	  - Supplies: reduction in supplies
	  - Overhead: reduction in space, support, and other overhead costs
	  - Other: all other reduced costs
	
	- Benefit category 2 - cost avoidance
	  - Personnel: reduction in personnel costs due to not having to hire more people
	  - Computer time: reduction in computer time costs as the amount of processing has not increased
	  - Supplies: fewer supplies needed
	  - Overhead: decrease in new hires, supplies, overhead
	  - Other: all other categories of cost avoidance
	
	- Benefit category 3 - intangible benefits
	  - Good will: improved acceptance of the organization by vendors and customers
	  - Improved service: ways in which the organization improved their performance with their customers
	  - Other: all other intangible benefits

o Total	The cost to implement, the cost of operations, and the benefits received are to be totaled both in the hours and dollars column.
o Prepared by	The name of the individual that completed the form.
o Date	The date on which the form was completed.

FIGURE 7-12

MAINTENANCE APPROVAL FORM

APPLICATION SYSTEM	NUMBER	MAINT IDENT #

DESCRIPTION OF CHANGE

RISK IF CHANGE NOT MADE

COST/BENEFIT ANALYSIS

    COST TO IMPLEMENT $ _____
    COST TO OPERATE $ _____
    BENEFITS $ _____
    YEARS OF USEFUL LIFE   _____
    CFRR OR ROI   _____

EDP COMMENTS

APPROVAL SECTION

ACTION REQUESTED

    DO NOTHING
    IMPLEMENT THE CHANGE
    ALTERNATIVE SOLUTION REQUESTED

DATE WANTED	DOLLARS AUTHORIZED	PRIORITY

COMMENTS

APPROVED BY	DATE

FORM COMPLETION INSTRUCTIONS

Figure 7-12 - Maintenance Approval Form

FIELD	INSTRUCTIONS FOR ENTERING DATA
o Application system	The name by which the application is known.
o Number	The number that is used to identify the application system.
o Maintenance Identification #	The sequential number used to identify and control the maintenance need.
o Description of change	A brief description of the proposed change used to familiarize the user with the change for which user approval is being requested.
o Risk if change not made	A description of the types of problems that can be expected if the change is not implemented. The risk should be as specific as possible, and it should be expressed in terms of the annual dollar risk. The risk analysis procedures previously described can be used in estimating this risk.
o Cost/benefit analysis	The information from Figure 7-11 entitled Cost/Benefit Analysis Form should be transferred to this section. In addition, the years of useful life for the maintenance change should be added and the percent of cash flow rate of return (CFRR) or the return on investment (ROI) should be indicated.
o EDP comments	Any information the data processing department would like to add may affect the decision made by the user.
o Action requested	The user can indicate which of the following actions they desire the data processing department to take: - Do nothing - Implement the recommended change - Develop an alternative solution
o Date wanted	If the change is approved, this is the due date.
o Dollars authorized	If the change is approved, this is the amount of money authorized for making the change.
o Priority	If the change is approved, this is the priority of the change.
o Comments	Any information the user would like to transfer back to the data processing department to help them with the implementation.

FORM COMPLETION INSTRUCTIONS

Figure 7-12 – Maintenance Approval Form

FIELD	INSTRUCTIONS FOR ENTERING DATA
o Approved by	The name of the individual who is approving the change.
o Date	The date on which the change is approved.

STEP 6 - DETERMINE ALTERNATIVE SOLUTION

The user may find the solution unacceptable for many reasons. When this happens, the user should have the option of requesting alternative solutions. Some organizations automatically provide users with alternative solutions. However, in a data processing environment this can frequently be confusing. It is recommended that the systems maintenance analysts provide the user with the solution which the analysts consider to be the best solution. If this is unacceptable to the user, then the analyst can offer alternative solutions.

To develop alternative solutions, the systems maintenance analyst repeats the same steps again. The systems maintenance analyst performs the analysis steps, using the new information, and finally presents it to the user for reconsideration. Frequently, the systems maintenance analyst has already considered several alternatives, and the process is merely one of documenting the alternative solution.

STEP 7 - ESTABLISH MAINTENANCE PRIORITIES

The last step of the analysis and estimate phase is for the user to establish priorities for implementing the approved changes. This provides the user with the capability of resequencing changes each time a new change is approved. The priority system can be as simple or elaborate as is necessary to maintain user control.

The types of priority systems the user may wish to establish are:

    o   Priority categories - A series of categories that place changes into strata. Within the strata they are implemented on a first-come, first-served basis. All the changes in the highest strata will be implemented before any change in a lower strata is implemented.

    o   First come, first served - Changes are implemented in the order in which they are approved.

    o   Individual priority - Each change is individually given a priority.

Periodically, users may wish to review all of the changes and reorder priorities. As conditions change, so does the need to change priorities. For example, a change that is not needed for two months will have a very low priority when first entered into the change queue, but then slowly increases in priority as the two-month grace period begins to expire.

ANALYZE AND ESTIMATE PHASE FEEDBACK

The key to monitoring each phase of the systems maintenance process is obtaining good feedback. Management establishes controls that both direct and assess the maintenance process. Feedback provides data about the effectiveness of these controls.

Feedback information is provided by feedback mechanisms or a mini report writer that provides data at each control point. The type of information that should be collected during the analysis and design phase includes:

    o   <u>Number of changes impacting other systems</u>

The scope of systems maintenance can be partially determined by how that maintenance impacts other systems. This shows data processing management what some of the systems integration and maintenance problems are. It also indicates the amount of time and effort required to make maintenance changes. As the number of changes impacting multiple systems increases, data processing management can anticipate that the time and effort required to perform maintenance will also increase.

    o   <u>Number of error alerts</u>

An error alert is a potentially dangerous and time-consuming condition. Each systems analyst must review the alert condition and then determine if his or her system was impacted. If so, the analyst may have to make changes in the affected system.

    o   <u>Projected CFRR/ROI on maintenance</u>

The objective of a department's systems maintenance function should be to increase the profitability of data processing applications. Systems maintenance, as well as new systems development, should be considered a profit center. If organizations are performing maintenance and not gaining a positive return on their investment, the program should be reassessed. Obviously, not all maintenance efforts can be profitable, such as complying with government regulations. However, by monitoring the profitability of maintenance, data processing management will acquire valuable information for determining whether to increase, decrease, or support the maintenance function.

o   Maintenance disposition analysis

Data processing departments are given many requests for maintenance. Some are implemented, some are rejected until more facts are known, while others are restudied for alternative solutions. Knowing the disposition of maintenance requests can aid data processing management in developing an effective maintenance process. When management rejects too many maintenance requests, it may indicate that users have a poor understanding of what data processing can and cannot do. Because developing a maintenance solution involves time and effort, data processing management may wish to conduct user training sessions if they find that users reject a significant percent of maintenance solutions.

o   Priority given to changes

The normal workload of the data processing department can be affected by a series of high priority changes. Data processing management should monitor the priority assigned to various changes. In addition to disrupting workload, systems maintenance priority assignments can indicate application systems problems, especially if users continually demand high-priority changes. On the other hand, having a reasonable mix of priorities may indicate the organization's maintenance process is effective.

o   Cost reduction when alternative solutions are requested

It has been suggested that systems analysts provide alternative solutions if the user is not satisfied with the recommended solution. Data processing management should monitor the additional savings of alternative solutions. If there is a significant difference in cost between the solution recommended and the accepted alternative solution, it may mean that the systems maintenance analysts are not devoting sufficient effort to developing the initial estimate.

o   Disposition of alternative solutions

Another indicator of the value of initial estimates is the disposition of alternative solutions. If alternative solutions are rejected then the primary solution was, in fact, the best solution. This category of feedback should also indicate the number of users that return to the recommended solution after they have seen the alternative solution.

ANALYZE AND ESTIMATE PHASE CHECKLIST

The analysis and estimate phase assesses the economics and usefulness of the systems maintenance effort. (See Figure 7-13.) Data processing management should periodically assess the effectiveness of this phase to ensure that the systems maintenance function is a cost-effective function. The assessment should also provide management with insight

FIGURE 7-13

ANALYZE AND ESTIMATE PHASE FEEDBACK DATA

#	FEEDBACK DATA	SOURCE	PURPOSE
1	Number of changes impacting other systems	Systems maintenance documentation forms	To evaluate scope of maintenance and inner relationship of data and processing between application systems
2	Number of error alert	Error alert forms	To determine the number of serious problems, assess the scope of common errors on the department and identify vendors causing problems
3	Projected CFRR/ROI on maintenance	Systems maintenance documentation forms	To determine whether maintenance is making or losing money for the organization and to identify areas for review for improving the maintenance process
4	Maintenance disposition analysis	Systems maintenance documentation forms	To determine the effectiveness of the recommended solution through evaluating potentially unnecessary requests from users
5	Priority given to changes	Systems maintenance documentation forms	To assess the impact of high-priority changes on the normal flow of work of the organization and to assess the effectiveness of applications in meeting user needs if a large number of high-priority changes are requested
6	Cost reduction when alternative solutions are requested	Comparison of the two systems maintenance documentation forms showing cost/benefit analysis	To evaluate whether the recommended solution is the most cost-effective solution. A significant reduction of cost may indicate the application people are not spending sufficient effort on the first estimate
7	Disposition of alternative solutions	Systems maintenance documentation forms	To determine the value and user acceptance of making alternative solution recommendations

into data processing/user relationships.

A senior member of data processing management should perform the assessment of the analysis and estimate phase. The objective of the assessment is to identify both good and bad analysis procedures for the analysis and estimate phase. The result of this analysis should be improved systems maintenance practices. A checklist is provided (see Figure 7-14) to assist data processing management in making this assessment.

CONCLUSIONS

Requests for systems maintenance originate in many locations. The request, if not originated in the data processing project area, will be sent there for analysis and estimation purposes. The systems maintenance analyst must determine how to implement the change and then must provide an estimate of the cost/benefit of making that change.

The systems maintenance process may be more complex than the systems development process because a solution must be developed and it must be a solution that can be implemented within the existing system structure. The constraints placed upon the systems maintenance analyst affect the economics of making changes. Unless the calculation is performed, management -- both user and data processing -- can never be sure they are expending their maintenance dollars on the right changes.

This chapter has provided the methods and tools for analyzing and estimating changes to application systems. In addition, the control concerns present in the phase have been identified for action by data processing management. These control concerns, together with a management checklist, can help in the assessment of the effectiveness of the phase in order to implement new and improved practices.

FIGURE 7-14

ANALYZE AND ESTIMATE PHASE CHECKLIST

NUMBER	MANAGEMENT QUESTION	RESPONSE			COMMENTS
		YES	NO	N/A	
1.	Have the control concerns in the analyze and estimate phase been addressed?				
2.	Have formal procedures been established to conduct the analyze and estimate phase?				
3.	Do the procedures include both forms and control mechanisms to ensure that procedures are followed?				
4.	Are maintenance changes controlled through a unique maintenance identification number?				
5.	Are the changes to data documented?				
6.	Are the changes to programs documented?				
7.	Are the changes to job control language documented?				
8.	Are the changes to operations and operating manuals documented?				
9.	Are the changes to user procedures and user manuals documented?				
10.	Are training courses or sessions developed where appropriate?				
11.	Are data changes coordinated with data dictionary changes?				
12.	Is each change assigned to an individual who is responsible for implementation of that change?				
13.	Does the program change documentation indicate what source statements are affected?				

FIGURE 7-14

ANALYZE AND ESTIMATE PHASE CHECKLIST (Cont'd)

NUMBER	MANAGEMENT QUESTION	RESPONSE			COMMENTS
		YES	NO	N/A	
14.	Is a new version number assigned to each program in which a change will occur?				
15.	Has the impact on interfaced systems been documented?				
16.	Has the impact on nonrelated applications been documented?				
17.	Do procedures ensure that interface systems affected will be changed?				
18.	Do the control procedures ensure that interfaced systems changed will be coordinated for the same time period?				
19.	Has the impact on interfaced applications been documented?				
20.	Are error alert forms prepared for common errors?				
21.	Does the error alert form describe the potential risks if the error is not corrected?				
22.	Does the error alert form identify the type of application system or specific application system affected by the common error?				
23.	Does the error alert form both identify the error symptoms and recommended solution?				
24.	Are error alert forms controlled by a control number so that project personnel will know they have received all of the error alert forms?				

FIGURE 7-14

ANALYZE AND ESTIMATE PHASE CHECKLIST (Cont'd)

NUMBER	MANAGEMENT QUESTION	RESPONSE			COMMENTS
		YES	NO	N/A	
25.	Is a cost/benefit procedure required for maintenance?				
26.	Does the cost/benefit procedure include all of the costs involved in implementing the new change?				
27.	Does the cost/benefit procedure include all of the costs involved in operating the new change?				
28.	Does the cost/benefit procedure include all of the benefits associated with installing a change, which would include cost reductions, cost avoidance and intangible benefits?				
29.	Is risk analysis used to estimate the difficult to estimate benefits?				
30.	Must users approve all changes?				
31.	Is the user provided with sufficient data in order to make a business-like decision on whether or not to approve a change?				
32.	Can a user request that an alternate solution be prepared?				
33.	Does the user establish the priority for each approved changed?				
34.	Is feedback information for the analyze and estimate phase identified?				
35.	Is the identified feedback information collected and analyzed by data processing management?				
36.	Does data processing management periodically assess the effectiveness of the analyze and estimate phase?				

Chapter 8
Phase 3—Preparing the Change

CHAPTER OVERVIEW

The Phase 3 objectives are to satisfy a maintenance need as quickly, effectively, and economically as possible. The objectives for installing the system change are basically the same as when one builds a new applicaiton -- user satisfaction. The major difference is that a maintenance change is installed in an operating environment and thus it may impede processes that currently perform properly. A new application generally does not impact current operations; often it replaces them.

The two previous phases should be of short duration. In many organizations much of this work is completed in a single day. Therefore, it may not be until Phase 3 that the user and project team resolve how to maintain the application in an operational status until the change is installed. This may require as much time and effort as effecting the change itself.

This chapter provides a detailed step-by-step approach to implementing the change. In actual practice some of the steps may be combined; however, understanding the differences in the steps helps maintenance personnel install controls in a manner that significantly increases the probability of success.

The chapter also discusses two problems related to implementing changes. The first is what to do when the project team believes it is not in the best interest of the application and/or the organization to implement the change. The second area is maintaining the system in an operational status while the change is being installed.

OBJECTIVES OF INSTALLING THE CHANGE PHASE

Personnel working on each phase of the systems maintenance life cycle should clearly understand the objectives of that phase. This helps orient them to the basic tasks that must be achieved during the phase. There are four major objectives for the change implementation phase:

1.   Install the change as specified

The systems maintenance analyst should require that needs be specified in such a way that they can be measured. Having agreed to these changes, the systems maintenance analyst must implement those changes according to the agreed upon specifications.

2.   Document changes

The application system documentation should be kept current while changes are made to the application system. This means that a part of making the change is changing the documentation to reflect the new operational status of the application system. The change should not be considered complete until the documentation is complete. The documentation includes system documentation, operations documentation, user documentation, and control documentation.

3. Keep old system operational

During the time that the change is being implemented, the old system must be maintained in an operational status. This may require following some special procedures to ensure either that the system can run and/or that the new requirements are incorporated through manual or other means until the change is implemented.

4. Install change on time and within budget

Good management practices dictate that a maintenance request is a contract between the user and the project personnel for the performance of specified data processing tasks. The contractual agreement should specify the implementation dates and implementation costs. While it is not always possible to achieve either, it should be a high-priority objective of the maintenance team to achieve the time and budget requirements.

PHASE 3 CONTROL CONCERNS

Each phase of the systems maintenance life cycle poses risks or control concerns for the data processing department. Data processing management must ensure that there are adequate controls to reduce these concerns.

When management addresses the control concerns, they significantly reduce the likelihood that problems will occur during that phase. Thus, the time and effort required to develop the methods, procedures, and controls for the phase should result in more trouble free, more effective, and more economical maintenance.

The control concerns in the making the change phase include:

o   Will the change process be planned?

Many organizations install changes on a crash basis and hope they work. Some plan changes, but many do not. This high-risk approach to systems maintenance unnecessarily subjects the data processing project and department to avoidable problems.

o   Will access violations occur?

The processing programs and the data used by those programs should be a controlled resource of the data processing department. If anyone can freely access programs and data, data processing management has, in effect, lost control over their departmental resources. If program and data access is controlled, so is much of the systems maintenance process.

o   Will serious problems occur before the change is installed?

The application systems are an extension of the user area. When changes are needed, they may be needed even before the installation date. This can be true when problems are encountered in the existing system if new policies or legislation necessitate quick changes, or if the organization would gain a competitive advantage through the installation of the change. As the time extends between the request for the change and the installation of the change, so may the problems resulting from not having that need implemented. For example, if a product was priced incorrectly, all billings for that product would be incorrect until the change was made.

o   <u>Will it be known if the change achieves the change objectives?</u>

If the objectives for installing the change are not clearly specified, it will be difficult to verify whether or not those objectives have been achieved. Lacking proof, data processing management and user management will be uncertain as to the success of the systems maintenance program.

o   <u>Will systems maintenance testing process be adequate?</u>

Many systems maintenance analysts gamble, thinking they can properly install a change without testing it. This may be either because of the urgency of installing the change, or because of the willingness of the analyst to gamble. Regardless of the reason, when testing is inadequate or missing altogether, the data processing project and department are subjected to unnecessary risks.

o   <u>Will the change be reflected in updated documentation?</u>

Making the change to the system documentation may require more time than making the change to the programs. For this reason, many analysts bypass the documentation process or they do it poorly. In either case, the risk is that future changes may not be installed correctly because the documentation is out of date. Relying on inadequate documentation can cause people to make false assumptions when they change, operate, use, or control the application system.

The recommended methods for the making the change phase are designed to alleviate these control concerns. Through using the necessary forms, approval methods, and feedback, data processing management can be assured that the phase is being performed properly. Thus, it behooves data processing management to install and encourage the use of the proper maintenance procedures.

STEPS INVOLVED IN MAKING THE CHANGE PHASE

At the completion of the prior phases, the change has been specified, and the priority for implementing it has been established. The change phase itself is divided into seven steps.

In addition to the seven steps, a strategy is presented for avoiding making changes. There are many reasons why a maintenance analyst may not want to make a change. For example, the analyst may know that the program will be rewritten within a short period of time, and at that time it will be much more economical to install the change. Analysts may use this evasion strategy to avoid making the change temporarily or permanently, even though it has been approved by the user.

The steps that are normally executed in making a change include (see Figure 8-1):

o   Step 1 - Planning the change process

o   Step 2 - Operating the system until the change is made

o   Step 3 - Obtain needed access

o   Step 4 - Establish performance criteria

o   Step 5 - Implement the change

o   Step 6 - Test the change

o   Step 7 - Document the change

These seven steps are depicted in Figure 8-1. Each one of these steps will be discussed individually after deleting unnecessary changes is discussed.

DELETING UNNECESSARY CHANGES

The data processing group is normally a service group for application users. As such, it should install whatever changes users request. On the other hand, data processing is a group of professional personnel whose opinions and attitudes should be heard during the change process.

Users normally have the prerogative to and the mechanism for requesting changes and assigning priorities. The systems maintenance analyst should also have the prerogative of attempting either to eliminate the change or to adjust the priority. While this process can be performed formally or informally, the latter is normally the preferred method.

The reasons that a systems maintenance analyst may wish to delete or delay a change include:

o   Timing - The requested timing may not fit into the analyst's plans for modifying an application system. For example, changes might be installed more economically if they were installed in an order different from the order the user requested. In other words, some changes may facilitate the implementation of other changes.

o   Intersystem conflicts - A change to one application system may have a negative impact on many other application systems. The user may not be aware of this, but the maintenance analyst is.

o   Departmental plans - The department may have a shortage of personnel, or higher priority changes in other application systems which may force the maintenance analyst to choose between application system user priorities and departmental or organizational priorities.

o   Inappropriate change - The maintenance analyst may, through experience, believe that the change is unnecessary as specified.

o   Better alternative procedures - The maintenance analyst may wish to suggest other procedures, such as manual procedures, which can accomplish the change with much less effort and cost.

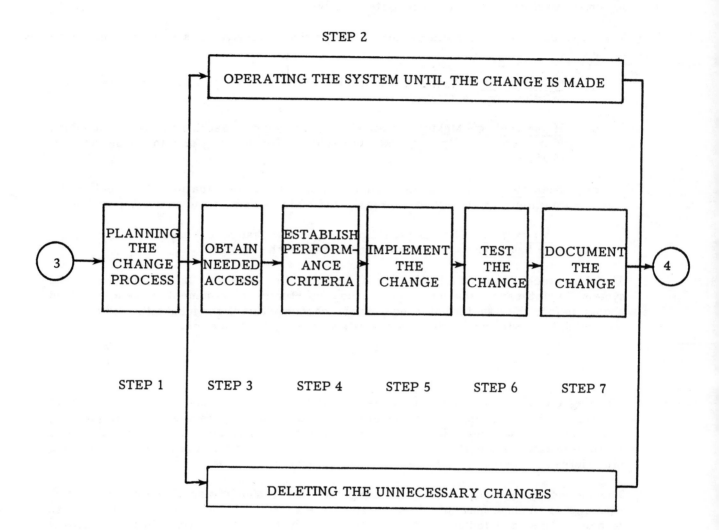

FIGURE 8-1

OVERVIEW - MAKING THE CHANGE

Under the formal method, the systems analyst would have to file a protest or equivalent with the user explaining why the change should not be installed or why it should be given a different priority. This would be the equivalent of an appeal and the user, having the responsibility and the budget for the application system, would have to formally consider and act upon that appeal. However, having an informal process allows for more negotiating on the part of the maintenance system analyst.

The type of bargaining methods that have proved effective in systems maintenance include:

o   Cost/benefit analysis - Recalculating the cost/benefit to show new alternatives or other considerations.

o   Horse trading - Making a swap with a user to get something the user wants done more economically or quicker in exchange for delaying or eliminating another change.

o   Scenarios - Giving the user a new perspective of the situation. This enables the maintenance analyst to use reason and logic to support the analyst's position.

o   Stall tactics - The analyst simply sits on the change and does nothing until the user begins pressuring the analyst to install the change.

The above techniques are all effective if they are used sparingly. In many instances, the systems maintenance analyst is given the opportunity to comment upon a proposed change before the user formally requests the change. This is the ideal situation and it is one which the systems maintenance analysts should try to encourage.

STEP 1 - PLANNING THE CHANGE PROCESS

Planning for a systems change involves marshalling the people and resources needed to complete the job. Normal systems maintenance does not require the elaborate planning necessary for new applications. However, large systems maintenance changes, such as those requiring six months or more to complete, should utilize the normal new system procedures as opposed to those designed for systems maintenance.

The individual in charge of implementing the change should also plan for the change. Planning for change normally does not require elaborate planning, such as critical path planning. Most maintenance changes will be relatively small in terms of hours of effort; thus, the planning effort is one of getting the needed people to make the change and then providing them with what they need at the right time. If the people are given the start and due date, they can normally do most of the detailed planning for their effort within the allotted time, and they can do it by themselves.

The documents outlining the problem and the recommended solution should provide sufficient specifications so that the change can be implemented without further program specification. The project leader and the individual making the change should review those specifications to determine their completeness. Where additional design information is necessary, they should be added to the forms described in Phase 2. However, in addition, there may be some information needed for job control language and other supportive efforts.

FIGURE 8-2

PLANNING THE CHANGE WORKSHEET

APPLICATION NAME _____ NUMBER _____	CHANGE IDENT # _____

ASSIGNED TO _____

START DATE _____ DUE DATE _____ BUDGET _____

TYPE OF INFORMATION	NEEDED	WHERE TO OBTAIN	RECEIVED	DATE
SPECIFICATION DATA Data changes Processing changes Job control changes Intersystem changes Other _____ Other _____ PRODUCTION RESOURCES New program(s) version Data for testing Needed software systems Computer time Other_____ PEOPLE SUPPORT Programmers User assistance Technical support Vendor assistance Data entry Other_____ SUPPLIES Forms Computer media Other_____				

PREPARED BY _____ DATE _____

FORM COMPLETION INSTRUCTIONS

Figure 8-2 - Planning the Change Worksheet

FIELD	INSTRUCTIONS FOR ENTERING DATA
o Application name	The name by which the application is known.
o Number	The application identifier.
o Change ident #	The sequential number controlling the change.
o Assign to	The individual who will make the change in the application system.
o Start date	The date in which the assigned individual should begin making the change.
o Due date	The date on which the change should be completed and ready to be placed into production.
o Budget	The number of hours/dollars allocated for this change.
o Type of information	The resources needed to implement the change.
o Needed	A column to check whether the resources specified in the column on the left are needed for this specific change.
o Where to obtain	The location where resources are stored, or the name of the contact who will obtain necessary people, or the name of the individual who will implement the change.
o Received	A checkmark indicating that the needed information has been received or that the person is available to help in making the change.
o Date	The date on which the information or confirmation of a person's availability was received.
o Prepared by	The name of the individual who prepared the form.
o Date	The date on which the form was initially prepared.

FORM COMPLETION INSTRUCTIONS

Figure 8-2 - Planning the Change Worksheet

FIELD	INSTRUCTIONS FOR ENTERING DATA
Type of Information/ People Support	The type of information column contains the more common types of resources required for making a change. In addition, space is provided for resources needed, but not included on the worksheet. The individuals preparing the form must first determine what resources are needed and then indicate them on the form. They next must decide where to obtain those resources and then begin the process of obtaining them. It is assumed that in most changes all the resources would be needed on or about the start date.
o Date changes	The description of data elements, records, or files that need to be changed.
o Processing changes	A description of the changes that need to be made to programs.
o Job control changes	The specification of the changes that need to be made to the operating system parameters.
o Intersystem changes	The description of changes that must be made to applications other than the one listed on this form.
o New program(s) - version	The number that will be assigned to the new program(s).
o Data for testing	The source of data that will be used to test the change.
o Needed software systems	Description of any new software that will be used either in making the change or as part of the change.
o Computer time	Description of the amount and frequency of computer time needed to make the change.
o Programmers	The number and time commitments of programmers needed to make the change.
o User assistance	Description of the user role in making the change.

FORM COMPLETION INSTRUCTIONS

Figure 8-2 – Planning the Change Worksheet

FIELD	INSTRUCTIONS FOR ENTERING DATA
o Technical support	Description of assistance needed by systems programmers.
o Vendor assistance	Description of the role of any of the hardware or software vendors in the change.
o Data entry	Description of the types and quantities of data that must be entered.
o Forms	Description of special forms needed for making the change or testing the change or running the system in production after the change.
o Computer media	Description of media needed to make, test, or run the change in a production mode.
o Other	Space to provide resources not indicated above.

A Planning the Change Worksheet (see Figure 8-2) provides a planning document for gathering resources. This document should be completed by the maintenance systems analyst in charge of the project. The document is used to record the type of information, the resources needed, where those resources can be obtained, and whether or not they have been received. The information included on the worksheet is shown on the form's completion instructions sheet.

STEP 2 - OPERATING DURING CHANGE PERIOD

The system minus the change must be maintained in an operational status during the implementation and testing of any change. This may or may not pose a challenge to the maintenance team. In many cases, the old system can run as is until the requested change is installed. However, in some instances the system cannot run as is.

Some of the conditions that require immediate action are:

o   Hang-ups - The system does not run at all in its current status. Potential temporary fixes are to eliminate specific types of data, to provide a temporary solution using a patch, and to operate the system in a manual mode.

o   Installation deadline has passed - The change may be delayed. For example, a federal regulation may require that a change, such as new federeal tax withholding tables, be installed. Alternate solutions include patching the system, running the system in the current version to produce most of the data, and then rerunning it at a later point in time to provide the correct output. Another solution is to run it in the old mode and then do special programming later to make the necessary corrections.

o   Detected error condition - If the system is operating but producing known errors, those errors should be corrected in future runs until the requested change is implemented. Solutions include manual searching and correcting of the error, developing a special program to search and correct an error, and inserting a patch in the program.

The systems maintenance analyst must determine whether or not changes impact the current production status of the application. If they do, then provisions must be made to assure that the production version of the application will produce the proper results during the period when the change is being installed. This is an essential part of the systems maintenance process. The above types of urgent problems and the recommended solutions are typical of the problems the maintenance analyst will encounter during this interim period.

STEP 3 - OBTAIN NEEDED ACCESS

Access to programs and data should not be automatic. Even though a systems maintenance team is assigned to maintain an application system, they are not authorized to have free and unrestricted access to the application programs and data. Restricting access is essential if the systems maintenance process is to be controlled.

Each change or group of changes should require a new version of the program. Once that version has been tested and installed in production, the program maintenance team should no longer have access to that program, or any other version of the program, until access is again authorized. This access can be controlled by data processing management or a security officer.

When management has authorized a change, they then can authorize access to a new program version. The approved change request form should be used to authorize access to a program. Access to data should require special forms because production data normally is not needed to make or test a program change. When conditions warrant using production data for testing, authority to use that data should be obtained from the individual or department resonsible for the data.

In automatically-controlled environments, access can be gained through passwords or other automated access methods. In these automated environments, access authorization should be entered into the system by management. The easiest way to control access is through the use of a standard form. In automated systems, approval is achieved by entry of authority to access into the password control system. In manual systems, access authority consists of a signature on the form.

A recommended Access Authorization Form is provided as Figure 8-3. This form should be prepared by the project team and sent to sent to the individuals or departments who can authorize access to the needed resources. The information contained on the form is outlined in the form's completion instructions sheet.

STEP 4 - ESTABLISH PERORMANCE CRITERIA

Users, data processing management, and project personnel need criteria which can be used to measure the success of the change. It is also unrealistic to design a test plan if the performance criteria have not been established.

"Performance" is used in the broad sense to indicate that the system performs in accordance with user requirements. The four specific areas of performance that need to be measured are:

o   Functional - The system performs those functions specified by the user. This includes accuracy, completeness, reliability, consistency, and protection against input data which does not comply with the system specifications.

o   Regression - The change does not negatively impact unchanged portions of the application system.

o   Stress - The system can handle all the specified data volumes without problems.

o   Economy/efficiency/effectiveness - The operating characteristics of the system, such as response time or turnaround time, before user needs are met.

The performance criteria for the appropriate areas should be specified in measurable terms. For example, specify expected volumes for stress testing, specify response time for effectiveness, list type of transactions rejected for functional requirements, and specify any allowable tolerances for regression of other previously accepted performance.

FIGURE 8-3

ACCESS AUTHORIZATION FORM

INDIVIDUAL
REQUESTING ACCESS _____ IDENT #_____

INDIVIDUAL

APPLICATION
NAME_____ NUMBER ____IDENT #_____

CHANGE

AREA	INDIVIDUAL CONTROLLING ACCESS	ACCESS DATES		ACCESS APPROVED BY	DATE	ACCESS DIS-APPROVED BY
		FROM	TO			
PROGRAMS (and version)						
DATA/FILES USE						
DATA/FILES DOCUMENTATION						
OTHER						

PREPARED BY_____ DATE _____

FORM COMPLETION INSTRUCTIONS

Figure 8-3 – Access Authorization Form

FIELD	INSTRUCTIONS FOR ENTERING DATA
o Individual requesting access	Normally the application system maintenance project leader name
o Individual Ident #	The employee number or equivalent number used in the automated access systems, or equivalent for a manual system.
o Application name	The name by which the application is known.
o Number	The application identifier.
o Change Ident #	The sequence number that uniquely identifies the change.
o Area	The resources to which access is requested. The areas in which resources are most frequently needed include: - Programs (and versions): the version number of the programs to which access is requested so that modifications can be made. - Data/files used: data elements, records, or files that need to be used for test purposes during the testing of the change. - Data/files documentation: the data, records, or files whose attributes or characteristics will be altered during the change process. - Other: other areas to which access is requested, such as the use of privileged facilities such as SUPER ZAP.
o Individual controlling access	The name of the individual to whom the request for access is addressed.
o Access date	The start and stop dates for which access is requested.
o Access approved by	The signature or other method of granting approval for the access.
o Date	The date on which the access was approved or disapproved.
o Access disapproved by	The signature or other method by which access is disapproved.
o Prepared by	The name of the individual who prepared the form.
o Date	The date on which the form was prepared.

FIGURE 8-4

SYSTEM CHANGE PERFORMANCE CRITERIA

APPLICATION NAME _____ CHANGE NUMBER ____ IDENT # _____

ADMINISTRATIVE CRITERIA

#	CRITERIA	HOW TO MEASURE	ACHIEVED YES	NO
1.	Installed on time	Compare completion date to due date		
2.	Installed within budget	Compare budget to actual cost		
3.	System maintenance procedures followed	Develop list of procedures compliance		
4.	Other:_____			
5.	Other:_____			

TECHNICAL CRITERIA

#	CRITERIA	HOW TO MEASURE	ACHIEVED YES	NO
1.	Input edits prevent problems	Verify against specification		
2.	Processing is correct	Verify against specification		
3.	Data files/database is correct	Verify against specification		
4.	Output reports are correct	Verify against specification		
5.	Modified system achieves effectiveness goals	Establish performance goals		
6.	User personnel perform new functions correctly	Establish performance goals		
7.	Operating personnel perform new functions properly	Establish performance goals		
8.	Controls achieve control objectives	Establish performance goals		
9.	Other:_____			
10.	Other:_____			

PREPARED BY_____ DATE _____

FORM COMPLETION INSTRUCTIONS

Figure 8-4 - System Change Performance Criteria

FIELD	INSTRUCTIONS FOR ENTERING DATA
o Individual requesting access	Normally the application system maintenance project leader name.
o Individual Ident #	The employee number or equivalent number used in automated access systems.
o Application name	The name by which the application is known.
o Number	The application identifier.
o Change Ident #	The sequence number that uniquely identifies the change.
o Administrative	Included within administrative criteria on the form are the most common criteria for measuring the management of installing the system change, together with recommendations on how to measure those criteria. For example, Figure 8-4 lists installed on time as an administrative criterion. In actual practice, a date would appear here, such as November 18. Prior to installation, the application would then be rated according to whether or not the agreed upon criteria had been achieved. Typical administrative criteria are the following: - Installed on time: the date on which the change was to be installed. This can be determined by comparing the actual installation date with the scheduled completion date. - Installed within budget: budgets can be expressed in terms of dollars or hours. Compare the budgeted expenses with the actual expenses. - Systems maintenance procedures followed: the project team should follow the system development life cycle procedures. This can be determined by checklisting the project against the required procedures.

Figure 8-4 - System Change Performance Criteria

FIELD	INSTRUCTIONS FOR ENTERING DATA
o Technical criteria	The functional, regression, stress, effectiveness, efficiency, and economy characteristics associated with installing the system change. These need to be specified as well as how to measure those criteria. Again, the example lists generalized criteria, but for a specific application these criteria should be the quantified criteria agreed to by the project and user personnel. Examples of the type of criteria that should be considered include: - Input edits prevent problems: the type of edits included in the change and the problems they are designed to prevent. - Processing is correct: the changes to processing rules perform as specified. - Data file/data base is correct: changes to the file structure or data base have been correctly implemented. - Output reports are correct: the headings column, data, instructions, and totals relating to output reports are correct. - Modified system achieves performance goals: the system performs as effectively, efficiently, and economically as specified. - User personnel perform new functions correctly: people working with the system can use the new features in the performance of their work. - Operating personnel perform new functions correctly: operators, both data processing and users, can effectively operate the new system. - Controls achieved specified control objectives: both the internal and external controls function properly.
o Prepared by	The name of the individual who prepared the form.
o Date	The date on which the form was prepared.

Determining measurable performance criteria can be difficult for users and project personnel. However, once an organization has established the criteria, both the implementation of the change and the testing become much easier. It also provides a basis for monitoring performance so the user can continually assess how effectively the application achieves its objectives.

A suggested form for documenting program change performance criteria is presented as Figure 8-4. This form should be completed by the systems maintenance project leader in conjunction with user personnel. The result of this process is a contract between the user and the project personnel, which describes the expected performance.

The information contained on the form is divided into administrative criteria and technical criteria. Both are important in measuring the performance of the change process. The information contained on the form is described in the form's completion instructions sheet.

The performance criteria should be established before the change is implemented. These criteria are useful in determining the type of logic and the type of controls needed in the application system. To develop performance criteria after the change has been implemented would reduce some of the value of this exercise.

STEP 5 - IMPLEMENT THE CHANGE

Implementing the change includes designing detailed systems specifying programs and coding. During this step, the concerns are:

1. That the change be installed in the proper part of the application system

2. That all segments of this and other application systems impacted by the problems be changed

3. That the functions currently being performed correctly continue to be performed correctly

The following tips and techniques are provided to assist systems maintenance analysts and maintenance programmers in the performance of their function:

o   Identify affected data elements - Determine all the data elements impacted by the change.

o   Identify programs using those data elements - Determine all the places that the change can impact.

o   Identify the programs that either create, modify, or delete the affected data elements - This normally will indicate the program(s) in which the change should be made. An obvious exception is a change to the use of the data and output reports.

o   Identify the external controls over the data element - A change to the data element, or processing of that data element, may impact some of the external controls.

o   Idenfity the programs that edit or audit the affected data element - Changes to the attributes of data may require changes to audit and edit routines related to that data element.

o   Code the change in a single module if possible - Isolating all of the instructions involved in a change in a specific module minimizes the probability of negatively impacting another module.

o   Contain the entire change in one program if possible - The fewer programs affected by the change the less the probability of negatively impacting other parts of the application system.

Time spent in determining where in the application the change should be installed is usually well spent. Also, determining potential areas of impact (such as all of the areas using the affected data element) reduces maintenance problems and reduces the need for tests.

STEP 6 - TEST THE CHANGE

It is only through complete testing that the systems maintenance analyst can be assured that the entire system will function properly after the change is made. While this is a time-consuming task, it is the only effective method for minimizing system change problems.

One large corporation has established a base case testing system. The base case, consisting of an exhaustive set of test data, is established at the time the application system is developed. Data processing and user personnel prepare the base case to acceptance test the application after it has been developed.

Whenever a change is made, the base case test data must be adjusted to reflect the change. When the change is installed, the base case is again executed to verify the functioning of the entire application. The technique works best when the results produced by the test are automatically verified.

The rule of thumb is that 30% of the systems development effort must be expended developing and using the base approach. Other effective test approaches expend at least 20% of the development effort on base cases. These percentages can be expected to be the same during the systems maintenance effort.

The systems maintenance test plan should be documented before it is to be executed. Figure 8-5 provides a form for documenting the systems maintenance test plan. The instructions for how to complete the Systems Maintenance Test Work Plan form are contained on the form's completion instructions sheet.

STEP 7 - DOCUMENT THE CHANGE

The continued success of the application system requires that each change be incorporated into the system documentation. Unless this step is performed each time a change is implemented, the documentation quickly becomes outdated. Outdated documentation may do more to inhibit than help in making changes.

FIGURE 8-5

SYSTEMS MAINTENANCE TEST WORK PLAN

APPLICATION SYSTEM_____NUMBER_____ CHANGE IDENT #_____					
#	TEST WORK PLAN STEP	ASSIGNED TO	DATES		
			START	DUE	COMPLETION
1.					

PREPARED BY_____ DATE_____

FORM COMPLETION INSTRUCTIONS

Figure 8-5 – Systems Maintenance Test Work Plan

FIELD	INSTRUCTIONS FOR ENTERING DATA
o Application system	The name by which the application is known.
o Number	The application identifier.
o Change Ident #	The sequence number that uniquely identifies the change.
o Test work plan step	A detailed description of the tasks that are to be performed during the testing process. Examples of the type of tasks that might be included in the test work plan are: – Designing test data for each new function installed – Developing test data to verify the negative aspects of processing (e.g., erroneous transactions) – Testing each new function installed – Testing the adequacy of new security procedures – Testing the impact on hardware and systems software – Testing the job control language – Testing the restart/recovery/backup data – Testing the adequacy of audit trail – Testing the procedures used should the system fail – Testing the error message correction procedures – Testing the manual procedures – Testing response time – Testing the intersystem connections
o Assigned to	The name of the individual who will perform or verify the effectiveness of the test plan.
o Dates	The dates on which the work plan step: – Will start – Is due for completion – Is actually completed
o Prepared by	The name of the individual who prepared the test work plan.
o Date	The date on which the work plan was prepared.

FIGURE 8-6

SYSTEMS MAINTENANCE DOCUMENTATION WORK PLAN

APPLICATION
SYSTEM _____ NUMBER _____ CHANGE IDENT # _____

#	DOCUMENTATION WORK PLAN STEP	ASSIGNED TO	DATES		
			START	DUE	COMPLETION

PREPARED BY _____ DATE _____

FORM COMPLETION INSTRUCTIONS

Figure 8-6 – Systems Maintenance Documentation Work Plan

FIELD	INSTRUCTIONS FOR ENTERING DATA
o Application system	The name by which the application is known.
o Number	The application identifier.
o Change Ident #	The sequence number that uniquely identifies the change.
o Documentation work	The documentation area and/or form that must be changed. This section would use the form numbers and descriptions familiar to the maintenance systems analyst in documenting the change. The types of documentation that may be affected include: - Data description forms - Program specification statements - Program listing description statements - System narrative description - User operating procedures - Error description procedures - Operator documentation - Record retention description - Control group procedures
o Assigned to	The name of the individual who will perform or verify the documentation work plan step.
o Dates	The dates on which the documentation work plan step: - Will start - Is due for completion - Is actually completed
o Prepared by	The name of the individual who prepared the documentation work plan.
o Date	The date in which the work plan was prepared.

Performing the documentation step is normally not a complex process. It merely involves updating all the documentation that is affected by the change. This can best be accomplished if the maintenance team develops a checklist that indicates all of the areas requiring change. When the change has been tested, the documentation can then be updated to reflect the change.

It is normally better to update the documentation after the change has been tested than before. The reason is that testing may alter the way in which the change is installed. If problems occur during testing, the correction process may impact the documentation process. Thus, after the change has been made and tested the documentation requirements are known.

A Systems Maintenance Documentation Work Plan Form is illustrated as Figure 8-6. This work plan should be completed by the systems maintenance analyst. The objective of the work plan is to identify all the areas of documentation that need to be changed, as well as the individual responsible for making the change. The information included on the Systems Maintenance Documentation Work Plan form is shown on the form's completion instructions sheet.

FEEDBACK

Feedback provides data processing and user management the information needed to monitor the performance of the change process. The feedback provided during the making the change phase can be used by data processing management to improve the change procedures. The same feedback information can be used by users to evaluate the changes made to their application.

The types of feedback that should be considered for collection during this phase include:

o   Number of making the change forms completed - This type of feedback information helps the systems maintenance analyst analyze the types of changes and the compliance with the making the change procedures.

o   Number of program compiles - The amount of computer resources consumed in compiling programs for program changes can be measured by this data.

o   Number of data elements changed - This number provides insight into the interdependency of the various elements of the system.

o   Number of tests - The number of tests required to implement system changes provides a measure of the data processing resources consumed in making changes.

o   Number of operator problems during the change process - The problems in operations associated with systems maintenance.

o   The type of operations problems during the change process - This data provides an indication of the difficulties encountered in operation because of making systems changes.

o   Extent of documentation changes - This data provides insight into the amount of effort expended on documenting systems maintenance changes.

o   Changes cancelled during implementation phase - This data indicates whether data processing personnel are cancelling requested systems maintenance changes.

o   Late implementation - This data monitors the effectiveness of project personnel in installing system changes on schedule.

o   Cost overrun - This data provides a means of monitoring the effectiveness of project personnel in installing systems maintenance changes within budget.

The proper use of feedback by data processing management will facilitate the process of implementing the change. Without information, any changes made by data processing management will use intuition as a basis for deciding on change. Having factual data, management can authorize changes according to weaknesses identified in the change process. The feedback for this phase is summarized in Figure 8-7.

MAKING THE CHANGE CHECKLIST

Data processing management has the responsibility of monitoring the effectiveness of the change process. This requires data processing management to periodically assess the effectiveness of the process. A checklist is included as Figure 8-8 to assist data processing management in the fulfillment of this responsibility.

The checklist is designed to aid data processing management in reviewing the making the change phase. "Yes" answers on the checklist indicate favorable responses, while "no" answers indicate areas requiring management investigation. Additional questions should be added to this checklist to verify compliance with specialized organizational change procedures.

SUMMARY

The making the change phase has two purposes: first, to keep the application system operational during the change process; and second, to install the change as specified. This chapter has provided recommendations on keeping the system operational and it has broken the implementation of changes into seven steps.

Implementing the changes begins with the planning the change process. Once the change has been planned, the systems maintenance analyst must gain access to the needed resources to implement the change. The next step is to establish performance criteria so that the success of the implementation process can be measured. Lastly, the analyst must implement the change, test the change, and document the change.

The systems maintenance analyst has an obligation to counsel the user on the appropriateness of the change. If the systems maintenance analyst believes it is not within the best interest of the department or the organization to install the change, he/she should advise the user of that fact. However, the maintenance systems analyst should be prepared to substantiate why he/she requested that the change not be implemented.

FIGURE 8-7

MAKING THE CHANGE FEEDBACK DATA

FEEDBACK DATA	SOURCE	PURPOSE
Number of making the change forms completed	Summarization of the forms	To quantify the amount of effort being expended on systems maintenance and to verify compliance with the systems maintenance procedures
Number of program compiles	Job accounting systems	To determine the amount of effort going into systems maintenance through program compilations
Number of data elements changed	Data dictionary or equivalent	To assess the impact of systems maintenance on data element attributes
Number of tests	Job accounting systems	To determine the amount of computer resources going into testing systems maintenance
Number of operator problems during change process	Operations logs	To identify the amount of operations time expended due to systems maintenance problems
Type of operator problems incurred during the change process	Operator logs	To identify the cause of operator problems
Extent of documentation changes	Documentation change work plan	To quantify the amount of effort going into maintaining documentation due to system changes
Changes cancelled during impelmentation process	Implementation form	To determine how many changes the system maintenance personnel are able to cancel
Late implementation	System maintenance schedule	To determine service to users in implementing system maintenance needs
Cost overrun	Job accounting systems	To determine both the effectiveness of estimating changes and the efficiency of project personnel in installing systems maintenance changes

FIGURE 8-8

MAKING THE CHANGE CHECKLIST

NUMBER	MANAGEMENT QUESTION	RESPONSE			COMMENTS
		YES	NO	N/A	
1.	Is the systems maintenance analyst required to develop plans prior to installing system changes?				
2.	Does the planning process include determining new data specifications?				
3.	Does the planning process include determining what production resources are needed?				
4.	Does the planning process include determining what people are needed to make the change?				
5.	Does the planning process include determining what special forms or media are required for the change process?				
6.	Are provisions made to keep the application system operational until the change is implemented?				
7.	Must access be approved prior to using data or programs in the change process?				
8.	Is access restricted to specific calendar dates?				
9.	Are performance criteria established for each change?				
10.	Are the performance criteria established for change administrative functions?				
11.	Are performance criteria established for the technical functions of the system?				

FIGURE 8-8

MAKING THE CHANGE CHECKLIST

NUMBER	MANAGEMENT QUESTION	RESPONSE			COMMENTS
		YES	NO	N/A	
12.	Are systems maintenance programmers instructed in the most effective methods of implementing changes?				
13.	Is a systems maintenance test work plan established for each change?				
14.	Have specific individuals been assigned each step of the test work plan?				
15.	Is a systems maintenance documentation work plan established for each change?				
16.	Is each step of the documentation work plan assigned to a specific individual?				
17.	Has the needed feedback data been identified?				
18.	Is the needed feedback data collected?				
19.	Does data processing management regularly review the feedback data?				
20.	Does data processing management regularly assess the effectiveness of making the change phase?				

Chapter 9
Phase 4—Testing and Training Phase

CHAPTER OVERVIEW

There are two types of testing. One involves the data processing department and confirms that the change complies with their specifications. The second, involving users, tests the intent of the change. This phase deals with the latter type of testing. This chapter outlines a testing and training methodology for systems maintenance.

Testing and training are as important to systems maintenance as they are to new systems development. Frequently, even small changes require extensive testing and training. It is not unusual to spend more time testing a change and training users to operate a new facility than to incorporate the change into the application system. This chapter explains the steps that should be performed during testing system changes.

Too frequently, systems maintenance has been synonomous with "quick and dirty" programming, which is rarely worth the risk. Frequently, it takes considerable time to correct problems that could have been prevented by adequate testing and training. If testing is properly conducted, it should not take longer to do the job right.

Data processing management has the responsibility to establish the testing and training procedures for systems maintenance. Many organizations establish change control procedures but do not carry them through the testing and training phase. A checklist is provided for management to review the effectiveness of their testing.

OBJECTIVES OF THE TESTING AND TRAINING PHASE

The overall objective of the testing and training phase is to ensure that the changed application will function properly in the operating environment. This includes both the manual and automated segments of the computerized application. The specific objectives of the training and testing phase include:

o   Develop tests to detect problems prior to placing the change in production

o   Correct problems prior to placing the change in production

o   Develop the needed training material

o   Train affected personnel prior to the change

o   Involve users in the testing and training phase

PHASE 4 CONTROL CONCERNS

Data processing management should be concerned about the implementation of the testing and training phase objectives. These concerns need to be addressed during the development and execution of the systems maintenance testing and training. The first step in addressing the control concerns is identifying those concerns that impact the phase.

The major control concerns of the testing and training phase are:

o   <u>Will the testing process be planned?</u>

Inadequate testing is synonymous with unplanned testing. Unless the systems maintenance analyst plans the test, there is no assurance that the results will meet change specifications.

o   <u>Will the training process be planned?</u>

People rarely decide on the spur of the moment to hold a training class or develop training material. What tends to happen is that training is given one-on-one after problems begin to occur. This is a costly method of training.

o   <u>Will systems problems be detected during testing?</u>

Even the best training plans rarely uncover all the potential systems problems. What is hoped is that the serious problems will be detected during testing.

o   <u>Will training problems be detected during testing?</u>

How people will react to production situations is more difficult to predict than how computerized applications will perform. Thus, training that prepares people for all possible situations should be the training objective.

o   <u>Will already detected testing and training problems be corrected prior to the implementation of the change?</u>

An unforgivable error is to detect a problem and then fail to correct it before serious problems occur. Appropriate records should be maintained and controls implemented, so that detected errors will be immediately acted upon.

STEPS INVOLVED IN THE TESTING AND TRAINING PHASE

The testing and training phase does not appear to provide the same mental challenge as the analyzing and implementing changes phase. However, the phase is essential to ensuring the successful operation of a computerized application. Much of the systems maintenance process involves testing changes and training people in how to use those changes.

Testing and training occur concurrently during this phase. During any lull in testing, training procedures can be established. For this reason, the steps are numbered to show concurrent steps with a prefix (i.e., the letters A and B) to differentiate between the testing and the training.

FIGURE 9-1

OVERVIEW – TESTING AND TRAINING PHASE

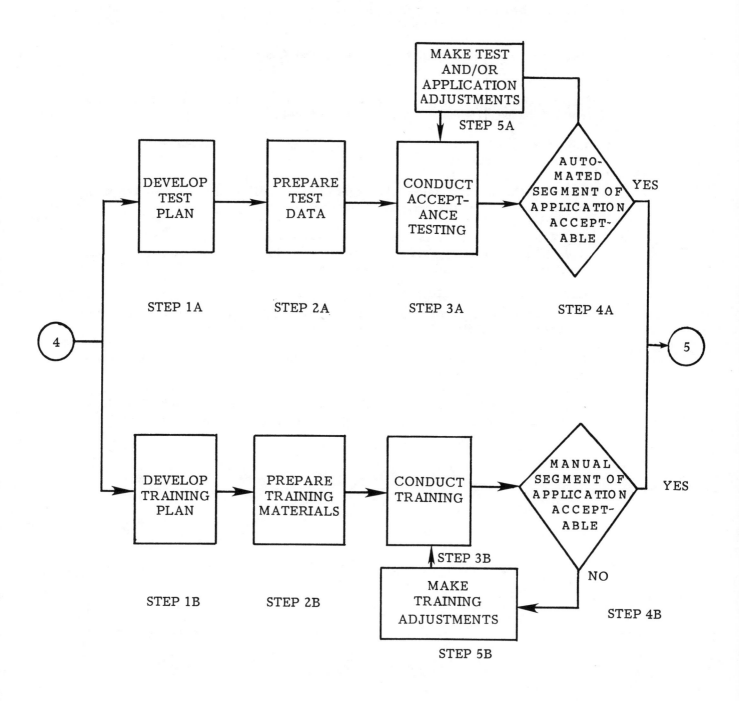

Steps included in the testing and training phase are (see Figure 9-1):

o   Step 1A: Develop testing plan - Prepare a detailed plan to ensure that the change has been implemented correctly.

o   Step 1B: Develop training plan - Prepare a detailed plan to ensure the change has been implemented correctly.

o   Step 2A: Prepare test data - Develop the transactions that will test the change.

o   Step 2B: Prepare training materials - Develop the written material and courses that will be used to instruct people affected by the change.

o   Step 3A: Conduct acceptance testing - User and data processing personnel jointly test the change.

o   Step 3B: Conduct training - The users of the application are instructed what they must do differently because of the change.

o   Step 4A: Determine if the automated segment of the application is acceptable.   The test results must be reviewed and a determination made concerning whether or not they achieved the change specifications.

o   Step 4B: Determine whether the manual segment of the application system is acceptable - An assessment needs to be made whether the involved parties have the needed materials and are adequately trained.

o   Step 5A: Make adjustments to the test and/or application - If testing or the application is not acceptable, make the necessary changes.

o   Step 5B: Make training adjustments - If the training material is inadequate or the people inadequately trained, the necessary adjustments should be made.

STEP 1A - DEVELOP TEST PLAN

The test plan for systems maintenance is a shorter, more directed version of a test plan used for a new application system. While new application testing can take many weeks or months, systems maintenance testing often needs to be done within a single day or a few hours.

Because of time constraints, many of the steps that might be performed individually in a new system are combined or condensed into a short time span. This increases the need for planning so that all aspects of the test can be executed within the allotted time.

The types of testing will vary based upon the implemented change. For example, if a report is modified, there is little need to test recovery and backup plans. On the other hand, if new files are created or processing procedures changed, then restart and recovery should be tested.

The preparation of a test plan is a two-part process. The first part is the determination of what types of tests should be conducted, and the second part is the plan on how to conduct them. Both parts are important in systems maintenance testing.

Among the types of testing that need to be considered are:

o   Testing changed transactions

o   Testing changed programs

o   Testing operating procedures

o   Testing control group procedures

o   Testing user procedures

o   Testing intersystem connections

o   Testing job control language

o   Testing interface to systems software

o   Testing execution of interface to software systems

o   Testing security

o   Testing backup/recovery procedures

The test plan should list the testing objective, the method of testing, and the desired result. In addition, regression testing might be used to verify that unchanged segments have not been unintentionally altered. Intersystem connections should be tested to ensure that all systems are properly modified to handle the change.

An Acceptance Test Plan Worksheet is included as Figure 9-2. This worksheet should be completed by the systems maintenance analyst and countersigned by the individual responsible for accepting the changed system. The information contained on the form is described in the form's completion instructions sheet.

FIGURE 9-2

ACCEPTANCE TEST PLAN WORKSHEET

APPLICATION NAME _____	NUMBER_____	CHANGE IDENT #_____

INDIVIDUAL RESPONSIBLE FOR TEST_____

TEST PLAN

CHANGE OBJECTIVE	METHOD OF TESTING	DESIRED RESULTS

REGRESSION TEST PLAN

INTERSYSTEM TEST PLAN

COMMENTS

INDIVIDUAL WHO ACCEPTS TESTED APPLICATION_____ DATE_____

FORM COMPLETION INSTRUCTIONS

Figure 9-2 - Acceptance Test Plan Worksheet

FIELD	INSTRUCTIONS FOR ENTERING DATA
o Application name	The name by which the application is known.
o Number	The application identifier.
o Change Ident #	The sequence number that uniquely identifies the change.
o Individual responsible for test	The name of the individual or individuals who will be conducting the test. This normally is the user and the application systems analyst/programmer.
o Test plan	The steps that need to be followed in conducting the test. For the functional, regression, stress, and performance types of testing, the following test characteristics need to be defined: - Change objective: the description of the objective of the change that was installed. This should be specific so that test planning can be based on the characteristics of the objective. - Method of testing: the type of test that will be conducted to verify that the objective is achieved. - Desired result: the expected result from conducting the test. If this result is achieved, the implementation can be considered successful, while failure to meet this result means an unsuccessful implementation.
o Regression test plan	The tests and procedures to be followed to be assured that unchanged segments of the application system have not been inadvertently changed by systems maintenance.
o Intersystem test plan	The tests to be conducted to assure that data flowing from and to other systems will be correctly handled after the change.
o Comments	Additional information that might prove helpful in conducting or verifying the test results.
o Individual who accepts tested application	The name of the individual who should review this test plan because of the responsibility to accept the change after successful testing.
o Date	The date on which the form was completed.

STEP 1B - DEVELOP TRAINING PLAN

Training is an often overlooked aspect of systems maintenance. Many of the changes are small; this fosters the belief that training is not needed. Also, the fact that many changes originate in the user area leads the systems maintenance analyst to the conclusion that the users already know what they want and have trained their staff accordingly. All these assumptions may be wrong.

The systems maintenance analyst should evaluate each change for its impact on the procedures performed by people. If the change impacts those procedures, then training material should be prepared. However, changes that increase performance and which have no impact on users of the system do not require training unless they affect the operation of the system. In that case, computer operations personnel would need training. Training cannot be designed by someone who is unfamiliar with existing training material. The systems maintenance change is incorporated into the application system. The training requirements are likewise incorporated into existing training material. Therefore, it behooves the application project personnel to maintain an inventory of training material.

Training Material Inventory Form

Most application systems have limited training material. The more common types of training material include:

o   Orientation to the project narrative

o   User manuals

o   Illustrations of completed forms and how to complete them

o   Explanation and action to take on error listings

o   Explanations of reports and how to use them

o   Explanation of input data and how to enter it

A form for inventorying training material is included as Figure 9-3. The form should be completed and filed with the systems maintenance analyst. Whenever a change is made, the form can be duplicated, and at that point the "needs updating" column can be completed to indicate whether or not training material must be changed as a result of incorporating the maintenance need.

The columns to be completed on the form are explained on the form's completion instructions sheet.

Training Plan Worksheet

The Training Plan Worksheet is a why, who, what, where, when, and how approach to training. The individual developing the plan must answer those questions about each change in order to determine the scope of training programs.

FIGURE 9-3

TRAINING MATERIAL INVENTORY

APPLICATION NAME_____	NUMBER_____	CHANGE IDENT #_____	
AREA NAME	TRAINING MATERIAL DESCRIPTION	NEEDS UPDATING YES	NO

PREPARED BY_____ DATE _____

FORM COMPLETION INSTRUCTIONS

Figure 9-3 - Training Material Inventory

FIELD	INSTRUCTIONS FOR ENTERING DATA
o Application name	The name by which the application is known.
o Number	The application identifier.
o Change Ident #	The sequence number that uniquely identifies the change.
o Training material name	The name or number by which the training material is known.
o Training material description	A brief narrative description of what is contained in the training material.
o Needs updating	Columns to be completed whenever a change is installed. The columns provide an indication of whether the training material needs updating (yes column) or does not need updating (no column).
o Prepared by	The name of the individual responsible for maintaining the inventory.
o Date	The last date on which the inventory was updated.

The points to ponder in developing training programs are:

o   Why conduct training? Do the changes incorporated into the application system necessitate training people?

o   Who should be trained? If training needs to be given, then it must be determined which individuals, categories of people, or departments require that training.

o   What training is required? The training plan must determine the content of the necessary training material.

o   Where should training be given? The location of the training session, or dissemination of the training material, can impact how and when the material is presented.

o   When should training be given? Confusion might ensue if people are trained too far in advance of the implementation of new procedures. For example, even training provided a few days prior to the change may cause confusion as people might be uncertain as to whether to follow the new or the old procedure. In addition, it may be necessary to conduct training both immediately before and immediately after the change to reinforce the new procedures and to answer questions immediately after the new procedures are installed.

o   How should the training material be designed? The objective of training is to provide people with the tools and procedures necessary to do their job. The type of change will frequently determine the type of training material to be developed.

o   What are the expected training results? The developers of the training plan should have in mind the behavior changes or skills to be obtained through the training sessions. They should also determine whether or not training is effective.

A worksheet is included as Figure 9-4 to document the training plan. This is designed to provide space to indicate the above types of information. In addition, the responsible individual and the dates needed for training can also be documented on the form. The information contained on the Training Plan Worksheet is described on the form's completion instructions sheet.

STEP 2A - PREPARE TEST DATA

Data must be prepared for testing all the areas changed during a systems maintenance process. For many applications, the existing test data will be sufficient to test the new change. However, in many situations new test data will need to be prepared.

In some cases, the preparation of test data can be significantly different for systems maintenance than for new systems. For example, when the system is operational it may be possible to test the application in a live operational mode. This eliminates the need for technical test data, and enables maintenance systems analysts to use the same input the users of the application prepare. Special accounts can be established to accumulate test data processed during testing in a production mode. The information in these accounts can then be eliminated after the test, which negates the effect of entering test data into a production environment.

It is important to test both what should be accomplished, as well as what can go wrong. Most tests do a good job of verifying that the spcifications have been implemented properly. Where testing frequently is inadequate is in verifying the unanticipated conditions. Included in this category are:

o   Transaction with erroneous data

o   Unauthorized transactions

o   Transactions entered too early

o   Transactions entered too late

o   Transactions that do not correspond with master data contained in the application

o   Grossly erroneous transactions, such as transactions that do not belong to the application being tested

o   Transactions with larger values in the fields than anticipated

These types of transactions can be designed doing a simple risk analysis scenario. The risk analysis scenario involves brainstorming with key people involved in the application, such as users, maintenance systems analysts, and auditors. These people attempt to ask all the questions, such as, "What if this type of error were entered? What would happen if too large a value were entered in this field?"

STEP 2B - PREPARE TRAINING MATERIAL

The material judged necessary to the training plan must be prepared. The tasks required to perform this step are similar to those used in making a change to an application system. In most instances, training material will exist, but will need to be modified because of the change. Changes in the program must be accompanied by changes in the training material.

Individuals responsible for modifying training should consider the following tasks:

o   Identifying the impact of the change on people

o   Determining what type of training must be unlearned (people must be stopped from doing certain tasks)

o   Determining whether "unlearning" is included in the training material

o   Making plans to delete outmoded training material

o   Determining what new learning is needed (this should come from the training plan)

FIGURE 9-4

TRAINING PLAN WORKSHEET

APPLICATION NAME _____ NUMBER _____		CHANGE IDENT #_____
INDIVIDUAL RESPONSIBLE FOR TRAINING_____		
TRAINING PLAN		

#	GROUP NEEDING TRAINING	TRAINING APPROACH	DESIRED RESULT
1.	Transaction origination staff		
2.	Data entry clerk		
3.	Control group – EDP		
4.	Control group – user		
5.	Computer operations		
6.	Records retention		
7.	Third party customers		
8.	User management and staff		
9.	Other:_____		
10.	Other:_____		

TRAINING DATES

Date training material prepared _____
Date training can commence_____
Date training to be completed_____

COMMENTS

INDIVIDUAL WHO ACCEPTS TRAINING AS SUFFICIENT_____ DATE_____

FORM COMPLETION INSTRUCTIONS

Figure 9-4 - Training Plan Worksheet

FIELD	INSTRUCTIONS FOR ENTERING DATA
o Application name	The name by which the application is known.
o Number	The application identifier.
o Change Ident #	The sequence number that uniquely identifies the change.
o Individual responsible for training	The individual with the overall responsibility for ensuring that all the training material is prepared, taught, and evaluated prior to the implementation of the change.
o Training plan	The details of why, who, what, where, when, how, and the results to be derived from the training plan. The remainder of the form deals with this plan.
o #	A sequential number indicating the number of the group to be trained.
o Group needing training	The name of the individual, type of person, or department requiring training. Figure 9-4 lists some representative groups of people. In practice, the names of the actual people or groups to be trained would be substituted. The groups to consider include: - Transaction origination staff: the people who originate data into the application system. - Data entry clerk: the person that transcribes data to computer media. - Control group - EDP: the group responsible for ensuring that all input is received and that output is reasonable. - Control group - user: the group in the user area responsible for the accuracy, completeness, and authorization of data. - Computer operations: the group responsible for running the application on computer hardware. - Records retention: the group or groups responsible for saving backup data.

FORM COMPLETION INSTRUCTIONS

Figure 9-4 - Training Plan Worksheet

FIELD	INSTRUCTIONS FORM ENTERING DATA
Group needing training (Cont'd)	- Third party customers: people with unsatisfied needs or people who are the ultimate recipients of reports, such as invoices. - User management and staff: the group responsible for the application. - Other: any other involved party requiring training.
o Training approach	The why, what, where, when, and how of the training plan.
o Desired results	The expected result, behavior change, or skills to be gained from the training material.
o Training dates	Important dates for implementing the training plan; the most common dates are: - Date training material prepared - Date training can commence - Date training to be completed
o Comments	Any material helpful in designing, teaching, or evaluating the training material.
o Individual who accepts training as sufficient	The name of the individual or department who must agree if the training is adequate. This individual should also concur with the training plan.
o Date	The date the training plan was developed.

o   Determining where in the training material that new learning should be inserted

o   Preparing the training material that will cause people to learn the new skills (this should be specified in the training plan)

o   Designing that material

o   Determining the best method of training (this should be documented in the training plan)

o   Developing procedures so that the new training material will be incorporated into the existing training material on the right date, and that other supportive training will occur at the proper time

An inventory should be maintained of the new/modified training modules. This is in addition to the training material inventory, which is hard copy material. The training modules are designed to be supportive of that training material. This helps determine what modules need to be altered to achieve the behavior changes/new skills required because of the change.

A training module inventory form is included as Figure 9-5. This should be completed by the individual responsible for training. The information contained on the form is described on the form's completion instructions form.

STEP 3A - CONDUCT ACCEPTANCE TESTING

Acceptance testing is normally conducted by both the user and systems maintenance team. The testing is designed to provide the user assurance that the change has been properly implemented. The role of the systems maintenance project team is to aid the user in conducting and evaluating the test.

Acceptance testing for systems maintenance is normally not extensive. In an on-line environment the features would be installed and the user would test them in a regular production environment. In a batch environment, special computer runs must be set up to run the acceptance testing (because of the cost, these runs are sometimes eliminated).

An effective method for conducting acceptance testing is to prepare a checklist providing both the administrative and technical data needed to conduct the test. This ensures that everything is ready at the time the test is to be conducted. A checklist for conducting a systems maintenance acceptance test is illustrated in Figure 9-6. This form should be prepared by the systems maintenance analyst as an aid in helping the user conduct the test. The information contained on the Conduct Acceptance Test Checklist is described on the form's completion instructions sheet.

STEP 3B - CONDUCT TRAINING

The training task is primarily one of coordination in that it must ensure that everything needed for training has been prepared.

FIGURE 9-5

NEW/MODIFIED TRAINING MODULES

APPLICATION NAME _____ NUMBER _____ CHANGE IDENT # _____
TRAINING MODULE INVENTORY

TRAINING MODULE DESCRIPTION	DESCRIPTION OF CHANGE	TRAINING MATERIAL	WHO SHOULD BE TRAINED	METHOD OF TRAINING					
				Meeting	Classroom	Self-study	New procedure	Supervisor	Other

PREPARED BY_____ DATE _____

FORM COMPLETION INSTRUCTIONS

Figure 9-5 - New/Modified Training Modules

FIELD	INSTRUCTIONS FOR ENTERING DATA
o Application name	The name by which the application is known.
o Number	The application identifier.
o Change Ident #	The sequence number that uniquely identifies the change.
o Training module inventory	The remainder of the information on the form describes the modules.
o Training module description	A brief narrative of the training module. The location of the training material should be identified so that it can be easily obtained.
o Description of change	As the training module becomes modified, this column should contain a sequential listing of all the changes made to the training module. In effect, it is a change history for the training module.
o Training material	The course material included in the training module.
o Who should be trained	The individual(s) to whom the training module is directed.
o Method of training	The recommended way in which the training module should be used. The most common methods of training, which are included on the form, are: - Meeting - Classroom training - Self-study - New procedure - Supervisor given - Other
o Prepared by	The name of the individual who prepared the inventory form.
o Date	The date on which it was last updated.

The coordination normally involves the following tasks:

o   Scheduling training dates

o   Notifying the people who should attend training

o   Obtaining training facilities

o   Obtaining instructors

o   Reproducing the material in sufficient quantity for all those requiring the material

o   Training instructors

o   Having the classroom or meeting room set up in a desired fashion

Many times training will be provided through manuals or special material delivered to the involved parties. The type of training should be determined when the training plan is developed and the material is prepared.

A training checklist should be prepared. A sample checklist for conducting training is illustrated in Figure 9-7. The individual responsible for training should prepare this checklist for use during the training period to ensure all the needed training is provided. The information included on the Conduct Training Checklist is described on the form's completion instructions sheet.

STEP 4A - AUTOMATED APPLICATION ACCEPTABLE?

The automated segment of an application is acceptable if it meets the change specification requirements. If it fails to meet those measurable objectives, the system is unacceptable and should be returned for additional modification. This requires setting measurable objectives, preparing test data, and then evaluating the results of those tests.

The responsibility for determining if the application is acceptable belongs to the user. In applications with multiple users, one user may be appointed responsible for all users. In other instances, all users may test their own segment or they may act as a committee to verify whether or not the system is acceptable. The poorest approach is to delegate this responsibility to the data processing department.

Test results can be verified through manual or automated means. The tediousness and effort required for manual verification has caused many data processing professionals to shortcut the testing process. When automated verification is used, the process is not nearly as time consuming, and tends to be performed more accurately.

A difficult question to answer on acceptability is whether 100% correctness is required on the change. For example, if 100 items are checked and 99 prove correct, should the application be rejected because of the one remaining problem? The answer to this question depends upon the importance of that one remaining item.

FIGURE 9-6

ACCEPTANCE TEST CHECKLIST

| APPLICATION NAME _____ | NUMBER _____ | CHANGE IDENT # _____ |

ADMINISTRATIVE DATA

Date of test _____

Location of test _____

Time of test _____

DP person in charge of test _____

User person in charge of test _____

Computer time available _____

TECHNICAL DATA

#	RESOURCE NEEDED	LOCATION	AVAILABLE		
			YES	NO	N/A
1.	Test transactions				
2.	Master files/data base				
3.	Operator instruction				
4.	Special media/forms				
5.	Acceptance criteria				
6.	Input support personnel				
7.	Output support personnel				
8.	Control group				
9.	External control proof				
10.	Backup/recovery plan				
11.	Security plan				
12.	Error message actions				

PREPARED BY_____ DATE _____

Figure 9-6 - Acceptance Test Checklist

FIELD	INSTRUCTIONS FOR ENTERING DATA
o Application name	The name by which the application is known.
o Number	The application identifier.
o Change Ident #	The sequence number that uniquely identifies the change.
o Administrative data	The administrative data relates to the management of the test and normally includes the following information: - Date of test - Location of test - Time of test - DP person in charge of test - User person in charge of test - Computer time - Other: any other administrative data needed in order
o Technical data	The resources needed to conduct the acceptance test and the location of those resources. The information that should be documented about the needed resources include: - #: the sequential number of the resources needed - Resource needed: the exact resource needed - Location: the physical location of that resource. In many acceptance tests the resources are marshalled in a common area to await the conducting the test.

FIELD	INSTRUCTIONS FOR ENTERING DATA
	- Available: an indication as to whether or not the information has been gathered. A checkmark in the "yes" column indicates the information is available at the indicated location; a "no" indicates the information is not available and if it is needed it must be obtained; while a "N/A (not applicable)" indicates that the resource noted on the form is not needed for this test. The more common type of resources which are needed for acceptance testing and which are included on the form are: a. Test transactions b. Master file/data base c. Operator instructions d. Special media/forms e. Acceptance criteria f. Input support personnel (time) g. Output support personnel (time) h. Control group (time) i. External control proof j. Backup/recovery plan k. Security plan l. Error message action m. Other: any other resource needed
o Prepared by	The name of the individual preparing the form.
o Date	The date on which the form was prepared.

FIGURE 9-7

CONDUCT TRAINING CHECKLIST

APPLICATION NAME _____			NUMBER ____	CHANGE IDENT # _____			
TRAINING CHECKLIST							
NAME OF INDIVIDUAL REQUIRING TRAINING	DEPARTMENT	TRAINING REQUIRED	DATES		LOCATION	INSTRUCTOR	COMMENTS
			Sched-uled	Taken			

PREPARED BY _____ DATE _____

Figure 9-7 - Conduct Training Checklist

FIELD	INSTRUCTIONS FOR ENTERING DATA
o Application name	The name by which the application is known.
o Number	The application identifier.
o Change Ident #	The sequence number that uniquely identifies the change.
o Training checklist	The remainder of the form contains the checklist information, which is: - Name of individual requiring training: whenever possible, actual names should be used, as opposed to groups of people, so records can be maintained as to whether or not the people actually took the training. - Department: the department/organization with which the individual is affiliated. - Training required: the training modules and/or material to be given the individual. - Dates: the dates on which the course is to be given or the training material to be disseminated to the individual. The scheduled dates should be listed, as well as the date that the individual actually took the course or received the material. - Location: the location of the course or the location to which the training material should be distributed. - Instructor: the name of the responsible individual should be listed. - Comments: any other information that would verify that training took place. In classroom situations where examinations are given, the space could be used to record that grade.
o Prepared by	The name of the individual preparing the form who should be the one responsible for ensuring the training is given.
o Date	The date on which the form was prepared.

Users should expect that their systems will operate as specified. However, this may mean that the user may decide to install the application and then correct the error after implementation.

The user has two options when installing a change known to have an error. The first is to ignore the problem and live with the results. For example, if a heading is misplaced or misspelled, the user may decide that that type of error, while annoying, does not affect the user of the output results. The second option is to make the adjustments manually. For example, if necessary, final totals could be manually calculated and added to the reports. In either case, the situation should be temporary.

Automated Application Segment Failure Notification

Each failure noted during the testing the automated segment of the application system should be documented. If it is known that the change will not be corrected until after the application is placed into production, then the problem identification form as described in Phase 1 of the systems maintenance process should be completed to document the problem. However, if the change is to be corrected during the testing process, then a special form should be used for that purpose.

A form for notifying the systems maintenance analyst that a failure has been uncovered in the automated segment of the application is illustrated in Figure 9-8. This form is to be used as a correction vehicle within the test phase. This form should be prepared by the individual uncovering the failure and then sent to the systems maintenance analyst in charge of the change for correction. The information contained on the Automated Application Segment Test Failure Notification form is described on the form's completion instructions sheet.

STEP 4B - MANUAL SEGMENT ACCEPTABLE?

Users must make the same acceptability decisions on the manual segments of the application system as they make on the automated segments. Many of the manual segments do not come under the control of the maintenance systems analyst. However, this does not mean that the correct processing of the total system is not of concern to the maintenance systems analyst.

The same procedures that are followed in verifying the automated segment should be followed in verifying the manual segment. The one difference is that there are rarely automated means for verifying manual processing. Verifying manual segments can take as much - if not more - time than verifying the automated segment.

The more common techniques to verify the correctness of the manaual segment include:

o   Observation - The individual responsible for verification observes people performing the tasks. That individual usually develops a checklist from the procedures and then determines whether or not the individual performs all of the required steps.

FIGURE 9-8

AUTOMATED APPLICATION SEGMENT TEST FAILURE NOTIFICATION

APPLICATION   CHANGE

NAME _____ NUMBER _____ IDENT # _____

DESCRIPTION OF FAILURE

TEST DATE _____ FAILURE # _____

SYSTEM CHANGE OBJECTIVE FAILED _____

_____

DESCRIPTION OF FAILURE _____

_____

_____

RECOMMENDED CORRECTION

PROGRAMS AFFECTED _____

_____

DATA AFFECTED _____

_____

DESCRIPTION OF CORRECTION _____

_____

_____

CORRECTION ASSIGNMENTS

CORRECTION ASSIGNED TO _____

DATE CORRECTION NEEDED _____

COMMENTS _____

_____

_____

_____

PREPARED BY _____ DATE _____

Figure 9-8 - Automated Application Segment Test Failure Notification

FIELD	INSTRUCTIONS FOR ENTERING DATA
o Application name	The name by which the application is known.
o Number	The application identifier.
o Change Ident #	The sequence number that uniquely identifies the change.
o Description of	A brief description of the condition that is believed to be unacceptable. In most instances, the detailed information would be presented orally as would the documentation supporting the failure. The purpose of the form is to record the problem and control the implementation. The information contained in this section includes: - Failure #: A sequentially increasing number used to control the identification and implementation of problems. If a form is lost or mislaid, it will be noticed because a failure number will be missing. - Test date: the date of the test. - System change objective failed: the measurable change objective that was not achieved. - Description of failure: a brief narrative description of what is wrong.
o Recommended correction	Corrections suggested by the individual uncovering the failure or the systems maintenance analyst after an analysis of the problem. The type of information included in the recommendation is: - Programs affected: all the programs that contributed to the failure. - Data affected: all the data elements, records, or files that contributed or were involved in the failure. - Description of correction: a brief description of the recommended solution.
o Correction assignments	This section is completed by the systems maintenance analyst to assign the correction of the failure to a specific individual. At a minimum, this should include: - Correction assigned to (name of individual) - Date correction needed - Comments (suggestions on how to implement the solution)
o Prepared by	The name of the individual who uncovered the failure.
o Date	The date the failure was uncovered.

o   Examination - The people performing the task need to evaluate whether or not they can correctly perform the task. For example, in a data entry operation, the data entry operator may be asked to enter that information in a controlled mode.

o   Verification - The individual responsible for determining that the training is correct examines the results of processing from the trained people to determine whether or not they comply with the expected processing.

If the training is not acceptable, the user must decide again whether or not to delay the change. In most instances, the user will not delay the implementation of change if there are only minor problems in training but, instead, will attempt to compensate for those problems during processing. On the other hand, if it becomes apparent that the users are ill-equipped to use the application, then the change should be delayed until the individuals are better trained.

The methods that users can incorporate to overcome minor training deficiencies include:

o   Restricted personnel - The new types of processing are only performed by people who have successfully completed the training. Thus, those who need more skills have time to obtain them before they begin using the new procedures or data.

o   Supervisory review - Supervisors can spend extra time reviewing the work of people to be assured that the tasks are performed correctly.

o   Data processing assistance - The systems maintenance analysts/programmers can work with user personnel during an interim period to help them process the information correctly.

o   Overtime - Crash training sessions can be held in the evening or weekends to bring the people up to the necessary skill level.

Training Failure Notification Form

Training failures should be documented in the same level of detail as failures of the computerized segment of the application are. However, procedural errors can cause as many serious problems as incorrect computer code can. Unless these failures are documented, people can easily overlook the problem and assume someone else will correct it.

Each failure uncovered in training should be documented on a Training Failure Notification form. This form should be completed by the individual who uncovers the problem, and then presented to the individual responsible for training for necessary action. A form that can be used to document training failures is illustrated in Figure 9-9. The information contained on the Training Failure Notification form is described on the form's completion instructions sheet.

FIGURE 9-9

TRAINING FAILURE NOTIFICATION

APPLICATION
NAME _____ NUMBER _____

CHANGE
IDENT # _____

DESCRIPTION OF FAILURE

FAILURE # _____

TEST DATE _____

PEOPLE NOT ADEQUATELY TRAINED _____

_____

_____

FAILURE CAUSED BY LACK OF TRAINING _____

_____

RECOMMENDED CORRECTION

TRAINING MATERIAL NEEDING REVISIONS _____

_____

_____

NEW METHOD OF TRAINING NEEDED _____

_____

PEOPLE NEEDING TRAINING _____

_____

DESCRIPTION OF CORRECTION _____

_____

CORRECTION ASSIGNMENTS

CORRECTION ASSIGNED TO _____

TRAINING MATERIAL NEEDING CORRECTION _____

COMMENTS _____

_____

PREPARED BY _____ DATE _____

FORM COMPLETION INSTRUCTIONS

Figure 9-9 - Training Failure Notification

FIELD	INSTRUCTIONS FOR ENTERING DATA
o Application name	The name by which the application is known.
o Number	The application identifier.
o Change Ident #	The sequence number that uniquely identifies the change.
o Description of failure	The details of the training failure need to be described. As a minimum, this would include: - Failure number: a sequentially increasing number used to control the failure form. - Test date: the date on which the test occurred. - People not adequately trained: the name of individuals, categories of people or departments who could not adequately perform their tasks. - Failure caused by lack of training: a description of why the training was inadequate.
o Recommended correction	Suggestions for correcting the failure. This section can be completed either by the individual uncovering the failure and/or by the maintenance systems analyst. The type of information helpful in correcting the training failure includes: - Training material needing revisions: the specific material that should be modified to correct the problem. - New method of training needed: suggestions for varying the training method, such as going from issuing training bulletins to holding a training class. - People needing training: all of the people that may need new training. - Description of (recommended) correction: a brief narrative explanation of the recommended solution.

Figure 9-9 - Training Failure Notification (Cont'd)

FIELD	INSTRUCTIONS FOR ENTERING DATA
o Correction assignments	Assignments made by the individual responsible for training. At a minimum, each assignment would include: - Correction assigned to: name of individual who will make the necessary adjustments to training material. - Training material corrections needed: the specific training document(s) that need changing. - Comments: recommendations on how to change the training material.
o Prepared by	The name of the individual who uncovered the failure.
o Date	The date in which the failure occurred.

STEP 5A - MAKING TEST ADJUSTMENTS

Corrections to problems should be implemented in the application system and then the system should be retested. The suggestions outlined in the implementing the change phase are equally applicable to making corrections during the test phase. The recommendations for testing an application system likewise apply to testing corrections made during the testing phase.

When a new change is entered to the application system (even a change made during the testing phase), the maintenance systems analyst should not assume that previously tested segments will work correctly. It is quite possible that the new change has caused problems to nonchanged portions. Unfortunately, it may mean that much of the testing already completed may have to be repeated.

STEP 5B - MAKING TRAINING ADJUSTMENTS

Identified training adjustments can be made in numerous ways. The methods selected will obviously be dependent upon the type of failure uncovered. In some instances, a single individual may have been overlooked and the training can be presented to them individually. In other cases, new training material may have to be prepared and taught.

The procedures described in this section for developing training materials apply equally to correcting training materials. In addition, if people have been improperly instructed, steps may have to be taken to inform them of the erroneous training and then to provide them with the proper training.

PHASE 4 - FEEDBACK

Without feedback, it is difficult to continually improve the training and testing procedures. The feedback is a byproduct of executing the phase.

The incorporation of feedback mechanisms into the training and testing procedures should be specified by data processing management. They should determine the types of feedback they want included to monitor the phase and then take the steps necessary to ensure that they get it. The frequency with which data processing management sees feedback information is a function of the effectiveness of the phase.

The types of feedback information that have proved beneficial in monitoring testing and training include (see Figure 9-10):

o   Number of tests

Number of acceptance tests conducted for each change. It should also show which changes have not conducted acceptance tests. This will provide data processing management with insight into the effectiveness of acceptance testing and the use of acceptance testing.

o   Number of problems detected during test

FIGURE 9-10

PHASE 4

TESTING AND TRAINING

FEEDBACK DATA	SOURCE	PURPOSE
Number of tests	Job accounting systems	To determine effectiveness of acceptance test plan and to identify changes not acceptance tested
Number of problems detected during test	Test failure notification form	To determine effectiveness of testing during the change phase
Size of changes to training manuals	Inquiry of individuals responsible for training material	To determine the amount of data processing resources going into training, and to justify cost of changes
Training problems detected during test	Training failure notification form	To determine the effectiveness of the training plan and the implementation of the plan
Testing/training schedules missed	Change planning sheets showing dates	To determine the effectiveness of conducting the acceptance test phase
Testing/training cost overrun	Job accounting system	To determine the effectiveness of the testing/training team in completing the phase within the allocated costs
Number of training sessions	Inquiry to individual responsible for training	To determine the amount of effort expended on training associated with systems maintenance

The success of program testing can be determined by the number of problems detected during acceptance testing. However, the number of errors may be attributable to poor user specifications or misunderstanding of user specifications.

   o   Size of changes to training manuals

The number of pages of training material which need to be developed should be monitored. This helps identify the allocation of data processing resources and helps explain the cost of making changes.

   o   Training problems detected during testing

The frequency that training problems occur indicates the quality of material and training sessions provided. However, it too, can be attributable to making generally poor user specifications.

   o   Testing/training schedules missed

This feedback data indicates when changes fall behind scheduled implementation dates because of the acceptance testing phase. Obviously, many of the problems may be attributable to problems in the previous phases.

   o   Testing/training cost overruns

This feedback data indicates when acceptance testing costs exceed acceptance testing budgets. This can be due to problems in the previous phases or improperly planned testing/training.

   o   Number of training sessions

This feedback data measures the amount of time and effort that go into conducting training because of system changes. Again, it measures the use of data processing resources.

PHASE 4 - REVIEW CHECKLIST

Data processing management should periodically review the effectiveness of the testing and training phase for two reasons: first it indicates management's interest in testing and training to the members of the department; and second, it enables management to determine if existing procedures are being followed and if those procedures are effective. If the procedures are found to be ineffective, they should be adjusted.

A checklist is included to review the phase (see Figure 9-11). This checklist is designed to be used by data processing management. The review should occur periodically, probably once per year unless serious problems have been encountered in either testing or training, or both.

SUMMARY

At the completion of the testing and training phase, the change is ready to be placed into production. If problems are not detected, they will be carried into the production system. In production, these problems can result in losses to the organization.

Testing and training associated with systems maintenance is frequently minimal or nonexistent. This is particularly true with small system changes. At the same time, many problems occur because the testing is inadequate.

This chapter has outlined the steps necessary to develop an effective testing and training process for systems maintenance. The chapter has outlined the control concerns that need to be addressed in designing these processes, and to provide the forms and procedures necessary to deal with those control concerns. The use of feedback and a management checklist will enable data processing management to continually monitor the effectiveness of this phase.

FIGURE 9-11

TESTING AND TRAINING REVIEW CHECKLIST

NUMBER	MANAGEMENT QUESTION	RESPONSE			COMMENTS
		YES	NO	N/A	
1.	Are systems maintenance analysts required to develop a test plan?				
2.	Must each change be reviewed to determine if it has an impact on training?				
3.	If a change has an impact on training, do procedures require that a training plan be established?				
4.	Is an inventory prepared of training material so that it can be updated?				
5.	Does the training plan make one individual responsible for training?				
6.	Does the training plan identify the results desired from training?				
7.	Does the training plan indicate the who, why, what, where, when, and how of training?				
8.	Does the training plan provide a training schedule, including dates?				
9.	Is an individual responsible for determining if training is acceptable?				
10.	Are all of the training modules inventoried?				
11.	Does each training module have a history of the changes made to the module?				
12.	Is one individual assigned responsibility for testing?				

FIGURE 9-11

TESTING AND TRAINING REVIEW CHECKLIST (Cont'd)

NUMBER	MANAGEMENT QUESTION	RESPONSE			COMMENTS
		YES	NO	N/A	
13.	Does the test plan list each measurable change objective and the method of testing that objective?				
14.	Does the training plan list the desired results from testing?				
15.	Does the training plan address regression testing?				
16.	Does the training plan address inter-system testing?				
17.	Is someone responsible for judging when testing is acceptable?				
18.	Is an acceptance testing checklist prepared to determine the necessary resources are ready for the test?				
19.	Does the acceptance testing checklist include the administrative aspects of the test?				
20.	Is a training checklist prepared which indicates which individuals need training?				
21.	Is a record kept of whether or not individuals receive training?				
22.	Is each test failure documented?				
23.	Is each training failure documented?				
24.	Are test failures corrected before the change goes into production?				
25.	Are training failures corrected before the change goes into production?				

FIGURE 9-11

TESTING AND TRAINING REVIEW CHECKLIST (Cont'd)

NUMBER	MANAGEMENT QUESTION	RESPONSE			COMMENTS
		YES	NO	N/A	
26.	If the change is put into production before testing/training failures have been corrected, are alternative measures taken to assure the identified errors will not cause problems?				
27.	Is feedback data identified?				
28.	Is feedback data collected?				
29.	Is feedback data regularly reviewed?				
30.	Are control concerns identified?				
31.	Does data processing management periodically review the training and testing phase?				

Chapter 10
Phase 5—Installing the Change

CHAPTER OVERVIEW

The previous phase prepared for the change in the operating environment. The steps involved in this phase relate to that operating environment. These steps ensure not only that the change is installed, but also that it will continue to operate successfully.

Computer operations personnel execute most of the functions in the installing the change phase. These involve the mechanics of installing the new version and deleting unwanted versions. However, the maintenance systems analyst should install procedures to monitor production data to ascertain that the production results are the desired results.

This chapter provides the methods, forms, tips, and techniques for installing system changes. Many production departments have developed elaborate control procedures to ensure that the right version is in production at the right time. Unfortunately, others are still struggling with this type of control. These latter organizations may need to devote extensive resources to designing and installing controls.

OBJECTIVES OF INSTALLING THE CHANGE PHASE

It is data processing management who establish both the systems maintenance phases for their department and the objective for each phase. The establishment of clear-cut objectives helps the systems maintenance analyst and operation personnel understand some of the procedures they are asked to follow. This understanding often results in a better controlled operation.

The primary objective of this phase is to get the right change installed at the right time. The previous phases should have resulted in properly designed and tested changes. In addition, the affected personnel should have received the appropriate training. However, a cautious systems maintenance group still guards against undetected potential problems.

The specific objectives of the installing the change phase are:

    o   <u>Put changed application system into production</u>

Each change should be incorporated through a new version of a program. The production system should have the capability of moving these versions in and out of production on prescribed dates. To do this it is necessary first to uniquely identify each version of a program and second to pinpoint the dates when individual program versions are to be placed in and taken out of production.

    o   <u>Assess the efficiency of changes</u>

If a change results in extensive time and effort to do additional checking, or to locate information not provided by the system, additional changes may be desirable.

o   Monitor the correctness of the change

People should not assume that testing will uncover all of the problems. For example, they may encounter problems in untouched parts of the application. People should be assigned the responsibility to review output immediately following changes. If this is a normal function, then those people should be notified that a change has occurred and should be informed where in the system the change is and what potentially bad outputs might be expected.

o   Keep systems library up to date

When programs are added to the production and source library, other versions should be deleted. This will not happen unless specific action is taken. The application system project team should ensure that unwanted versions in the source and object code libraries are deleted when they have fulfilled their purposes.

PHASE 5 - CONTROL CONCERNS

When the change is put into production, data processing management can never be sure what type of problems may be encountered shortly thereafter. The concerns during the change process deal with properly and promptly installing the change. It is during the installation phase that the results of these change activities become known. Thus, many of the concerns culminate during the installing the change phase.

Data processing management must identify the concerns in each phase so that they can establish the proper control mechanisms to deal with those concerns. The most common concerns during the installing the change phase include:

o   Will the change be installed on time?

When the testing and training phase has been completed, an actual installation date can be established. Data processing management wants the version to go into production on the date specified.

o   Is backup data compatible with the changed system?

Each time an application system is changed, the backup data required for recovery purposes may also have to be changed. Because this step occurs outside the normal change procedures, it may be overlooked. Backup data includes the new program versions, the job control language associated with those programs, and other documentation procedures involved in making the system operational after a problem occurs.

o   Are recovery procedures compatible with the changed system?

Modifying an application system may also require modifying the recovery procedures. If new files have been established, or if new operating procedures or priorities have been designed, they must be incorporated into the recovery procedures.

o   Is the source/object library cluttered with obsolete program versions?

Large source and object libraries negatively impact operations performance. If these libraries are not regularly reviewed and cleared of obsolete programs, resources will be

libraries are not regularly reviewed and cleared of obsolete programs, resources will be unnecessarily consumed.

o   Will errors in the change be detected?

Attempt to detect remaining program errors prior to using the new version to conduct business. This may require extra monitoring to ensure that the output data is accurate and complete.

o   Will errors in the change be corrected?

If an error is detected, it should be corrected. A continual concern of all levels of management is that problems will be recognized but not acted upon.

This chapter provides guidance to data processing management in addressing these control concerns. In addition, the chapter will recommend gathering data to help monitor these situations. Data processing departments installing controls which anticipate problems are normally better run departments.

STEPS INVOLVED IN THE INSTALLING THE CHANGE PHASE

The installing the change phase consists of those steps that take a change from completion of testing through installation and monitoring of the output. The installation of the change is normally quick and routine, but the monitoring of the output may be time consuming and complex. However, monitoring provides the controls necessary for anticipating problems before they become serious (see Figure 10-1).

The installing the change phase is divided into six steps. Some of these are manual and some are heavily automated. Each will be explained in detail in the chapter.

The six steps involved in installing the change phase are:

o   Step 1 - Develop restart/recovery plan

o   Step 2 - Enter change into production

o   Step 3 - Delete unneeded version

o   Step 4 - Operate application

o   Step 5 - Monitor production

o   Step 6 - Document problems

STEP 1 - DEVELOP RESTART/RECOVERY PLAN

Restart and recovery are an important part of application system processing. Restart means computer operations begin from a point of known integrity. On the other hand, recovery occurs when the integrity of the system has been lost. In a recovery process, the system processing must be backed up to a point of known integrity, and then transactions must be rerun to the point where the problem was detected.

FIGURE 10-1

OVERVIEW – INSTALLING THE CHANGE

STEP 4

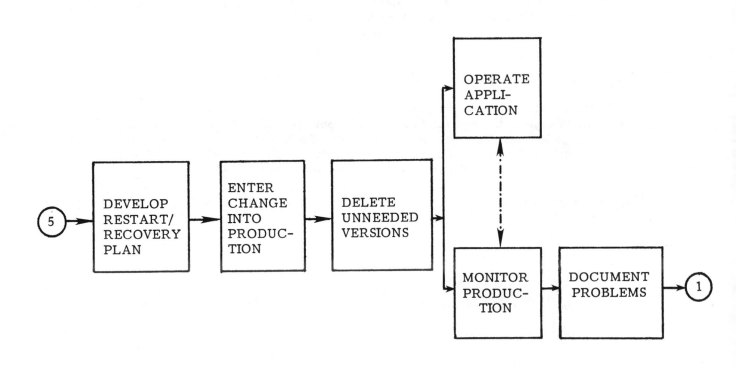

STEP 1   STEP 2   STEP 3   STEP 5   STEP 6

Many aspects of system changes impact the recovery process. Among the changes that should be evaluated for their impact on recovery are:

o   Addition of a new file

o   Change of job control

o   Additional use of utility programs

o   Change in retention periods

o   Change in computer programs

o   Change in operating documentations

o   Introduction of a new or revised form

The systems maintenance analyst should assess each change to determine its impact on the recovery process. If a program is changed, the systems maintenance analyst must ensure that those changes are included in backup data. Without having the latest version of the program, the systems maintenance analyst may not be able to correctly recover computer processing.

If the systems maintenance analyst determines that recovery has been impacted by the change, he/she must update the recovery plan. A worksheet is illustrated in Figure 10-2 for the restart/recovery planning process. This worksheet should be prepared by the systems maintenance analyst and forwarded to the individual responsible for recovery. The information contained on the Restart/Recovery Planning Worksheet is described on the form's completion instructions sheet.

STEP 2 - ENTER CHANGE INTO PRODUCTION

Some positive action must be taken to move a changed program from test status to production status. This action should be taken by the user responsible for approving the change. When the user department is satisfied with the change, the new program versions can be moved into production.

The production environment should be able to control programs according to production date. Each version of a program in the production library should be labeled when it is to go in and when it is to go out of production. If there is no known replacement, then the date to take that version out of production is the latest date that can be put into that field. When a new version has been selected, the date can be changed to the actual date the old version is to go out of production.

A history of changes should be available for each program. The change history provides a complete audit trail of everything that has happened to the program from the date it was first written. The change history, together with a notification to operations that a change is ready for production, provides the necessary controls during this step.

FIGURE 10-2

RESTART/RECOVERY PLANNING WORKSHEET

APPLICATION
SYSTEM _____ NUMBER _____ CHANGE
IDENT # _____

RESTART/RECOVERY PLANNING DATA

IMPACT ON ESTIMATED TOTAL DOWN TIME

IMPACT ON ESTIMATED DOWN TIME FREQUENCY

CHANGE IN DOWN TIME RISK

NEW PROGRAM VERSIONS FOR RECOVERY

NEW FILES/DATA NEEDED FOR RECOVERY

NEW RECOVERY INSTRUCTIONS/PROCEDURES

DATE NEW VERSION OPERATIONAL

COMMENTS

PREPARED BY_____ DATE_____

FORM COMPLETION INSTRUCTIONS

Figure 10-2 — Restart/Recovery Planning Worksheet

FIELD	INSTRUCTIONS FOR ENTERING DATA
o Application system	The name by which the application is known.
o Number	The application identifier.
o Change Ident #	The sequence number that uniquely identifies the change.
o Restart/recovery planning data	The information needed to modify the recovery procedures consumes the remainder of the form. The following worksheet data is helpful in planning needed changes to the recovery process: - Impact on estimated total downtime: one of the criteria used for developing the recovery process is the estimated total downtime. If the change affects the downtime, then the entire recovery process may have to be reevaluated. - Impact on estimated downtime frequency: the number of times that the recovery process will probably need to be executed is an important factor in determining backup data and other procedures. If the change will affect the frequency of downtime, then the entire recovery process may have to be reevaluated. - Change in downtime risk: the probable loss occurring when a system goes down may be a more important factor than either the total downtime or downtime frequency. If the loss is very low, the fact that the system is down may be unimportant; however, if the loss is potentially very high, management must establish strong controls to lessen the downtime risk. If the change causes a probable loss, then the entire recovery process may have to be reevaluated. - New program versions for recovery: each new program version must be included in the recovery plan. This section documents the needed changes.

Figure 10-2 — Restart/Recovery Planning Worksheet (Cont'd)

FIELD	INSTRUCTIONS FOR ENTERING DATA
	– New files/data needed for recovery: changes in data normally impact the recovery process. This section documents the data changes which impact recovery.
	– New recovery instructions/procedures: if operating procedures or instructions have to be modified, this section provides space to document those changes.
	– Date new version operational: this is the date the new programs, files, data, recovery instructions and procedures need to be included in the recovery process.
	– Comments: any additional information that may be helpful in modifying the recovery program to better reflect the changed application system.
o Prepared by	Normally the systems maintenance analyst.
o Date	The date the form was prepared.

History of Change Form

Changes to an application program can be documented using the form in Figure 10-3. The objective of this History of Change form is to show all of the changes made to a program since its inception. This serves two purposes: first, if problems occur, this audit trail indicates whether or not the changes have been made; and second, it discourages unauthorized changes. The information contained on the History of Change form is described in the form's completion instructions sheet.

Notification of Production Change Form

The procedure to move a version from a testing to production should be formalized. Telephone calls and other word-of-mouth procedures may not be sufficient to actually move a program into production. The formal process can be further enhanced by using the number to prevent the loss of notification forms. The systems maintenance project leader should prepare the Notification of Production Change form. The completed form should then be sent to the computer operations department to install a new version. A sample form to be used for this purpose is illustrated in Figure 10-4. The information contained on the Notification of Production Change form is described in the form's completion instructions sheet.

STEP 3 - DELETE UNNEEDED VERSIONS

It may or may not be desirable to delete old versions of programs at the time a new version is entered. The most obvious reason for not deleting an old version is to maintain a fallback version in case the new version proves defective.

Organizations should establish standards regarding at what point old versions should be automatically deleted from the library. Some organizations, while not automating this function, periodically notify the project team that older versions will be deleted unless they, the project team, take specific action to have them retained in the library. Still other organizations charge the projects a fee for retaining versions in libraries.

Do not delete programs from libraries without authorization. Some type of form should be prepared authorizing computer operations personnel to delete programs from a library. This authorization form provides a history of additions to the libraries.

A Source/Object Library Deletion Notice form is illustrated in Figure 10-5. This form is a more effective control if a sequential number is added to the form to control the form so that if it is lost someone will detect the loss. The form should be prepared by the systems maintenance project leader and sent to computer operations for action. The information contained on the Source/Object Library Deletion Notice form is described on the form's completion instructions sheet.

STEP 4 - OPERATE APPLICATION

The objective of the entire systems maintenance process is to satisfy the new need. This is accomplished by incorporating that need into the application system and running it in a production status. If all parts of the systems maintenance process have been properly performed, the production step becomes a mechanical step: the program library automatically calls in the correct version of the program on the proper day. However, if

FIGURE 10-3

HISTORY OF CHANGE

APPLICATION SYSTEM _____ NUMBER _____

| PROGRAM NAME _____ NUMBER _____ |

| CODED BY _____ |

| MAINTAINED BY _____ |

| DATE ENTERED INTO PRODUCTION _____ VERSION # _____ |

| PROGRAM CHANGE HISTORY |

CHANGE IDENT #	NEW VERSION #	CODED BY	DATE ENTERED INTO PRODUCTION	COMMENTS

FORM COMPLETION INSTRUCTIONS

Figure 10-3 - History of Change

FIELD	INSTRUCTIONS FOR ENTERING DATA
o Application system	The name by which the application is known.
o Number	The application identifier.
o Program name	A brief description of the program or its name.
o Number	The program identifier.
o Coded by	The programmer who originally coded the program.
o Maintained by	The programmer who now maintains the program.
o Date entered into production	The calendar date on which the program was first used in production status.
o Version number	The original version number.
o Program change	The information needed to provide an audit trail of changes to a program. The type of information recommended is: - Change ID # - The sequence number that uniquely identifies the change. - New version number - The program version number used to code the change. - Coded by - The name of the programmer who coded the change. - Date entered into production - The calendar date on which this version went into production. - Comments - Additional information valuable in tracing the history of change to a program.

FIGURE 10-4

NOTIFICATION OF PRODUCTION CHANGE

SENT TO _____	APPLICATION CONTROL # _____			
RE: APPLICATION NAME _____ NUMBER_____	CHANGE IDENT # _____			
PRODUCTION CHANGE INSTRUCTIONS				
RESOURCE	TASK		EFFECTIVE DATES	COMMENTS
	ADD	DELETE		
Program #				
Program #				
Program #				
Program #				
JCL statements #				
JCL statements #				
Operator manual procedure #				
Operator manual procedure #				
Other:_____				
Other:_____				
Other:_____				
PREPARED BY_____ DATE_____				

FORM COMPLETION INSTRUCTIONS

Figure 10-4 - Notification of Production Change

FIELD	INSTRUCTIONS FOR ENTERING DATA
o Sent to	The name of the individual in operations who controls the application system being changed.
o Application control #	A sequentially issued number used to control the changes to each application system.
o RE: Application name	The name by which the application is known.
o Number	The application identifier.
o Change Ident #	The sequence number that uniquely identified the change.
o Production change	Instructions to computer operations to move programs, job control statements, operator manual procedures, and other items associated with a program change into a production status. The specific instructions provide for both adding and deleting information. The following information is needed: - Resource: the resource that needs to be added or deleted to the production environment. The most common resources involved in a production change include: a) Programs b) JCL statements c) Operator manual procedures - Task: computer operations needs to be instructed whether to add or delete the resource from the production status. The add column indicates that it is to be moved from a test status to production status, while the delete column indicates that it is to be removed from production status. - Effective date: the date on which the tasks are to be performed. - Comments: additional instructions which help computer operations personnel perform their assignment. For example, this column might include the location or the source of new pages for the operator's manual.
o Prepared by	Normally the name of the systems maintenance project leader.
o Date	The date on which the form was prepared.

FIGURE 10-5

SOURCE/OBJECT LIBRARY DELETION NOTICE

APPLICATION NAME _____ NUMBER _____	DELETION CONTROL # _____

SENT TO _____ DATE _____

FROM _____ DEPARTMENT _____

DELETION INSTRUCTIONS

LIBRARY	PROGRAM VERSION TO DELETE	DELETION DATE	COMMENTS

PREPARED BY _____ DATE _____

FORM COMPLETION INSTRUCTIONS

Figure 10-5 - Source/Object Library Deletion Notice

FIELD	INSTRUCTIONS FOR ENTERING DATA
o Application name	The name by which the application is known.
o Number	The application identifier.
o Deletion control number	A sequentially increasing number used to control the form.
o Sent to	Normally the individual in computer operations responsible for the application having a program deleted.
o Date	The date on which the form was prepared.
o From	Normally the name of the systems maintenance project leader.
o Department	The organization or department authorizing the deletion of the program.
o Deletion instructions	The information needed by computer operations to delete the unwanted program versions. The information includes: - Library: the name or number that identifies the library in which the program resides. - Program version to delete: the program number and version of that program which is to be deleted. - Deletion date: the date on which the program version can be deleted. - Comments: any additional information that may be helpful to computer operations in performing the desired tasks.

there are special operator instructions, the operator should be alerted to that change on the appropriate day. Most data processing organizations have procedures for this purpose.

STEP 5 - MONITOR PRODUCTION

Application systems are most vulnerable to problems immediately following the introduction of new versions of a program(s). For this reason, many organizations monitor the output immediately following the introduction of a new program version. In organizations that normally monitor output, extra effort or attention may be applied at the time a change program version is first run.

The following groups may monitor the output of a new program version:

o   Application system control group - An individual or group that normally monitors the output of an application system

o   User personnel - Special user personnel assigned to monitor the output for a limited period of time

o   Systems maintenance personnel - Selected systems and programming personnel assigned to monitor output for a limited time

o   Computer operations personnel - Selected people assigned to monitor the output for a limited period of time

Regardless of who monitors the output, the systems maintenance analyst and user personnel should provide clues as to what to look for. User and systems maintenance personnel must attempt to identify the specific areas in which they believe problems might occur.

The types of clues that could be provided to monitoring personnel include:

o   Transactions to investigate - Specific type of transactions, such as certain product numbers, which they should monitor

o   Customers - Specific customers or other identifiers to help them locate problems on specific pages of reports

o   Reports - Specific outputs that should be reviewed

o   Tape files - Data records or files that have been changed which they may need to examine by extracting information to determine if data was properly recorded

o   Performance - Anticipated improvements in the effectiveness, efficiency, or economy of operations which they should review

This process is normally more effective if it is formalized. This means documenting the type of clues to look for during the monitoring process. A Program Change Monitor Notification Form is illustrated in Figure 10-6. This form should be completed by the

FIGURE 10-6

PROGRAM CHANGE MONITOR NOTIFICATION

APPLICATION SYSTEM _____ NUMBER _____ CHANGE IDENT # _____

DESCRIPTION OF CHANGE	DATE OF CHANGE _____

MONITORING GUIDELINES			
AREA POTENTIALLY IMPACTED	PROBABLE IMPACT	ACTION TO TAKE IF PROBLEM OCCURS	COMMENTS

PREPARED BY _____ DATE _____

FORM COMPLETION INSTRUCTIONS

Figure 10-6 - Program Change Monitor Notification

FIELD	INSTRUCTIONS FOR ENTERING DATA
o Application system	The name by which the application is known.
o Number	The application identifier.
o Change Ident #	The sequence number that uniquely identifies the change.
o Description of change	A description which helps the people monitoring the application gain perspective on the areas impacted.
o Date of change	The date on which the change goes into production. This is the date when the monitoring should commence.
o Monitoring	The description of the type of problem to be anticipated. The information should be descriptive enough to tell the monitors both what to look for and what action to take if they find problems. Obviously, those potential problems which are identified are those most likely to occur. However, the monitors should be alert to any type of problem that might occur immediately following introduction of a new program version. The information about the high probability items is: - Area potentially impacted: the report, transaction, or other area in which the individuals monitoring should be looking. - Probable impact: this section describes the type of problems that are most likely to occur within the impacted area. - Action to take if problem occurs: the people to call, correction to make, or any other action that the individual uncovering the problem should take. - Comments: any additional information that might prove helpful to the monitors in attempting to identify problems associated with the program change.
o Prepared by	The name of the individual who prepared the form, normally the systems maintenance analyst.
o Date	The date on which the form was prepared.

user and/or systems maintenance personnel and then given to the people monitoring the transaction. The information contained on the Program Change Monitor Notification Form is outlined in the form's completion instructions sheet.

STEP 6 - DOCUMENT PROBLEMS

Individuals detecting problems when they monitor changes in application systems should formally document them. The formal documentation process can be made even more effective if the forms are controlled through a numbering sequence. This enables systems maintenance personnel to detect lost problem forms. The individuals monitoring the process should keep a duplicate copy of the form on hand, in case the copy sent to the project is lost.

The individual monitoring the process should be asked both to document the problem and to assess the risk associated with that problem. Although this individual may not be the ideal candidate to make a risk assessment, a preliminary assessment is often very helpful in determining the seriousness of the problem. If the initial estimate about the risk is erroneous, it can be corrected at a later time.

A form to record a system problem caused by a system change is illustrated in Figure 10-7. This form should be completed by the individual monitoring the application system. The completed form should be given to the systems maintenance analyst for correction. The information contained on the System Problem Caused By System Change form is described on the form's completion instructions sheet.

This type of problem report is similar to that described in earlier phases. The major difference is that because of the program change monitor notification the individual can associate the problem with a specific program change. This additional piece of information is usually invaluable in correcting the problem.

PHASE 5 - FEEDBACK

Feedback enables data processing management and users to monitor each phase of the systems maintenance process. The feedback information relates to the processes and controls operational during that phase. During the installing the change phase, management is able to measure the overall success of the systems maintenance process. The information gathered during this phase is some of the most valuable data gathered.

The types of feedback information that have proved most valuable includes the following (see Figure 10-8):

o   Number of changes installed

One of the more meaningful pieces of information is the number of changes actually installed. This piece of feedback data can be monitored by individuals or by system changes within time spans such as changes per week. This piece of data shows the end result of the change process.

o   Number of changes installed by application

FIGURE 10-7

SYSTEM PROBLEM CAUSED BY SYSTEM CHANGE

APPLICATION   CHANGE
NAME _____ NUMBER_____ IDENT #_____

                                                     PROBLEM
PROBLEM DATE_____ PROBLEM TIME___ CONTROL #_____

DESCRIPTION OF PROBLEM

AREA OF APPLICATION AFFECTED

IMPACT OF PROBLEM

If not fixed within 1 hour:

If not fixed within 1 day:

If not fixed within 1 week:

RECOMMENDATION

PREPARED BY_____ DATE_____

FORM COMPLETION INSTRUCTIONS

Figure 10-7 - System Problem Caused by System Change

FIELD	INSTRUCTIONS FOR ENTERING DATA
o Application name	The name by which the application is known.
o Number	The application identifier
o Change Ident #	The sequence number that uniquely identified the change.
o Problem date	The date on which the problem was located.
o Problem time	The time within the day the problem was encountered if the time is meaningful.
o Problem control #	A sequential number that controls the form.
o Description of problem	A brief narrative description. Normally, examples of the problem are attached to the form.
o Area of application affected	This segment is designed to help the systems maintenance analyst identify the source of the problem. If it is one of the problems outlined on the program change monitor notification form, the individual completing the form can be very specific regarding the affected area. Otherwise, the individual should attempt to identify areas such as report writing or input validation where the problem seems to originate.
o Impact of problem	The individual identifying the problem should attempt to assess the impact of that problem on the organization. This information is very valuable in determining how fast the problem must be fixed. Ideally this risk would be expressed in quantitative units, such as number of invoices incorrectly processed, dollar loss, number of hours lost because of the problems. It is often helpful to divide the problem into various time periods. This is because some risks are not immediately serious but become serious if they are not corrected by a certain time or date. Some suggested time spans included on the form are: - If not fixed within one hour - If not fixed within one day - If not fixed within one week

Figure 10-7 - System Problem Caused by System Change (Cont'd)

FIELD	INSTRUCTIONS FOR ENTERING DATA
o Recommendation	The suggestions from the individual uncovering the problem as to what should be done to fix it. This recommendation can either be to correct the errors that have occurred and/or to correct the problems in the application system.
o Prepared by	The name of the individual who uncovered the system problem caused by the system change.
o Date	The date on which the form was prepared.

FIGURE 10-8

PHASE 5

INSTALLING THE CHANGE

FEEDBACK DATA	SOURCE	PURPOSE
Number of changes installed	Job accounting system	To identify the volume of changes being installed in the operations area
Number of changes installed by application	Job accounting system	To determine the frequency of change by application in order to evaluate application workload
Number of problems encountered with installed changes	System problem encountered due to system change form	To determine the effectiveness of the systems maintenance process
Number of old program versions deleted	Job accounting system	To determine the effectiveness of the systems maintenance process
Number of new program versions installed	Source job accounting system	To determine the magnitude of the change effort as measured by number of new program versions installed
Number of conditions monitored	Program change monitor notification form	To determine the efforts undertaken to detect problems before they become serious
Number of changes not installed on time	Departmental job scheduling system	To determine the frequency with which user requirements are not achieved

This piece of feedback information indicates the maintenance activity for each application. It shows data processing management the volume of changes occurring from an installation perspective.

o Number of problems encountered with installed changes

This piece of data helps measure the success of the systems maintenance process. If few problems are encountered after changes are installed, data processing management can assume that the systems maintenance procedures are effective.

o Number of old program versions deleted

This piece of feedback information provides insight into the maintenance being performed on the data processing libraries. If more programs are being added than deleted, data processing management may wish to take action to reduce the size of the program libraries.

o Number of new program versions installed

This is another measure of the size of the change process. A single installed change may involve many new versions of a program. This should take more time and effort than a change involving only a single program.

o Number of conditions monitored

Monitoring installed changes is a measure to help reduce the seriousness of problems. The more monitoring that occurs, the greater the assurance to data processing management that problems will be detected before they become serious. This type of feedback could be stratified by individual application.

o Number of changes not installed on time

It is expected that changes will be installed on schedule. What data processing management must monitor are conditions where the expected norm is not achieved, such as late implementation of changes. This feedback does not indicate cause, and thus a large number of late installations would warrant investigation to determine the cause.

PHASE 5 - REVIEW CHECKLIST

Periodically data processing management should review the effectiveness of each phase of the systems maintenance process. A checklist for Phase 5 is included as Figure 10-9 for this purpose. The checklist is to be used by data processing management to periodically review the effectiveness of the installing the change phase.

Data processing management may wish to review all the phases simultaneously. Thus, they would use the five checklists for the phases of the systems maintenance at the same time. This overall assessment would give them a much better appreciation of the effectiveness of systems maintenance processes in their organization than if they assessed each phase individually. However, if particular phases (such as testing and training) are causing problems, data processing management may wish to review that phase individually in order to improve the processes and controls in that phase.

FIGURE 10-9

INSTALLING THE CHANGE CHECKLIST

NUMBER	MANAGEMENT QUESTION	RESPONSE			COMMENTS
		YES	NO	N/A	
1.	Is each change reviewed for its impact upon the restart/recovery plan?				
2.	If a change impacts recovery, is newly estimated downtime calculated?				
3.	If the change impacts recovery, is the new downtime risk estimated?				
4.	Are the changes that need to be made to the recovery process documented?				
5.	Is the notification of changes to the production version of an application documented?				
6.	Are changes to application systems controlled by an application control change number?				
7.	Are there procedures to delete unwanted program versions from the source and object library?				
8.	Are program delete requests documented so that production is authorized to delete programs?				
9.	Are procedures established to ensure that program versions will go into production on the correct day?				
10.	Are operators notified of the date new versions go into production if their procedures are changed?				
11.	Are procedures established to monitor changed application systems?				

FIGURE 10-9

INSTALLING THE CHANGE CHECKLIST (Cont'd)

NUMBER	MANAGEMENT QUESTION	RESPONSE			COMMENTS
		YES	NO	N/A	
12.	Do the individuals monitoring the process receive notification that an application system has been changed?				
13.	Do the people monitoring changes receive clues regarding the areas impacted and the probable problems?				
14.	Do the people monitoring application system changes receive guidance on what action to take if problems occur?				
15.	Are problems detected immediately following changes documented on a special form so they can be traced to a particular change?				
16.	Are the people documenting changed program problems asked to document the impact of the problem on the organization?				
17.	Is data identified and collected for the installing the change phase?				
18.	Does data processing management review and use the feedback data?				
19.	Does data processing management periodically review the effectiveness of the installing the change phase?				

SUMMARY

The installing the change phase ends the systems maintenance process. The previous phases have been designed to make this phase successful. It is only through the installation of the change that the data processing department can satisfy the users' maintenance needs.

The complexity of data processing makes it difficult to continually install changes without problems. Therefore, some — if not all — changes should be monitored. The objective of the monitoring process is to detect problems that have escaped the scrutiny of testing.

The success of the systems maintenance process can be measured by determining whether changes have been installed on time and without problems in order to meet the users' needs. It is for this reason that data processing management should collect, analyze, and act upon feedback. All systems maintenance processes should change over time in order to better meet user needs. The monitoring and adjustment of the system maintenance process allows this to happen.

Chapter 11
Evaluating Systems Maintenance

CHAPTER OVERVIEW

This chapter will propose three yardsticks for measuring maintenance: first is making subjective judgment, second is weighing the benefits of maintaining an application versus rewriting it, and third is using metrics to measure the effectiveness of the performed maintenance. Data processing management should utilize these three yardsticks to measure the effectiveness of the maintenance function.

Unlike subjective evaluations, quantitative evaluations are consistent, defensible, and explainable. However, while the results are indisputable, the criteria used to reach those conclusions may not be acceptable. The success of the quantitative method for evaluating maintenance depends on the reasonableness of the criteria used in reaching the conclusion.

OBJECTIVES IN MEASURING SYSTEMS MAINTENANCE EFFECTIVENESS

Senior management should periodically question the value received for each data processing dollar expended on maintenance. As the amount of data processing resources going into maintenance increases, the questions regarding maintenance benefits should increase. In order to answer these questions, management needs yardsticks for measuring the maintenance function.

Justifying most new applications involves making a cost/benefit analysis. If the benefits of a new application do not exceed the cost of a new application, management normally disapproves the proposal. Many organizations have spent a great deal of effort on developing reliable cost/benefit procedures.

On the other hand, maintenance is frequently considered a necessary evil. Because the product was built, it is intuitively obvious to many that it should be maintained. However, maintenance -- like new development efforts -- should be justified or it should not be performed.

The same cost/benefit logic that is used to justify new systems may not apply to routine maintenance. For example, when a payroll system goes down because of a hang-up, it could be argued on a cost/benefit basis that all the benefits of the payroll would be lost if maintenance were not performed. Thus, the cash flow or rate of return, or return on investment, would be huge if those types of procedures and thought processes were used.

What needs to be measured is the effectiveness of the maintenance process. Measures are needed for differentiating between good or effective maintenance and poor or ineffective maintenance. In our payroll example, ineffective maintenance would still result in a very large cash flow rate of return. Thus, new yardsticks are needed to measure the effectiveness of systems maintenance.

Some of the questions management might ask about the maintenance process include:

1. Should an installation spend money to maintain an application system or should it rewrite or redesign the system?

2. Does systems maintenance increase systems performance?

3. Are the techniques used for systems maintenance effective?

4. Are system changes being effectively installed?

5. Is the application system structured so that it can be effectively maintained?

SUBJECTIVE CRITERIA

For years data processing management has been making subjective judgments about the effectiveness of the function. The problems with making subjective judgments are:

o   The judgment is not supportable.

o   The judgment may be biased.

o   The judgment may be oriented more toward a point in time than a period in time. The maintenance need of the moment overshadows those of the past and future.

o   Two people probably would not make the same judgments.

o   It is difficult to explain subjective statements to the individual or group being judged.

Some measures of effective maintenance are difficult to quantify. These are primarily attitudinal measures which need to be done on a Likert scale. A Likert scale asks people to judge a specific measurement criterion and place it somewhere between two opposite poles on a scale. The Likert scale is frequently a five-point scale divided as follows:

o   Very good rating

o   Good rating

o   Neither good nor bad rating (average)

o   Poor rating

o   Very poor rating

The evaluator is then given a series of criteria and asked to rate them on this scale. In the user satisfaction area, the evaluator may determine that the satisfaction of the user is good. This then becomes the rating.

The types of attitudinal maintenance measurements that might be performed on the maintenance function include:

o   User satisfaction - The degree of satisfaction expressed by the user regarding systems maintenance.

o Maintenance team morale - The enthusiasm with which the maintenance team maintains an application system.

o Peer assessment - How other maintenance teams view the effectiveness of a maintenance project effort.

o Complexity of maintenance environment - A comparison of this maintenance environment with other maintenance environments in the data processing area.

CRITERIA FOR MEASURING IF THE SYSTEM SHOULD BE REWRITTEN

Many organizations have been developing application systems since the late 1950's. In some organizations many of the operational systems are twenty years old in structure, if not in code. A difficult question to answer is when these systems should be deemed obsolete and rewritten or redesigned.

Data processing technology continues to change at a rapid pace. Systems concepts that were uneconomical five years ago can now be economically designed. The question that needs to be answered about these older systems is when the systems should be redesigned to take advantage of new data processing technology.

The dilemma that management faces is evaluating the cost differences between maintaining the old system and rewriting it. For example, system X may cost $25,000 to maintain during the current year, but it would cost $100,000 to rewrite it. Management views this as spending $25,000 versus spending $100,000. However, this thinking may be short-sighted. For example, the following factors also need to be considered:

o Is the annual cost of maintenance steady or is it increasing, and at what rate?

o Would the cost of operation drop significantly if it were redesigned?

o Would the cost of maintenance drop significantly if the system were redesigned?

o Would additional benefits be accrued if the system were redesigned?

o Would hardware and software costs drop if systems were redesigned using newer technology?

o Could obsolete hardware and/or software be eliminated if systems were redesigned?

Some of these questions could be answered if management analyzed the usefulness of the current system structure; other questions require an analysis of the operating environment. For example, to determine whether a specific piece of hardware or software could be eliminated, management has to analyze the operating environment. There are features and characteristics unique to each operating environment, and they are difficult to generalize.

This section presents criteria to use in determining whether an existing application system should be continued in production or whether it should be rewritten or redesigned. The criteria are designed to provide information helpful in making this analysis. The criteria should be considered as input to the decision process, and not the decision process itself.

The criteria are designed to help data processing management measure the health and well-being of an application system. As a system begins to deteriorate, the criteria help diagnose that deterioration. However, if an application system malfunctions, it does not mean that rewriting or redesigning is justified.

Management has two options when a system deteriorates in performance. One option is to rewrite or redesign the application system. The other option is to deal specifically with the characteristics causing the deterioration.

The criteria provided in this section to diagnose application system deterioration are provided as a representative, but not exhaustive, set of measurement criteria. Organizations should be able to add to this list of general criteria, as well as being able to add some specific criteria applicable only to their organization.

The criteria are described in Appendix A. Each criterion is described individually on a Criteria to Measure Need to Rewrite form which contains the following information about each criteria:

o   <u>Criterion name</u>

The specific criterion that can be used to measure the deterioration of performance of an application system.

o   <u>Description of criterion</u>

A narrative explanation of the characteristics of the criteria that need to be collected to measure how well or how poorly systems are performing.

o   <u>Data collection techniques</u>

The methods, tools, and techniques that can be used to collect the data used for measurement purposes.

o   <u>Criterion strength</u>

The value of the criterion in measuring application system deterioration.

o   <u>Criterion weaknesses</u>

The concerns or attributes associated with that criterion which may cause it to falsely represent the deterioration of the application system.

FIGURE 11-1

SYSTEM REWRITE SELF-ASSESSMENT

	SYSTEM BEING ASSESSED _____			
	BY _____ DATE _____			

CRI-TERION #	REWRITE CRITERION	ASSESSMENT		
		VERY APPLICABLE	APPLICABLE	NOT APPLICABLE
1.	Users stop making requests for changes			
2.	Number of errors detected by the application system			
3.	High number of requests for system change			
4.	High maintenance dollars			
5.	Difficulty in extracting data from the application system			
6.	Application system is difficult to change			
7.	Cost to process a transaction			
8.	Obsolete hardware/software			
9.	Application system is complex to operate			
10.	Application system structure out of synchronization with data processing plans			
11.	Cost of testing system changes			
12.	Problems encountered in placing changes into a production status			
	TOTAL CHECKED			

Using the Criteria

The system being evaluated for potential rewrite should be assessed using the "rewrite" criteria provided in Appendix A. This criteria may be supplemented by an organization's internally developed criteria. A self-assessment check is provided for this purpose (see Figure 11-1).

To use the checklist, the evaluator rates the application being assessed by each criterion for its applicability to that application. For example, criterion #1 asked if the user has stopped making requests for changes. If that is true or nearly true, the criterion should be rated "applicable," and if the number of changes being requested is consistent with prior periods, the criterion should be rated "not applicable." Each of the twelve criteria should be rated.

After all twelve criteria are rated, they should be scored as follows:

- o   Very applicable scores   = 3

- o   Applicable   = 2

- o   Not applicable scores   = 1

Add up the score. The following provides an indication of the rewrite potential of the assessed application.

Score	
12-16	Rewrite unnecessary
17-22	Some reworking required
23-27	Major reworking required
28-36	Scrap the system

MEASURING THE EFFECTIVENESS OF SYSTEMS MAINTENANCE

The effectivness of the system maintenance process for an application system can be measured using metrics. Metrics are produced by showing the relationship between two variables. For example, two variables in systems maintenance are 1) number of changes made in a period and 2) maintenance dollars expended during that period. The metric produced by these two variables is dollar cost per change made.

The reliability of the metric is dependent upon the correlation between the two variables. The higher the correlation, the higher the reliability. For example, there is a very high correlation between the absence of flaws in a diamond and the price of the diamond: the fewer the flaws, the higher the price. On the other hand, there is probably a very low correlation between the setting in which the diamond is placed and the price of the diamond. For example, a perfect diamond in an elaborate setting would probably not command much more money than that same diamond in a simple setting. The same analogy is true of metrics.

Organizations should develop metrics for systems maintenance measurement and then study them over a period of time to determine the correlation. Those metrics which appear to be good predictors of systems maintenance success should be continued, and those proving not to be good predictors should be discontinued. With experience, organizations will be able to develop a set of metrics that can be used to measure their maintenance function effectively.

Metrics should be used as input to the maintenance measurement process. Metrics coupled with subjective judgment may be more effective for measuring systems maintenance than either yardstick used individually.

The maintenance metrics described in this section are a representative, but not exhaustive, set of maintenance metrics. Organizations should select those which appear to be most representative of their organization. They should then be supplemented with metrics unique to their organization.

The metric descriptions are described on maintenance metric forms included in Appendix B (see Figure 11-2 for a sample form). The description of each metric includes:

o   Metric name

The two variables that represent a measure of systems maintenance effectiveness.

o   Description of metric

A detailed description of the two variables comprising the metric. Each variable will be described in sufficient detail to explain the meaning and type of information included in each variable.

o   Data collection technique

The methods, tools, and techniques that can be used to collect the data used for measurement purposes.

o   Metric strength

The value of the metric in measuring systems maintenance performance.

o   Metric weakness

The concerns or attributes associated with that metric which may cause it to falsely represent the effectiveness of systems maintenance.

Figure 11-3 explains the potential use of each metric in Appendix B.

SUMMARY

The goals and objectives of systems maintenance cause it to be measured differently than systems development is measured. New systems can be measured effectively using cost/benefit analysis. Systems maintenance requires yardsticks which take into account the correction of problems, condition of enhancements, and new requirements.

FIGURE 11-2

MAINTENANCE METRICS DESCRIPTION

METRIC		METRIC NUMBER	
DESCRIPTION OF METRIC			
DATA COLLECTION TECHNIQUES			
METRIC STRENGTH			
METRIC WEAKNESSES			

FIGURE 11-3

WHEN TO USE METRICS MATRIX

METRIC NUMBER	METRICS	USE OF METRICS
1.	Cost of maintenance divided by number of changes	Measures the cost of an average change.
2.	Benefit derived from changes divided by cost of changes.	Develops a ratio of benefits to cost. A metric over 1 is a cost-beneficial change.
3.	Data fields per screen last year divided by data fields per screen this year.	Measures the effectivenss of the use of screens.
4.	Number of lines of maintenance code divided by size of maintenance staff.	Measures the productivity of maintenance staff to write lines of code.
5.	Number of errors/problems/violations divided by number of terminals.	Measures the ease of use of terminals.
6.	CPU charges divided by application systems job steps.	Measures the economy and effectiveness of application systems job steps.
7.	Number of program changes divided by the number of failures the first time the changed program is run in production.	Measures the effectiveness of testing.
8.	Anticipated cost of maintenance divided by the actual cost of maintenance.	Measures the ability to stay within the maintenance budget.
9.	Anticipated days to install the system change divided by the actual days.	Measures the ability to meet maintenance schedules.
10.	Number of programming errors detected divided by the number of programs changed.	Measures the ability of programmers to write good program code.

FIGURE 11-3

WHEN TO USE METRICS MATRIX

METRIC NUMBER	METRICS	USE OF METRICS
11.	Size of new systems development staff divided by size of maintenance staff.	Measures the effectiveness of the developed system to meet user needs.
12.	Number of system errors detected divided by size of maintenance staff.	Measures the ability of maintenance staff to lower the number of problems encountered by users.
13.	Number of tests required divided by the number of systems errors.	Measures the proficiency of testing programs.
14.	Number of source code statements changed divided by the number of tests.	Measures the ability to write good source code statements.
15.	Cost to develop divided by the cost to maintain.	Measures the effectiveness of the developed system to meet user needs.
16.	Number of changes to a production system divided by the number of times the system becomes inoperable (e.g., a hang-up, invalid output, etc.)	Measures the effectiveness of system changes.
17.	Production operating hours divided by production rerun time.	Measures the effectiveness of systems maintenance.
18.	Maintenance manpower hours expended divided by maintenance manpower used to correct systems and programming errors.	Measures the effectiveness of maintenance personnel in performing their function.
19.	Cost to operate the production system divided by the cost to maintain the system.	Measures the effectiveness of systems maintenance.
20.	The assets controlled or processed by the application divided by the cost of maintenance.	Measures the effectiveness of systems maintenance.

FIGURE 11-3

METRIC NUMBER	METRICS	USE OF METRICS
21.	Total maintenance effort divided by total maintenance effort applied to converting the old version of the system to the new version.	Measures the effectiveness of systems conversion.
22.	Number of users using the application system divided by the number of programmers assigned to systems maintenance.	Measures the effectiveness of systems maintenance.
23.	Number of programs in the application system divided by the number of programmers assigned to maintenance.	Measures the effectiveness of a developed system to meet the needs of users.

The systems maintenance function can be evaluated using subjective criteria, criteria to measure the viability of the application system structure, and metrics to show relationships among systems maintenance variables. Each of the evaluation methods measures a different aspect of systems maintenance.

The concept of using metrics to measure systems maintenance effectiveness is a new concept. Data processing management normally judges maintenance by using subjective criteria. However, metrics can potentially provide the best measurement device. The use of metrics provides quantifiable and controllable measurements of a single application system over a period of time. Metrics also makes it possible to compare the maintenance efforts of two or more application systems.

Data processing organizations are encouraged to experiment with the use of metrics in measuring systems maintenance performed. It should be expected that early in the process some metrics will show a very high correlation between systems maintenance effectiveness, while others may not show the hoped for correlation. By eliminating the poor predictors, data processing management can develop a set of metrics that very accurately predict the effectiveness of maintenance in application systems.

Chapter 12
Maintaining Vendor Applications

CHAPTER OVERVIEW

Many organizations purchase the applications they use. Sometimes organizations purchase applications because they do not have sufficient time or staff to develop them in-house; or they purchase applications because the applications contain some unique capability; and other times organizations believe it is more economical to purchase applications than to develop them in-house.

Purchased applications, like in-house applications, must be modified so that the applications are consistent with the needs of the organization. Some of these modifications may be required prior to purchase, but the majority of changes normally occur over time. These purchased applications pose some unique maintenance problems. Among the problems associated with maintaining software purchased from vendors are obtaining contractual rights to maintain the software, obtaining source code, and in-house staff knowledgeable about the application structure. The maintenance information problems should be addressed before purchasing the application.

This chapter recommends an approach for maintaining applications purchased from vendors, which involves planning prior to purchasing, negotiating maintenance into the contract, and then including purchased applications in the organization's normal maintenance process.

MAINTENANCE PREPLANNING

Organizations that do not preplan maintenance on purchased applications may encounter severe problems. The organization that leases application software from vendors does not own those applications. Maintenance rights normally remain with the vendor. With rented software, the user of the application may not be able to make changes without the consent of the vendor.

Preplanning maintenance involves both obtaining permission to perform maintenance and preparing to process the maintenance changes. It may not be economical to do this planning after the contract for the leased or purchased application has been signed. Prior to signing the contract the user is in a good position to negotiate maintenance provisions. However, if the user requests new maintenance requirements after signing the contract, the vendor may seek additional payments.

The most common maintenance conditions included in contracts for vendor-produced applications are:

o   Vendor personnel must perform maintenance; contractee pays

o   The user is not able to obtain the source code listings as the contract does not cover modifications to source code

o   User can purchase source code; user maintains system

Vendors of widely-used leased applications systems normally resist attempts to modify the applications. This is because the vendor periodically issues a new version of the application system. The new version may be restrutured so that changes made to previous versions cannot be easily made to the new version. Therefore, maintenance already made may have to be made again if the user desires to purchase the new version of the application system with the previous modifications.

Most of these problems can be avoided through planning before signing the application contract. The maintenance options available at that point are substantially greater than after the contract is signed. Data processing departments should establish a maintenance policy on application systems obtained from vendors.

VENDOR-PRODUCED APPLICATION MAINTENANCE POLICY

A departmental policy on maintaining purchased application systems serves two purposes: first, it becomes the basis for contractual negotiations with vendors; and second, it informs data processing project and user personnel concerning the types and extent of maintenance that can be performed on vendor-produced software. The policy outlines departmental strategy for vendor-produced application maintenance.

An integral part of the vendor application system maintenance policy is the policy on purchasing applications. The data processing department must determine for which of the following purposes vendor-produced application systems will be obtained.

o   When unique processing approaches and capabilities are desirable

o   When a commercial package meets the organization's specifications

o   When vendors can provide applications more cheaply than the organization can develop them

o   When users request them

o   When insufficient time is available to develop the application in-house

o   When there is insufficient programming staff in-house to develop the application

o   Only vendor-produced applications will be used (no in-house developmental capability exists)

The strategy for obtaining vendor-produced applications leads to the maintenance policy. For example, if the prime reason for obtaining vendor applications is economics, then the ongoing maintainability of the application is an important element in the selective process. On the other hand, if an organization has no developmental staff and minimal maintenance personnel, it may wish that all maintenance be performed by vendor personnel.

The policy covering maintenance of vendor-produced application systems should include:

1.   Whether or not maintenance should occur on vendor-provided application sys-

tems

2. Who should perform the maintenance on vendor-supplied application systems

3. Whether or not source code listings should be obtained with vendor-supplied application systems

4. If all contracts with a vendor should include standard maintenance provisions

5. The data processing strategy on obtaining application systems from vendors

6. Maintenance expectations from in-house data processing personnel

Guidelines for employee maintenance of vendor-produced applications should be based on employee expectations. These guidelines may be as simple as to reconfirm that normal maintenance policies and procedures are applicable to vendor-provided applications. However, some of the unique characteristics of purchased software may make modifications to the normal maintenance policies necessary. For example, if vendor personnel are involved, special call-in guidelines may have to be established.

The development of a vendor application system maintenance policy is the responsibility of senior data processing management. The policy should be established prior to obtaining any application system from vendors. The following sections of the chapter will provide recommendations regarding contractual negotiations and provisions for maintenance.

OVERVIEW OF CONTRACTUAL CONSIDERATIONS

Three vendor considerations impact the contractual negotiations for systems maintenance. The major issues to the vendors are:

o   Issuance of new versions of application system - If the vendor continually issues new versions of application systems, it impacts maintenance. If the vendor permits special changes (i.e., special customer capabilities) then the vendor may be saddled with maintaining hundreds of versions of the same application system. If the vendor prohibits users from making changes, then it will be easier for the customer to switch over to new versions. In addition, customers who perform their own maintenance are reluctant to move to new versions unless those changes can be easily transferred.

o   Propriety of application system - The value of most purchased application systems is that they are fully designed and workable programs. If the system logic and approach were fully documented, others could implement the approach and not have to reimburse the vendor for their effort. In order to prevent this, many vendor-produced applications have routines which will no longer function properly if someone modifies the code.

o   Economics of maintenance - Vendors know that when they permit users to change application code the process can become time consuming and complex. The point may be quickly reached where it would have been more economical to design a special system for a user, rather than to attempt to modify a general package.

As users of vendor-produced applications request price quotations for changes, the vendors take into account these considerations. Some refuse to make changes, while others price them at a point where they are not economical for their customers. However, in packages with a limited customer base, vendors become more willing to make changes.

Before customers sign contracts, they are better able to modify vendor-produced applications than after they have signed contracts. Customers should discuss purchased application maintenance before discussing the specifics of maintenance contracts. The considerations are discussed individually and summarized in Figure 12-1.

Considerations Before the Contract Is Signed

Organizations should consider the following before signing a contract to obtain a vendor-produced application:

o   Who is responsible? Responsibility for maintenance should be determined and specified in the contract. There are two categories of maintenance that need to be specified. One type is the correction of errors, and the second type is user-requested new requirements and enhancements.

o   How quick is service? If the customer requests maintenance for any purpose covered in the contract, response time should be specified; that is whether the request is for critical maintenance or for new requirements and enhancements. In the area of new requirements and enhancements, the contract may specify when the vendor must respond with a proposal for undertaking the work.

o   Who owns the application? Normally the vendor owns the application, but for maintenance purposes the user may desire to own the application. If the customer owns the application, then the customer can perform any desired maintenance.

o   How extensive is documentation? Maintenance cannot be performed unless the vendor supplies sufficient documentation. The types and extent of the documentation needed for maintenance should be covered in the contract.

o   What will it cost? The customer should know from the contract what he will pay for needed maintenance.

o   Where will it be done? The contract should specify whether maintenance will be performed at the customer's place of business or whether the vendor can perform the maintenance at a location of the vendor's choice. It may be desirable to have the maintenance done at the user's place of business in order to train and inform customer personnel.

o   What are the penalties if it is not done? If emergency maintenance is required, the vendor should be penalized for poor or late maintenance. This should be spelled out in the contract either in terms of a daily penalty rate or a penalty for each occurrence.

FIGURE 12-1

PURCHASED APPLICATIONS MAINTENANCE CONSIDERATIONS

BEFORE CONTRACT SIGNED	AFTER CONTRACT SIGNED
o Who is responsible?	o What maintenance does the contract permit?
o How quick is service?	o What will the vendor do (for changes not specified in contract)?
o Who owns application?	o Around-the-application maintenance. When customer is unable to unwilling to make change.
o How extensive is documentation?	
o What will it cost?	
o Where will it be done?	
o What are the penalties if it is not done?	
o What does ongoing maintenance provide?	

o   What does ongoing maintenance provide? The contract should specify the types of maintenance and improvements that are included in the contractual agreements and those which must be independently negotiated.

Considerations After the Contract Is Signed

The customer is in a limited bargaining position after the contract has been signed and the application is operational. A few considerations not specified in the contract include:

o   What does the contract permit? Organizations leasing or purchasing applications may not be free to perform or obtain any type of maintenance they desire. The contractual provisions must be reviewed to determine what restrictions, if any, there are on making changes to the application system.

o   How will the vendor handle unspecified changes? If the desired change is not permitted or specified under the contract, then the customer must negotiate with the vendor for the change. Most vendors want to satisfy their customers, but unless something is included in the contract, the customer is dependent upon the vendor's good will.

o   Around the application maintenance - If the customer is unable or unwilling to change the application system, then some changes can be implemented outside the computer application. The options for maintaining around the application will be explained in a later section.

NEGOTIATING MAINTENANCE INTO CONTRACTS

An important part of a contract to purchase or lease an application system are provisions for maintaining that system. The process of contracting for maintenance consists of these steps:

1.   Step 1 - Determine the desired maintenance plan

2.   Step 2 - Negotiate the plan into the contract

3.   Step 3 - Develop procedures to ensure compliance with the maintenance plan

Each of these steps will be discussed individually.

Step 1 - Determine Maintenance Provisions

An organization should define the attributes of maintenance prior to negotiating a contract for an application system. The alternative is to review what the vendor offers and assess whether that is acceptable. However, unless an organization has determined what they want, they may accept something less than desirable because they don't have time to define needs.

The same problems that appear during the system development process appear in purchased applications. Customers who spend the time and effort to identify needs are usually satisfied with the end product. Also, well-defined needs tend to eliminate most of the disputes after the application has been purchased.

The provisions that need to be considered in specifying maintenance of a vendor-developed application system include:

o   Who is responsible for emergency maintenance? If the vendor application hangs up, whose responsibility is it to return the application to an operational status?

o   System problem - If the application system does not perform according to the written or implied specifications, who is responsible for making the application system comply with specifications?

o   What are the qualifications of vendor personnel? The vendor should inform the customer about the qualifications of vendor maintenance personnel. The vendor should list the names of specific individuals (and a procedure for replacing those people).

o   What system documentation aids will the vendor provide to aid in maintaining the application system? The documentation aids might include:

- Source code listings

- Data definition

- Data and file layouts

- System flowcharts

- Control flowcharts

- Error message description

- Manual of recommended actions to take for each error message

- Test data and test solutions

- Recommended job control (if applicable)

- System narratives

- System constraints (e.g., table sizes)

- Control matrices

- Transaction flow analysis

o   What is the vendor's commitment to customer support? In the contract, the vendor should document the size, caliber, and location of maintenance staff the vendor agrees to provide during the contractual period. The commitment should also indicate the expected time period to answer customer requests. The types of requests that might be individually addressed in the contract include:

- Emergency maintenance

- Problems

- Requests for price quotations

- Requests for application enhancements

o Vendor-guaranteed maintenance - Any application system can be improved. Improvements can include performance enhancements as well as new capabilities. Many of these would be a result of customer recommendation. Many vendors agree to provide new versions of application systems at specified periods of time, or at a minimum every X months.

o Technical guarantees - The vendor should agree to maintain the application on specified hardware and/or operating software provided by the mainframe vendor. For example, if the mainframe vendor changes to a new version of the operating system, the application vendor should guarantee to make whatever changes are necessary to ensure that the application will run under the new version of the operating system.

o Cost of services - During the life of the contract, the application vendor should specify the cost, both free and charged services. The more detailed the specification, the fewer the disputes over charges.

Some of the services that should be detailed include:

- Fixing unplanned critical maintenance

- Obtaining new versions of the application system

- Installing new versions of the application system

- Obtaining up-to-date maintenance documentation

- Receiving training on new enhancements and features (this may be according to the cost of materials or it may be on a per student basis)

- Hourly rate by type of vendor personnel

- RPQ proposals

- Answering telephone requests for information

o Problem identification - One of the problems that plague many data processing installations is the initial problem identification. Some vendors are reluctant to spend a lot of time and effort pinpointing the problem; thus, they blame another vendor and then leave. In a multivendor environment, one of the vendors must accept this responsibility of fixing the problem.

o Location of service - The contract should specify whether the vendor performs the analysis and system fix at the customer's location or at the vendor's location. For example, the vendor may require that the problem be diagnosed and shipped back to the vendor's location for analysis and correction. Whatever arrangement is selected, it should be mutually agreed upon.

o   Failure-to-perform penalties - The penalties for inability or unwillingness to perform maintenance should be specified in the contract. The type of penalties may include:

-   X dollars per day until the maintenance is performed

-   Fixed dollar amount

-   Forfeiture of future rental payments

-   Forfeiture of vendor good-faith deposit

o   Discontinuance of product - Frequently vendors either give up a product line, or the product becomes obsolete; consequently, the vendor decides to discontinue service. In either instance, the customer may wish to keep the product operational. However, because of the contractual agreements this may not be possible if the vendor refuses to give up copyright on the application, training manuals, and material or if the vendor refuses to provide the type of documentation needed to maintain the system (e.g., the customer normally does not, but should, receive source code if the product line is discontinued). The contract should outline how maintenance and documentation is to be handled if either the vendor goes out of business or the product is discontinued.

Step 2 - Negotiate Contract

Normal contract negotiation is a give and take proposition between the vendor and the customer. However, not only should customers know which maintenance provisions they want, but also customers should list the provisions in the order of importance. For example, if the vendor is unwilling to include all the desired provisions, the customer should know which ones are expendable and which are essential. It may be desirable to assign priorities as follows:

o   Priority 1 - Necessary to include in the contract

o   Priority 2 - Nice to include in the contract

o   Questionable whether to include in the contract (included for negotiation purposes)

Most lawyers recommend that the contract be fair. This is particularly true in the area of contractual penalties. In the desire to get a sale, the vendor may agree to provisions which, if the worst conditions were to occur, would cause the vendor to cancel the contract. In this instance, both parties lose. For example, if the contract calls for a $500 per day penalty for the failure to provide certain maintenance, the vendor, quickly reaching the point where the contract is no longer profitable, terminates it, taking a less severe penalty.

A fair contract is one which encourages both parties to adhere to the contractual provisions. A contract favoring one party at the expense of the other may not achieve the desired results. Thus, the customer should first establish the contractual maintenance objectives, which are normally to maintain the application in an operational and technically up-to-date status. Having heavy penalties or imposing excessive contractual restrictions may defeat the purpose of the contract.

Step 3 - Monitoring Procedures

A contract written should not be a contract forgotten. While a good contract gathers dust because the disputes are minimized, the contract provisions should still be enforced. Many times new personnel are unaware of all of the provisions included in the contract. Therefore, it becomes helpful to establish procedures to monitor the contract during the contractual period.

The types of procedures proved effective in monitoring application system contracts include:

   o   Periodically reviewing the terms of the contract with the vendor

   o   Analyzing each maintenance process to determine if it conforms to the contract

   o   Developing a maintenance contractual checklist to be completed at the end of each maintenance process

   o   Periodically auditing maintenance to determine if it conforms to the contractual provisions

TIPS AND TECHNIQUES FOR OBTAINING VENDOR SUPPORT

The only support the vendor is required to make to a customer is that provided in the contract. However, in many instances the vendor is willing to provide additional support for a variety of reasons. Customers can gain this free support by engaging in mutually cooperative ventures with a vendor.

Most vendors attempt to cultivate a strong customer base. In addition, vendors are continually looking for new customers. Using these two golden rules of marketing, customers can encourage vendors to aid them by adopting the following approaches:

   o   Form or join a users group that is organized to promote and improve the application system.

   o   Agree to provide an application system testimonial in return for new features and enhancements.

   o   Agree to work with vendor personnel in installing and testing a new feature or enhancement.

Most vendors of application systems welcome user groups. The user groups serve several very valuable purposes including being a forum for vendors to discuss changes and enhancements, promoting the application package, and providing training among the membership. It is difficult for the vendor's technical personnel to work with several users. It is a time-consuming and confusing process. If a users group can perform as a central spokesman for users, the probability of getting more maintenance quickly is improved.

MAINTAINING AROUND THE COMPUTER

Maintenance can be performed without changing the application system. Maintenance of vendor-supplied applications can be performed using two approaches. The first is for maintenance personnel to maintain through-the-application systems; this involves changes to programs within the application. The second method is to maintain around the application system, which means that maintenance personnel install changes without altering the application system code.

Often maintaining around the computer is as effective as maintaining through the computer. Because of the complexity of application code and the customer's unfamiliarity with the application, changing computer code can be a high-risk process. Also, if the vendor regularly issues new versions, the problem arises of repeating the maintenance in future versions. This problem is less likely when people use around the computer techniques maintenance procedures.

Five effective around the application systems maintenance processes which installations can utilize are:

o   Manual processing

o   Preprocessor

o   Interim processor

o   Postprocessor

o   User exits

Manual Processing

Many changes to the computerized segment of an application system can be accomplished by making changes to the manual areas of application processing. Maintenance personnel can make some of these changes using existing features for nonstandard purposes. Other changes require maintaining manual records.

Examples of maintenance through manual procedures include:

o   Using existing codes or work areas to convey new meanings. For example, if the system does not provide for negative numbers, then coding the negative number is a special transaction which may achieve the same results.

o   Manual logs - Keeping information that cannot be entered in the computer manually, and then appending it with output results.

Preprocessor

The desired processing results may be obtained if people process the data before entering the computer application. For example, if the user wants some analysis or additional edits of input, this can be accomplished by running the input through a user-developed preprocessor, and then sending the preprocessed data into the application system for normal processing.

Preprocessing programs are most valuable for the following type of changes:

o   New edits

o   Checking input to authorization tables or files

o   Counting input records

o   Analyzing input data

Interim Processors

If the desired changes require processing that cannot be provided by the vendor, customers can add programs within the processing logic that may perform the needed steps. These interim processors take the output records from one program of the vendor's application, perform some analysis or processing on that information, and then send the data to another application system program for continued processing.

The types of changes that can best be satisfied with interim processors include:

o   Verification of data relationships

o   Additional computations and reports

o   Elimination or modification of unacceptable interim processing results

Postprocessor

Special codes and limitations may be adjusted through postprocessing routines. For example, let's assume that an order entry system has a two-position field limitation on quantity. If it becomes necessary to exceed this limitation, it may be accomplishable by entering two transactions for values less than 100 which can fit within the two-character field. Then a postprocessing can be added which accumulates the two amounts to produce the desired results.

The type of maintenance that can be best performed with a postprocessor includes:

o   Decoding of information entered to circumvent processing restrictions

o   Combining output information

o   Editing output data

o   Inserting descriptive or other information not included in the application system into the output data

o   Reformatting output data

User Exits

User exits are options provided by vendors to insert in customer-produced routines. User exits normally provide a standardized linkage to customer-developed modules which can be incorporated into a program and executed during the execution of that program. Normally, the customer can code the module in the standard language of the organization, have it compiled, and then merge the object module with the vendor program via the user exits.

The types of processing that can be effectively performed through user exits include:

- o   Additional edits and audits on data being processed by the program

- o   Relationship checks between data being processed by the application system on an independent source of data

- o   Computational logic

- o   Creation of a special file for additional processing and/or creation of an audit

PATCH VERSUS RECOMPILE

The options regarding making changes in machine language or through recompilation vary depending on whether it is a vendor-produced application or an in-house produced application. The in-house argument is one that is based upon risk. The probability of making an error in a patched program is significantly higher than in a recompiled program. In addition, the audit trail is more complete when a program is recompiled.

In a vendor-produced application, the following criteria may cause an organization to make changes using machine language patches versus recompilations.

- o   The vendor chooses not to release the source code to the customer.

- o   The customer does not have the compiler in which the vendor wrote the application system.

- o   Customer personnel are not trained in the language in which the application system was written.

TRAINING/SKILLS/DOCUMENTATION

Successfully operating and maintaining a vendor-produced application requires a thorough understanding of that application. The needed skills are gained through training and documentation. Both the vendor and the customer share the responsibility for determining that the appropriate skills are mastered by customer personnel.

When an in-house application system is developed, the needed skills reside in-house. This does not mean that all the people who need the skills will have them but, rather, that if problems occur or answers are needed, someone who thoroughly understands the application will be available. When an application system is obtained from a vendor, that same level of skill does not necessarily reside in-house.

The skills required for maintenance are dependent upon the organization's maintenance strategy. If someone determines that no changes will be made to the application, except for emergency changes, then less skill is required than if the organization intends to make in-house modifications to a leased or purchased application.

At a minimum, a user of a vendor-produced application should possess the following training/skills/documentation in order to ensure that the system will remain operational:

o   Documentation providing the job control language statements and operating requirements of the application system.

o   A listing of all error messages produced with recommended corrective action.

o   At least one member of the customer organization should be trained in trouble shooting the application system. This training should cover an overview of the application system structure, the language in which it was written, processing idiosyncrasies, and tips and techniques on potential application restrictions and actions to take should those restrictions be violated.

o   Duplicate copies of object and source program if available.

The responsibility for maintenance of an application system should reside with a single individual. Having one individual responsible for a vendor-produced application provides both a focal point for the vendor and a focal point for maintenance. Experience has shown that assigning maintenance responsibility to a single individual is better than assigning maintenance responsibility to a group. A single maintenance coordinator should be designated, regardless of whether the individual performs maintenance routinely or whether the individual is only responsible for hang-up analysis.

UNPLANNED CRITICAL MAINTENANCE

A major concern with a vendor-produced application is hang-ups. If an organization relies upon the continual running of an application, any impediment to the successful execution of the application will negatively impact the organization. When the application is obtained from a vendor, the organization may or may not have the ability to return that system to an operational status without the assistance of the vendor.

Contracts and other considerations are of little importance when the operations of an organization grind to a halt. The first consideration is to restore operations, and then restitution from the vendor can be sought. Organizations should develop an emergency maintenance checklist for each vendor-produced application system. The objective of the checklist is to guide employees through a step-by-step process to restore the applications to operational status. The checklist should be developed in conjunction with vendor personnel and normally would include:

o   Problem documentation forms.

o   Problem diagnosis checklist. This should be prepared primarily by vendor personnel and it should be used to aid in pinpointing the cause of the problem.

o   Instructions on how to accomplish common type fixes. For example, if a value in a record has been determined to be the cause of the problem, then the correction procedure should explain how to back that record out or eliminate it without having to restart the entire application.

The execution of the critical maintenance procedures would be performed by the individual assigned maintenance responsibility for that application. That individual should execute the emergency procedures in an effort to restore the application to an operational status. However, should the individual be unable to fix the program, vendor maintenance personnel should be called. The organization should have a list of the people to call -- including their home telephone numbers.

The vendor should be responsible for problems resulting in hang-ups. Thus, even when the customer's personnel can fix the problem, the vendor should be called in to determine that the analysis and fix were properly performed. In addition, the vendor should permanently fix the application if required.

VENDOR-DEVELOPED APPLICATION MAINTENANCE PLANNING CHECKLIST

Maintenance of applications obtained from a vendor is as important as maintenance of applications developed in-house. When user personnel do not possess sufficient skills to provide complete maintenance, then the area assumes even greater importance. Maintenance decisions made during contractual negotiations and maintenance training of customer personnel normally pay dividends when the application becomes operational.

A planning checklist for assessing the adequacy of the maintenance provisions in applications obtained from vendors is included as Figure 12-2. This checklist summarizes the main points covered in this chapter. It is intended to aid in preparing to maintain vendor-produced application systems and in preparing for contract negotiations.

SUMMARY

Data processing management should establish a policy for maintaining vendor-produced application systems. This policy should be transcribed into a list of maintenance considerations to be incorporated into application contracts. Data processing management should arrange these considerations according to category, indicating which are essential and which are negotiable.

Data processing management should make one individual responsible for maintenance of each vendor-produced application system. This individual should receive adequate training and documentation from the vendor. The individual responsible for maintenance should also prepare checklists and procedures to facilitate returning the application system to operational status after a problem occurs.

The operation of the vendor application system should be monitored to ensure that the vendor complies with contractual provisions for maintenance. Provisions not being complied with should be brought to the attention of data processing management for appropriate action. The organization should also monitor vendor attitudes and service to assess the desirability of future contracts with the same vendor.

FIGURE 12-2

VENDOR-DEVELOPED APPLICATION MAINTENANCE PLANNING CHECKLIST

NUMBER	MANAGEMENT QUESTION	RESPONSE			COMMENTS
		YES	NO	N/A	
1.	Has a policy been established regarding maintenance of vendor-produced application systems?				
2.	Is a list of maintenance conditions established prior to negotiating a contract with a vendor for an application system?				
3.	Are the vendor's obligations for maintenance included in the application contract?				
4.	Do the maintenance provisions in the application contract include the following areas: a) The customer's right to modify the application system b) Issuance of source code to the customer c) The speed of service d) The cost of service e) The caliber of vendor personnel who will maintain the application system f) Where the maintenance will be performed g) Target dates for installing new versions of the application system h) Penalties if maintenance is not performed per the contractual agreements i) Ownership of copyrights and application should maintenance be discontinued j) Ownership of copyrights and applications should the vendor go out of business k) Types of maintenance documentation provided to customer l) Statement on the vendor's willingness to make enhancements and/or install new requirements into the application system				

FIGURE 12-2

VENDOR-DEVELOPED APPLICATION MAINTENANCE PLANNING CHECKLIST

NUMBER	MANAGEMENT QUESTION	RESPONSE			COMMENTS
		YES	NO	N/A	
5.	Does the application system provide user exits for user-initiated modifications?				
6.	Has around-the-application system maintenance been considered in lieu of vendor maintenance?				
7.	Was the contract developed with the vendor fair to both parties?				
8.	Does the vendor provide maintenance training for user personnel?				
9.	Has one individual been assigned the responsibility for maintaining the application system?				
10.	Have a checklist and procedures been established outlining the steps to be performed when emergencies occur?				
11.	Have procedures been established to monitor the provisions in the contract?				
12.	Have procedures been established to enforce the provisions in the contract should the vendor fail to perform properly?				
13.	Have procedures been established to monitor application system performance to determine satisfaction and interest in getting new ventures with the vendor?				

Chapter 13
Monitoring the Systems Maintenance Process

CHAPTER OVERVIEW

Good maintenance procedures don't just happen. First, they must be carefully planned; second, data processing management must continually monitor the process to ensure effective implementation of the plans.

Monitoring is an audit-related function designed to assess both the process and the compliance with the process. More effective, more effecient, and more economical systems maintenance will result in improved service to users.

This chapter is designed to help data processing management monitor the systems maintenance function in their department. Recommendations are provided about the type of feedback valuable in monitoring maintenance, as well as suggestions on how to have that information presented.

MONITORING OBJECTIVES

The responsibility for monitoring the performance of computerized applications resides with data processing management. User management must make sure that data is accurate and complete and that it has been authorized. This is the data-oriented aspect of monitoring, as opposed to the systems-oriented aspect of monitoring which resides with data processing management.

Monitoring the performance of systems is one segment of the systems maintenance process. The monitoring serves two purposes. First it is designed to evaluate the performance of an operational computerized application. The monitoring is performed to determine how effectively the application eliminates problems. The second part of monitoring is to provide sufficient information and direction so that the problem can be corrected.

Data processing management may also wish to monitor if the application effectively utilizes the organization's hardware and software. This is a highly technical aspect of monitoring which is not included in this book. However, if data processing management desires to monitor that aspect of application systems it should be incorporated into the monitoring program.

The major reasons for data processing management to monitor the computerized environment are:

o   Management responsibility

One of the responsibilities of management is to monitor the performance of the area for which they are responsible. For data processing management this is the computerized environment. Since data processing management organizes, plans, directs, and controls the data processing function, they should also determine if their plans and controls are functioning properly.

o   Improve performance

The objective of monitoring is to detect and correct problems in order to improve the overall performance of the data processing function. The longer problems exist, the more severe they become.

o   Improve user relations

Users want computerized applications that perform their specified functions. The fewer the problems, the greater the confidence of the user in the ability of the data processing function to perform specified tasks. As a result, user relationships improve. If users are unhappy, it may affect their relationships with the data processing function and can also affect the attitudes of others within the organization.

o   Improve EDP image

Data processing in many organizations is a scapegoat for organizational problems. Many departments blame data processing for both real and imaginary problems. An environment that is relatively trouble free gives data processing a better image within the organization.

MONITORING CONTROL CONCERNS

The functions of management involve planning, organizing, directing, and controlling. The systems maintenance life cycle is a vehicle for controlling systems maintenance. Monitoring of that process by data processing management is another means of controlling the process.

The discussion of each phase of the systems maintenance life cycle has included a list of control concerns regarding that phase. These are the types of concerns that need to be addressed as data processing management monitors the SMLC.

The failure to monitor the systems maintenance process adequately raises additional control concerns. Without monitoring, the status of the systems maintenance function may not be known. If management is unaware of potential problems, the problems continue to grow in scope.

The control concerns associated with the monitoring process include:

o   Are there unknown problems?

Data processing management may be unaware of problems in the systems maintenance process and the changes made by that process. Lower level personnel often fail to report problems. Hasty solutions are rushed into production, or procedures are averted so that the problems will not come to the attention of senior data processing management. Without a knowledge of the frequency and types of problems occurring in the systems maintenance process, data processing management cannot take the necessary action to alleviate those problems.

o   Are known problems corrected?

Problems are detected through various means in an operating environment. Some are detected by computer operators, some by project personnel, and others by users of application systems. The methods of reporting and correcting those problems vary, depending upon the individual detecting the problem. Without proper identification, reporting and monitoring of those problems, the correction may not be documented, given a priority, or implemented. The information necessary to avoid losses, or sometimes major disasters, can be known but not acted upon.

o   <u>Is the severity of problems known?</u>

Speed of correction of a problem, as well as the effort going into that correction, is dependent upon the severity of the problem. Problems that appear to have minimal impact on the organization receive relatively low implementation priority. On the other hand, problems that border on disaster for the organization receive very high implementation priority. If the methods of defining the severity of the problem are not specific, the wording of the problem may not indicate the potential impact on the organization. The ideal method of expressing the severity of a problem is to quantify the impact as an annual dollar loss. This piece of information enables management to address necessary maintenance in terms of cost/benefits.

o   <u>Have corrections been given priorities?</u>

The severity of the problem and the priority for implementation are closely interrelated. However, it is possible to know the severity of a problem without having a good method for assigning priorities to the implementation of changes. Some users operate as if every change is of extreme importance. Others have limited priority systems which only distinguish among classes but not within classes. The priority system must be sufficiently sensitive to ensure that users can control the implementation of each change. The system must also permit reordering of priorities each time a new change is entered into the queue.

o   <u>Can the cause of problem be identified?</u>

Whether one is able to identify the cause of a problem is normally dependent upon whether one has enough information describing the problem. Large amounts of time and effort can be wasted when someone attempts to find the cause of a problem when too few clues pointing to the cause of the problem have been identified and/or documented. In some instances, the cause is not located the first time the problem occurs, and the organization must wait until it occurs again before conducting a realistic investigation.

o   <u>Is it expensive to investigate the concern?</u>

Other problems are encountered, but the severity or cause of the problem cannot be determined because an investigator may need to perform extensive extracts in order to gather information which substantiates the cause or severity of the problem. For example, if the product master pricing file lists the wrong price for Item X, it may be necessary to examine hundreds of thousands of invoices to determine who was misbilled and for how many dollars. Someone might decide that the cost of making this investigation far exceeds the value to be derived from making the investigation. Without appropriate feedback mechanisms, similar investigations may prove to be uneconomical.

Long-Range Objective of Monitoring

Monitoring has both short-range and long-range objectives. The short-range objectives are to correct problems that have or are occurring in the computerized environment. For example, if a report contains erroneous information, both the application program and the erroneous data need to be corrected. This is a continuous process requiring immediate action when problems are detected.

The long-range objective of monitoring computerized applications is to improve the controls within those applications, as well as the controls governing maintenance of those applications. This second use of monitoring is the more valuable use in that it establishes an environment designed to prevent problems, as opposed to normal monitoring which is designed to detect and correct problems.

The long-range objectives for monitoring are listed in Figure 13-1. These objectives are related to the previously discussed control concerns. Monitoring can result in designing better methods for maintaining operational systems. Monitoring to anticipate unknown problems can result in better system design. Monitoring to know whether problems are corrected can result in the design of better controls to monitor the implementation of corrections. Monitoring can also result in the development of better methods of assigning priorities to the correction of problems. Monitoring problems whose cause cannot be identified can result in developing better methods for documenting and subsequently identifying problem causes. Monitoring to determine when it is too costly to investigate problems can result in determining when feedback mechanisms are needed.

Data processing management should use monitoring for both short-range and long-range purposes. Obviously, the short-range purpose of monitoring is to ensure the integrity of the operational environment. This must be the first priority of monitoring. However, to lose sight of the long-range objectives is to lose sight of one of the major benefits of monitoring.

THE MONITORING PROCESS

The process of monitoring systems maintenance is not very different from any other type of monitoring. What does vary are the tasks being monitored and the methods of monitoring. The previous sections have outlined the areas and tasks to be monitored in systems maintenance, and the following section will describe the monitoring techniques.

The monitoring process is illustrated in a flowchart in Figure 13-2. The process to monitor the system maintenance process is as follows:

o   Set monitoring objective

If data processing management wants to monitor systems maintenance documentation, then they should specify which aspects of systems maintenance documentation they will monitor. The details should be described as standards of performance.

o   Establish standards of performance

Monitoring is a very complex task until standards of performance have been established. In the previous example, until documentation standards have been set the individual monitoring the maintenance process can only make subjective judgments about the documentation.

-320-

FIGURE 13-1

LONG-RANGE MONITORING CONTROL CONCERNS OBJECTIVES

CATEGORY OF CONCERN	LONG-RANGE OBJECTIVE OF MONITORING
Problems unknown	To design better methods for monitoring operational systems
Known problems not corrected	To design better controls to monitor implementation of corrections
Severity of problems unknown	To determine better methods to identify and quantify severity of problems
Corrections not prioritized	To develop better methods of assigning priorities for the correction of problems
Cause of problem cannot be identified	To develop better methods to document problems to facilitate the identification of problem causes
Too costly to investigate concern	To determine when new feedback mechanisms are needed

FIGURE 13-2

MONITORING PROCESS

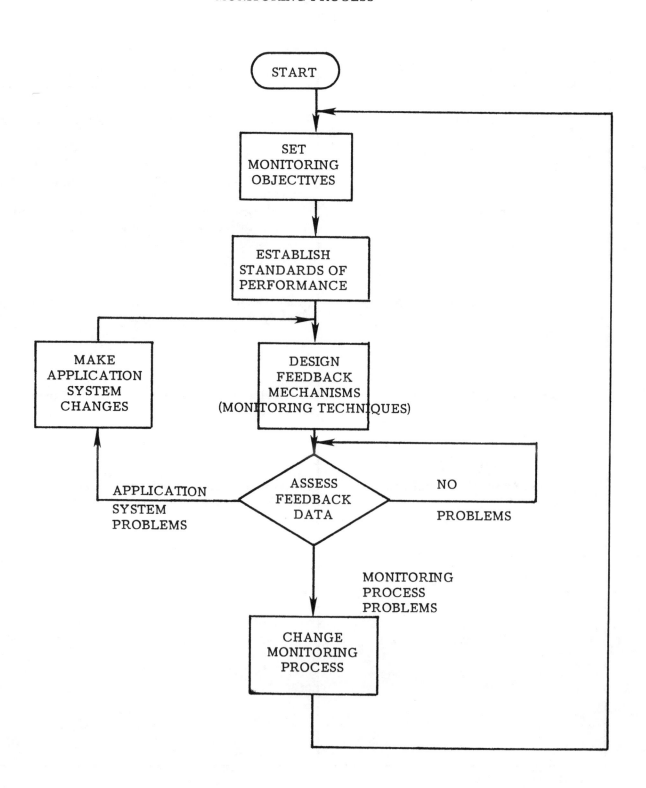

o   Design feedback mechanisms (monitoring techniques)

While the monitoring process remains relatively unchanged, the monitoring techniques may need to be uniquely constructed for the process. A detailed description of the more popular monitoring techniques are described later in this chapter.

o   Assess feedback data

The key step of the monitoring process is to use the feedback as a basis for decision making. If the data is inadequate, someone may need to perform additional investigation and analysis before management can determine which actions to take.

The key ingredient to a successful systems maintenance process is the active participation of data processing management in the monitoring process. While much of the collection, analysis, and presentation can be made by lower level data processing management, the final review and decision making are the responsiblity of senior data processing management. This is particularly true when serious problems occur either with the application or the monitoring process.

The three areas of decisions resulting from the analysis of feedback data are:

1.   No problems - The feedback data indicates that the system is functioning properly and thus no action is required. Monitoring should verify that the system continues to perform as specified.

2.   Application system problems - The application system fails to perform as specified. These problems normally result in a request for change to the application system. The new change may or may not affect the needed feedback mechanisms in the application system. If the feedback mechanisms are affected or if new analyses are required, then new feedback mechanisms must be designed. This might result in the installation of a new monitoring technique.

3.   Monitoring process problems - The information gathered may indicate that the monitoring process is ineffective. The data collected may be erroneous, incomplete, or the analysis process may be faulty. Any of these causes should result in changing the monitoring process. When this happens the methods of monitoring may have to be redesigned and the entire monitoring process may have to be changed.

MONITORING TECHNIQUES

Individuals should use monitoring techniques which are consistent with the monitoring objectives. Management should analyze the objectives together with the standards of performance supporting that objective in order to determine how best to monitor the operating environment and ensure that performance standards are achieved.

Data processing management uses a variety of techniques to monitor the systems maintenance process. These techniques can be categorized into the following eight categories (see Figure 13-3):

1.   Compliance with standards

FIGURE 13-3

MONITORING TECHNIQUES

#	TECHNIQUE CATEGORY	DESCRIPTION	ADVANTAGES	DISADVANTAGES
1	Compliance with standards	Verifies conformance to required methods of performance	Enforcement of DP standards	Standards may not be applicable to situation
2	Quality assurance group	Establishment of a group charged with monitoring	Full-time monitors	DP senior management may not get involved
3	Metrics	Quantitative comparison of two variables	Quantitative assessment	Metrics may not correlate with problem
4	Feedback reports	Presentation and analysis of feedback data in report format	Formal presentation	Takes time to prepare
5	Daily reviews	Scheduled meeting each day to discuss problems and actions	Keeps management on top of problems	Consumes management time
6	Segregation of duties/functions	One function monitors another	Continuous monitoring	DP senior management may not get involved
7	Approval (SMLC)	Each task must be approved	Continuous involvement of management	May become routine
8	Automated monitoring	Using the computer to monitor the process	Consistent and continuous	Costly and may not be complete

Data processing management verifies through examination of documentation that systems maintenance analysts use the established systems maintenance standards. This is primarily an audit function in which data processing management verifies through observation, examination, or testing that the maintenance people have used the standards when they have changed application systems. For example, if flowcharts are to be updated each time a program change is made, then data processing management would compare, at least on a test basis, program flowcharts with program listings to ensure that they are in agreement.

This monitoring technique ensures enforcement of data processing standards. If management doesn't use some kind of compliance technique, there may be a gradual erosion of standards. However, the compliance check should also verify that the standards are applicable to the application being reviewed. Poor standards can be worse than no standards at all.

2. Quality assurance group

A quality assurance group is an independent function established in the data processing department to assure that the quality of application systems remains high. Quality is defined by the organization. Thus, quality in one organization does not mean the same as quality in another organization. Quality can be expressed in terms of adherence to standards and goals, meeting schedules and budgets, and any other criteria management desires to establish as a measure of quality.

If quality is in compliance with standards, then the quality assurance group should verify that standards are complied with. If quality is measured in terms of meeting user needs, then a contract must be established between data processing and the user specifying those needs. The quality assurance group can then verify if the needs have been achieved in the application system. The systems maintenance process is one measure of quality, and the quality assurance group can verify that that process is used and is effective.

The quality assurance group has the advantage of being full-time systems maintenance monitors. Data processing management competes for their time and may not be able to perform sufficient monitoring in the limited time available. On the other hand, the establishment of a quality assurance group may mean that senior data processing management will no longer get involved in monitoring the systems maintenance process.

3. Metrics

Using metrics involves making a quantitative comparison of two variables. The metrics that are useful for monitoring maintenance are described in Chapter 11 which explains what metrics are effective, how to collect the data for those metrics, and how to use metrics.

The advantage of using metrics is that management is given a specific number which they can use to compare maintenance trends in one application over a period of time. They can also compare maintenance performance in different projects at a single point in time, or they can measure the performance of a single maintenance task. The disadvantage is that poorly constructed metrics may not relate to the problem; thus, the metrics are useless. Normally, metrics must be proved over a period of time.

4. Feedback reports

In each chapter of the systems maintenance life cycle is a description of the type of feedback valuable for monitoring that phase of the life cycle. In many cases the data must be organized, summarized and presented before management can make meaningful judgments about maintenance conditions.

Among the more common methods for reporting feedback data are:

o   Listing raw data: If management were monitoring the cost of changes, they would receive a listing of change numbers and the cost of each change. This is one of the simplest methods of presenting the feedback in report form.

o   Trend analysis: Feedback data can be presented over a period of time. This shows trends of events which may be more meaningful than the raw information. For example, it might be more useful to know whether the cost of making a change was increasing or decreasing over a period of time than to know the cost of a change itself. Trend analysis can be used for this purpose.

o   Columnar information: A variation of raw data presentation is to present that data in columnar format. Often, however, the information is summarized in the columns as opposed to being presented in true raw state. For example, a report may include columns for the number of changes, and the total cost of changes by project. Thus, one report lists all the projects showing the total number of changes made and the total number of dollars expended on those changes.

o   Graphics: Graphics present information in pictorial format as opposed to alphanumeric format. Examples of graphics include bar charts, line charts, pie charts, and other pictorial comparisons of variables. For example, a bar chart could present the average cost of making the change by project. It would then be visually obvious which project had the highest cost per change and which the lowest.

The advantage of written feedback is that the presentation is formalized. Oral presentation or poorly presented data may not achieve the desired objective. However, when management understands and accepts a specific report format they can use the reports to quickly assess the impact of systems maintenance. The disadvantage is that it takes time and effort to prepare formal reports on a regular basis. The benefit of those reports must be weighed against the cost of preparation.

5.   Daily reviews

Many organizations assemble their key supervisors first thing in the morning for a short meeting, which may last two or three minutes or longer, depending on the problem. The objective of this meeting is to review problems encountered the previous day and agree upon a course of action. This enables data processing management to schedule people and resources on a daily basis to satisfy current problems.

Using this concept, one member of data processing management is assigned the responsibility of preparing a briefing of events from the previous day. This individual normally comes to work ahead of the rest of data processing management to prepare the briefing. All parties involved in the data processing function need to be involved to plan the deployment of all the resources.

The advantage of a daily review is that it keeps all levels of data processing management on top of the problem. In large departments, managers present at the meeting can later inform their subordinates of the problems and actions taken during the meeting. The disadvantage is that it consumes management's precious time. Even if there are no problems, management should still come together and meet for a short period of time.

6. Separation of duties/functions

One of the most effective methods for monitoring an environment is to segregate the duties or functions among two or more people or activities. The object of segregating functions is so that one group or activity will monitor the other activity. For example, in a cash environment one individual may sign the checks, while another individual may reconcile the bank account. Thus, no one individual has the opportunity both to create and to conceal a problem.

Separation of duties is the division of activities among two or more people. The separation of functions in a computerized environment can be the division of tasks among two or more systems or programs. It may also be having people monitor the activities of the computer independent of the data used by the computer.

When duties or functions have been separated, the methods of cross-monitoring must be determined. Separation without monitoring does not achieve the desired objectives. Thus, as the functions are organized and assigned to people or systems, the methods by which those functions are to be monitored should be established at the same time.

The advantage of separation of duties or functions is that a continuous monitoring activity is established. One group is responsible for monitoring another group, and vice versa. The disadvantage is that senior management may become complacent about the effectiveness of separating duties or functions and therefore may not get involved in the monitoring process.

7. Approval (SMLC)

A well-designed systems maintenance life cycle involves approval to perform the tasks within the life cycle. The granting of the approval should come from a monitoring process. Approval should not be given until data processing management is satisfied that the process is being performed properly.

To implement the approval process, data processing management should have predetermined procedures for giving approval. Ideally the approval request would be documented, and management would use a checklist of events to determine that all the required tasks have occurred before they give approval. For example, prior to permitting a change to go into production, management should assure themselves that the change has been adequately tested, that users concur with the change being installed, that the documentation is up to date, and that the unchanged segments of the application are not negatively impacted. When this happens, the approval process instigates monitoring by data processing management.

8. Automated monitoring

Data processing management should utilize the power of the computer to monitor the computerized environment. As more and more functions become automated, the opportunity to automate the monitoring process increases. Properly done, this may be a very low-cost and effective way of incorporating monitoring procedures into the maintenance process.

There are many techniques used to monitor the data processing environment, including:

o   Job accounting systems: Systems that collect data for accounting purposes can also be used to provide information to monitor the environment. These systems not only include accounting information, but they also provide information about the use of data processing resources, frequency of application runs and reruns, invalid access attempts, and access to files.

o   User exits: Many vendor-produced operating software systems permit the entry of special coding through user exits. This allows management to enter small routines to monitor certain conditions that otherwise might be difficult or costly to monitor.

o   Communication/DBMS logs: Logs used for recovery purposes in large communication and data base management systems contain much information that can be used for monitoring the environment. The information in the logs primarily relates to activities occurring in that environment, such as performance, number of transactions processed, and problems in using the facilities of the system.

o   Source/object libraries: Programs used in the operating environment are stored in source and object program libraries. If data processing management wishes to monitor changes to programs, types of code used, or number of changes made, this information can be obtained from preprocesses or postprocesses attached to the object and/or source program libraries.

o   Test libraries: Test libraries used in the testing environment can provide statistics about the number of tests run and the cost of tests. Data needed about the testing processes can normally be obtained from the test libraries or testing systems.

These are but a few of the many methods of automating the monitoring process. It is inconsistent with the objections of data processing to establish labor-intensive monitoring procedures in an automated environment. Data processing management should review the opportunities within their operating environment to install techniques that can use the power of the computer to monitor the computer processes.

These automated monitoring processes provide consistent and continuous monitoring. All of the advantages of computerizing tasks are applicable to automating the monitoring process. The disadvantages are that the processes may be costly, and they may be incomplete if the necessary data is not available for automatic capture.

SUMMARY

Data processing management has the responsibility of monitoring the data processing environment. This monitoring can include monitoring any of the following activities:

o   Management and administration of change

o   Access to programs for maintenance

o   Quality of testing and specified needs

o   Recovery to a fallback position in the event the change is not successful

o   Production performance

o   Documentation of application system changes

o   Approval processes

Fulfilling this monitoring process involves the same planning and effort as required in any other part of the systems maintenance process. The objectives of monitoring systems maintenance are similar to the objectives of monitoring individual phases of the SMLC; however, the techniques used to monitor systems maintenance may be different than those used for monitoring other aspects of data processing. This chapter has explained both the concerns that need to be addressed in monitoring systems maintenance, as well as the tools and techniques that can be employed to alleviate those concerns.

Appendix A
Criteria to Measure Need to Rewrite

CRITERION   CRITERION #1

Users stop making requests for changes.

DESCRIPTION OF CHANGE

When systems become too unresponsive to user needs, users find alternative means to satisfy their needs. Some develop informal systems which maintain the needed information. When these conditions occur, users stop using the application system and rely upon their informal systems. Thus, they stop requesting changes to the system.

DATA COLLECTION TECHNIQUES

If an organization has a formal system change request form, count the number of requests made. If the number of requests is abnormally low, or dropping, user personnel should be interviewed regarding the usefulness of the system in their area.

CRITERION STRENGTH

Business conditions continually change, and application systems must stay in synchronization with business conditions. Therefore, needed systems will undergo a series of continual changes. If these changes stop or significantly decrease, it may indicate that the system is out of synchronization with the user function.

CRITERION WEAKNESS

Having few requests for system changes can also indicate that the user is completely satisfied with the application system. Systems that have antici-pated user needs may have built those capabilities into the system prior to the need. However, an interview with user personnel is a means of quickly pinpointing the cause of minimal (or no) system change requests.

CRITERIA TO MEASURE NEED TO REWRITE

CRITERION   CRITERION #2

Number of errors detected by the application system.

DESCRIPTION OF CRITERION

During computer processing, data is continually checked for errors. Errors can result from improper input, inconsistent data relationships, failure to meet system criteria, data source unlocatable (e.g., if an employee cannot be located in the employee master file), and improprieties in output preparations.

DATA COLLECTION TECHNIQUES

For each detected error in an application system one or more error messages is produced. Each error message should represent an error for the purposes of this criteria. The error messages should be counted to produce a total number of errors detected. This could be a routine added to the application system; or if errors are placed on a tape or disk file and then printed, it could be counted either automatically during printing or manually after printing.

CRITERION STRENGTH

Errors can be indicative of complexity or unresponsiveness of an application system. Errors can be made because the system does not readily fit into the day-to-day needs of the organization. The higher the number of detected errors, the greater the need to rewrite to simplify the system and to integrate it more into user processing.

CRITERION WEAKNESSES

Errors can also represent data preparation by unskilled people, or people who have sloppy or unsupervised work habits. These types of errors can be reduced with additional training and supervision.

CRITERIA TO MEASURE NEED TO REWRITE

CRITERION   CRITERION #3

   High number of requests for system change.

DESCRIPTION OF CRITERION

   If an organization has a formal system change request, the number of
   changes can be obtained by counting the requests. Without a formal system,
   the number of changes requested must be obtained from the application
   project team. The magnitude of the number of changes can be obtained by
   comparing two previous periods in the same system or other systems of
   similar size and complexity.

CRITERION STRENGTH

   A change request indicates that the system is not satisfactorily meeting the
   needs of the user. The more changes, the less satisfactory the system is in
   meeting user needs. The high frequency of change may represent a serious
   problem in systems structure in meeting user needs.

CRITERION WEAKNESS

   A great number of changes may also indicate changes in the conduct of
   business in the user area. In this instance the magnitude of change would not
   reflect upon the viability of the application system but, rather, indicates the
   volatility of procedures in the user area.

CRITERION   CRITERION #4

High maintenance dollars.

DESCRIPTION OF CRITERION

The magnitude of changes to an application system can be measured two ways. One way is the number of changes and the second way is to present the dollar cost of those changes. Dollar cost is perhaps more representative of the size and complexity of the changes than is the number of changes. One change in system X may cause considerably more than 25 changes in systetm B.

DATA COLLECTION TECHNIQUES

If project personnel charge their time and the computer time they consume to a maintenance budget, the cost of maintenance can be obtained from the budgetary process. The magnitude of the costs can be determined by comparing it to maintenance dollars for previous accounting periods on the same project, or measuring it against maintenance costs for other projects of similar size and complexity.

CRITERION STRENGTH

Maintenance costs are more indicative of the magnitude of change than is the number of changes. Thus, maintenance dollars should be a good predictor of the magnitude of change made to an application system.

CRITERION WEAKNESS

Maintenance dollars may be expended for error correction, system enhancements, and new requirements. The allocation of maintenance dollars among the three categories may indicate that new requirements and enhancements are consuming maintenance dollars to achieve new needs as opposed to correcting problems because the system is out of synchronization with the user area.

CRITERIA TO MEASURE NEED TO REWRITE

CRITERION   CRITERION #5

Difficulty in extracting data from the application system.

DESCRIPTION OF CRITERION

Many user needs are one-time needs. Special types of extracts or reports are prepared to meet a specific need, which may or may not be repeated at a future time. The difficulty in providing users with this special information is indicative of the responsiveness of the application system to meeting user needs.

DATA COLLECTION TECHNIQUES

One-time user requests for information should be identified. If the program change request system provides this information, it can be collected from the system change request procedure. However, if the system does not provide this information, then either interview the application project team or the user to determine which changes are of a one-time nature. For each of these changes, determine the days required for satisfaction. Compare this with the length of time required to make similar changes in previous periods, or against other application systems of the same size and complexity.

CRITERION STRENGTH

As the data processing systems become more integrated into the day-to-day processing in the user area, the user must be able to satisfy special needs quickly. The more responsive the system is in satisfying those needs, the more valuable it becomes to the user.

CRITERION WEAKNESS

The number of days required to satisfy a user need may be more dependent upon the complexity of the extract than on the ability of the application system to meet user needs. Likewise, requests quickly satisfied may be easily satisfied, even though the system is deteriorating.

CRITERION   CRITERION #6

Application system is difficult to change.

DESCRIPTION OF CRITERION

The difficulty of changing a system can be measured in the number of days required to make a change. The number of days should not include time in a queue awaiting systems and programming attention but, rather, the number of days from the time the change is started until it is ready to go into operation. The assumption is that in good systems changes can be installed quickly, while in poorly structured or poorly documented systems the change process becomes time consuming.

DATA COLLECTION TECHNIQUES

If a formal change process exists, and the project personnel record the day they start work on a change and the day that it is ready to go into operation, the information can be collected from those forms. Otherwise the information must be gathered by interviewing project personnel.

CRITERION STRENGTH

The amount of time to make a change is normally extensive if it is difficult to determine where to make the change, how to fit the change into the existing logic, and to test and document the change. The time required grows as the system deteriorates.

CRITERION WEAKNESS

The number of days to install a change can also be indicative of the magnitude of the change. Big changes can take a large number of days to install regardless of the effectiveness or ineffectiveness of the application systems structure.

CRITERIA TO MEASURE NEED TO REWRITE

CRITERION   CRITERION #7

DESCRIPTION OF CRITERION

The cost to process a transaction should be evaluated on a continuous basis. The criterion is really the cost trend to process a transaction. An increasing dollar cost is indicative of a deteriorating application system, while consistent or decreasing costs are indicative that the system is still viable and takes advantage of new technology.

DATA COLLECTION TECHNIQUES

The cost of processing a transaction requires two pieces of information: the number of transactions processed per run and the cost per run. Frequently, this type of information is available from job accounting systems. The complex part is to define what is meant by a transaction. For example, several computer records may encompass a single business transaction.

CRITERIA STRENGTH

As computer technology becomes more efficient, the cost to process a transaction should decrease. However, if the systems structure is obsolete, or not in synchronization with the hardware and software capabilities, the cost will increase. Thus cost to process a transaction should be a good predictor of systems obsolescence.

CRITERION WEAKNESS

The cost to process a transaction is also related to the complexity of the processing required for that transaction. Thus a change in the mix of transactions or an increasing complexity in processing may also result in increased cost.

CRITERIA TO MEASURE NEED TO REWRITE

CRITERION   CRITERION #8

Obsolete hardware/software

DESCRIPTION OF CRITERION

The hardware and software that an organization uses changes over a period of time. Systems developed using one generation of hardware and software may not operate effectively on a new generation of hardware and software. Each new generation makes many existing application systems obsolete.

DATA COLLECTION TECHNIQUES

To determine if changeovers in hardware and software have occurred, interview either computer operations personnel or a hardware/software acquisitions group if the organization has one. Interview project personnel to determine the type of technology required to operate their application system.

CRITERION STRENGTH

Operating systems using obsolete hardware and software may substantially increase the cost and complexity of operation. Occasionally these systems require special emulators or simulators which themselves may be costly to obtain and operate.

CRITERION WEAKNESS

Application systems which are written in high-level language and are device-independent can frequently be shifted to new hardware and software with minimal or no loss of performance.

CRITERION   CRITERION #9

Application system is complex to operate.

DESCRIPTION OF CRITERION

Difficult-to-operate application systems increase both the cost of operation and the potential for error. Complexity of operation can be due to poor systems design or change in operating methods both within the user area and the computer operations area. Thus, complexity can be a problem of computer operators and/or users of the application.

DATA COLLECTION TECHNIQUES

Statistics on complexity to operate normally have to be gathered from interviewing or observing computer operators and/or user personnel. However, occasionally reviewing the procedures required to accomplish work in the application system is sufficient to provide insight in the complexity of operation.

CRITERION STRENGTH

If a system is complex to operate, people may avoid using that system. Also, turnover in personnel will require extensive training and also subject the organization to a potentially high error rate.

CRITERION WEAKNESS

That a system is too complex to operate may be a subjective judgment. Items are only complex if there is an easier way to operate the application system.

CRITERION   CRITERION #10

Application system structure out of sequence with data processing plans.

DESCRIPTION OF CRITERION

Data processing organizations change methods, procedures and technology periodically. For example, an organization may move from batch to on-line data base systems. When these changes occur, application systems not using that technology cause problems for data processing management. For example, it is difficult keeping people interested in and adept at working with older methods and procedures.

DATA COLLECTION TECHNIQUES

The organization's long- and short-range plans should be studied and then a determination made which application systems are within the structure of those short- and long-range plans. This may require interviews with project managers and data processing management.

CRITERION STRENGTH

A change in methods, procedures or technology normally requires extensive investments of time and dollars. When there are exceptions to the normal procedures these continue to take an ever-increasing amount of effort over time.

CRITERION WEAKNESS

There may be little reason to change an effectively functioning application to a new method, procedure, or technology if that move cannot be cost justified.

CRITERIA TO MEASURE NEED TO REWRITE

CRITERION   CRITERION #11

Cost of testing system changes.

DESCRIPTION OF CRITERION

The cost of change may not be as indicative of obsolete systems structure as is the cost of testing. Testing provides insight into the complexity of getting changes operational. The more difficult the system is to maintain, the more difficult testing becomes.

DATA COLLECTION TECHNIQUES

The cost of testing can be measured in terms of number of tests, minutes of tests or dollar cost of tests. This information may be available from the departmental budgetary systems or computerized job accounting systems. The information collection technique should be the one simplest to perform.

CRITERION STRENGTH

The cost of testing provides a guide to the difficulty in making a successful change in an application system. The more difficult to make the change, the higher the probability that testing will become costly.

CRITERION WEAKNESS

A high cost of testing can also be attributable to sloppy programming or using programmers inexperienced in the application system or in the software systems in which the application and testing reside.

CRITERION   CRITERION #12

Problems encountered in placing changes into a production status.

DESCRIPTION OF CRITERION

The installation of a change in an application system has many risks associated with it. The change may not perform correctly, the changes may impact unchanged areas of the application, and users may not understand the change and therefore may make errors.

DATA COLLECTION TECHNIQUES

The amount of documentation recorded during the implementation process determines the ease of gathering data about encountered problems. Frequently this information must be gathered by interviewing users and operational and project personnel. In addition, project personnel should analyze error messages immediately following a change, additional change requests which may be related to correcting problems caused by the change, and changes taken out of production status for more testing.

CRITERION STRENGTH

The final success of the change process is a problem free conversion. Thus, if present personnel take shortcuts in making and testing changes, the change conversion process will be adversely affected. The application system may seem to be viable when in fact it is deteriorating. However, the test states of the system won't be apparent.

CRITERION WEAKNESS

Changes in the conversion process may be caused by conditions other than a deteriorating application systems structure. For example, it could be caused by unskilled operators and user personnel.

Appendix B
Maintenance Metrics Description

METRIC   METRIC #1

Cost of maintenance divided by number of changes.

DESCRIPTION OF METRIC

This metric provides the cost to make a change.

DATA COLLECTION TECHNIQUES

Annual maintenance should be paid out of the organization's budget and the number of changes from a formal change request process.

METRIC STRENGTH

The changes during a year should average into change of average size and complexity. Statistically this should be comparable to previous maintenance periods and other application systems.

METRIC WEAKNESS

A change in the mix of system changes, for example a series of very large or very small changes, could significantly impact the cost per change.

MAINTENANCE METRICS DESCRIPTIONS

METRIC   METRIC #2

Benefit derived from changes divided by cost of changes.

DESCRIPTION OF METRIC

The metric indicates the payback on dollars invested in maintenance. The higher the metric, the greater the payback.

DATA COLLECTION TECHNIQUES

The cost of maintenance should be included in the budget and presumably in the benefits from the system change request. However, it may be necessary to do additional investigation both to substantiate the benefits received or to document the benefits received.

METRIC STRENGTH

The metric is a strong predictor of value received from maintenance dollars.

METRIC WEAKNESS

The metric can be misleading if benefits are not accurately calculated.

MAINTENANCE METRIC DESCRIPTIONS

METRIC

Data fields per screen last year divided by data fields per screen this year.

DESCRIPTION OF METRIC

The metric indicates the usefulness per screen. A metric less than one indicates that the screens are becoming more useful, while a metric over one indicates that the screens are becoming less useful.

DATA COLLECTION TECHNIQUES

The data elements per screen should be totaled at various checkpoints, normally at one point each year.

METRIC STRENGTH

The metric indicates how maintenance is impacting the usefulness of screens.

METRIC WEAKNESS

Factors other than maintenance may impact the number of data elements per screen.

METRIC   METRIC #4

   Number of lines of maintenance code divided by size of maintenance size.

DESCRIPTION OF METRIC

   The metric indicates the number of lines of maintenance code coded by each
   maintenance programmer. This is a maintenance performance indicator.

DATA COLLECTION TECHNIQUES

   The number of maintenance programmers can be obtained from the organization chart or the departmental budgetary reports, and the number of lines
   of code entered by a maintenance programmer should be available from the
   source program library statistics.

METRIC STRENGTH

   Over an extended period of time, the size and complexity of changes should
   equal out so that the line of code is a good indicator of the viability of the
   structure of the application system.

METRIC WEAKNESS

   Factors other than systems structure may impact lines of code per period,
   such as programmer systems analysts skills.

MAINTENANCE METRICS DESCRIPTIONS

METRIC   METRIC #5

Number of errors/problems/violations divided by number of terminals.

DESCRIPTION OF METRIC

This metric shows the user problems incurred in operating on-line systems. The higher the metric, the greater the number of problems encountered (indicating poorly maintained systems).

DATA COLLECTION TECHNIQUES

The number of errors/problems/violations should be available from communication logs and the number of terminals from the operations supervisor.

METRIC STRENGTH

The metric provides insight into the frequency of errors averaged by the number of terminals.

METRIC WEAKNESS

The errors/problems/violations may have causes other than improper maintenance or systems design.

METRIC   METRIC #6

CPU charges divided by application system jobs steps.

DESCRIPTION OF METRIC

The metric provides an indication of the efficiency of the maintained system. The lower the metric, the more efficient the application. Note that CPU cost could be CPU time if it can be collected in a meaningful format.

DATA COLLECTION TECHNIQUES

The CPU time, or CPU cost, as well as the number of job steps should be available through job accounting systems.

METRIC STRENGTH

The metric provides an indication of the operational efficiency. It may be more appropriate to plot the metric over time to show whether maintenance is increasing or decreasing operational efficiency.

METRIC WEAKNESS

The metric does not take into account the complexity in size and job steps.

METRIC   METRIC #7

Number of program changes divided by the number of failures the first time the changed program is run in production.

DESCRIPTION OF METRIC

The metric provides an indication of the effectiveness of testing system changes. The higher the metric, the better the system testing; the lower the metric, the more ineffective the system change.

DATA COLLECTION TECHNIQUES

The number of programs changed can be obtained from either the source program or the object library. The number of failures should be available from documentation identifying problems.

METRIC STRENGTH

The metric shows the relationship of poorly implemented maintenance to total maintenance. It provides a positive indication that the effectiveness of testing changes.

METRIC WEAKNESS

The metric does not identify the cause of the failure or the pressures put on the project team to install the change.

METRIC   METRIC #8

Anticipated cost of maintenance divided by the actual cost of maintenance.

DESCRIPTION OF METRIC

The metric shows the effectiveness of the project team in installing changes within budget. The lower the metric, the poorer the maintenance performance; the higher the metric, the better the maintenance performance.

DATA COLLECTION TECHNIQUES

The anticipated and actual cost can be gathered from the departmental budget. In some organizations this information would be contained on the system change form.

METRIC STRENGTH

The metric shows the performance of the project team to install changes within the project.

METRIC WEAKNESS

The major weakness is the ineffectiveness of the budgetary process.

MAINTENANCE METRIC DESCRIPTIONS

METRIC   METRIC #9

Anticipated days to install the system change divided by the actual days.

DESCRIPTION OF METRIC

The metric indicates the effectiveness of the project team in installing the change within schedule. The lower the metric, the poorer the performance in meeting schedules; the higher the metric, the better the performance in meeting schedules.

DATA COLLECTION TECHNIQUES

The anticipated number of days can be obtained by using the time span between the date the change was scheduled to begin and the scheduled date of installation. The actual days to install would be the time span between the actual start date and the actual installation date.

METRIC STRENGTH

The metric shows the ability of the project team to meet schedules.

METRIC WEAKNESS

The metric does not explain the cause of success in meeting schedules; it is also dependent upon the effectiveness of the scheduling process.

METRIC   METRIC #10

Number of programming errors detected divided by the number of programs changed.

DESCRIPTION OF METRIC

The metric indicates the project team's proficiency in writing good program code. The lower the metric, the more proficient the project team; the higher the metric, the less proficient the project team is in writing good program code.

DATA COLLECTION TECHNIQUES

The number of programs changed can be obtained from the source program library, and the number of program errors obtained from compiler outputs.

METRIC STRENGTH

The metric indicates the programmer's knowledge and skill in writing program code.

METRIC WEAKNESS

The metric does not take into account the volume of work the programmer produces, as well as the programmer who debugs the program code.

MAINTENANCE METRIC DESCRIPTIONS

METRIC   METRIC #11

Size of new system development staff divided by size of maintenance staff.

DESCRIPTION OF METRIC

The metric indicates the proficiency of the maintenance staff in maintaining the application system. The higher the metric, the more proficient the maintenance group; while the lower the metric, the less proficient the maintenance group.

DATA COLLECTION TECHNIQUES

The number of people assigned to develop a new system and the number assigned to maintain the system after it has been developed can be obtained from departmental budgetary reports.

METRIC STRENGTH

The metric shows proficiency measured in terms of people.

METRIC WEAKNESS

The metric does not take into account the number of changes or volatility of the area involved.

METRIC   METRIC #12

Number of system errors detected divided by size of maintenance staff.

DESCRIPTION OF METRIC

The metric shows the number of system errors caused per person assigned to the maintenance staff. The higher the metric, the poorer the staff in eliminating system errors; while the lower the metric, the better the staff in eliminating system errors.

DATA COLLECTION TECHNIQUES

The size of the maintenance staff can be gathered from the departmental budget, and the number of errors from problem analysis documentation sheets.

METRIC STRENGTH

The metric relates errors to the number of people on the maintenance staff. It provides a positive indication of the average number of errors the maintenance staff makes in the system.

METRIC WEAKNESS

The metric does not take into account the application systems structure which may be a direct cause of errors.

METRIC   METRIC #13

Number of tests required divided by the number of systems errors.

DESCRIPTION OF METRIC

System errors are problems that require maintenance. The metric shows testing proficiency on the part of the maintenance staff. The lower the metric, the more proficient the maintenance staff in testing, while the higher the metric, the less proficient in testing.

DATA COLLECTION TECHNIQUES

The number of tests taken can be gathered from the job accounting system, and the number of detected errors in an application system causing changes to occur can be gathered from the change request form.

METRIC STRENGTH

The metric shows the number of tests occurring per detected error. This is valuable because several errors may be incorporated into a single test.

METRIC WEAKNESS

The metric does not take into account testing philosophy such as whether the computer or the programmer should find the errors.

METRIC   METRIC #14

Number of source codes statements changed divided by the number of tests.

DESCRIPTION OF METRIC

The metric provides insight into the efficiency of testing based upon the size
of the change. The higher the metric, the more efficient the testing process; while the lower the metric, the less efficient the testing process.

DATA COLLECTION TECHNIQUES

The number of source code statement changes can be obtained from the
source code library, and the number of tests made can be taken from the job
accounting systems.

METRIC STRENGTH

The metric shows the efficiency of testing in relationship to the size of the
test.

METRIC WEAKNESS

This does not take into account the complexity and type of source statements changed. For example, a lot of source statement notes may be entered which do not require testing.

METRIC   METRIC #15

Cost to develop divided by the cost to maintain.

DESCRIPTION OF METRIC

The metric shows the relationship between the dollars to develop and the dollars to maintain. The higher the metric, the more efficient the maintenance process; while the lower the metric, the less efficient the maintenance process.

DATA COLLECTION TECHNIQUES

Both the cost to develop and cost to maintain an application can be obtained from departmental budgetary statements.

METRIC STRENGTH

The metric relates developmental to maintenance costs in terms of total effort, including people, machine time and other chargeable expenses.

METRIC WEAKNESS

The metric does not take into account the complexity of changes and the volatility of the area serviced by the application.

METRIC   METRIC #16

Number of changes to a production system divided by the number of times
the system becomes inoperable (e.g., a hang-up, invalid output, etc.)

DESCRIPTION OF METRIC

Relates maintenance to systems problems. The higher the metric, the more
proficient the maintenance staff is in performing good maintenance; while
the lower the metric, the less efficient the maintenance staff is in successfully installing changes.

DATA COLLECTION TECHNIQUES

The number of changes to a production system can be obtained from the
system change forms, and the number of times the system becomes inoperable can be obtained from the problem documentation forms.

METRIC STRENGTH

The metric relates critical systems problems to the number of changes
made. The more changes that can be made without causing problems, the
greater the efficiency of good programming practices.

METRIC WEAKNESS

The metric does not take into account the amount of pressure under which
the maintenance staff operates.

METRIC   METRIC #17

Production operating hours divided by production rerun time.

DESCRIPTION OF METRIC

The metric is designed to consider rerun time from the perspective of total production time. The higher the metric, the more proficient the project team in ensuring that applications will run well; while the lower the metric, the poorer the maintenance team is in developing applications that perform properly.

DATA COLLECTION TECHNIQUES

Both the application run times and the application rerun times can be obtained from the job accounting system.

METRIC STRENGTH

The metric relates rerun problems to ineffective system performance. The higher the rerun time, the lower the metric rates performance.

METRIC WEAKNESS

The metric does not take into account the cause of the rerun, which could be hardware problems, for example.

METRIC   METRIC #18

Maintenance manpower hours expended divided by maintenance manpower used to correct systems and programming errors.

DESCRIPTION OF METRIC

The metric relates error correction time to total maintenance effort. The higher the metric, the more time allocated to new requirements and enhancements; while the lower the metric, the greater the likelihood of systems maintenance problems.

DATA COLLECTION TECHNIQUES

The time charged to maintenance can be gathered from data processing budgetary records, but the segment charged to error correction may have to be gathered from an analysis of the type of change which may or may not be available in the data processing accounting systems.

METRIC STRENGTH

The metric shows the amount of time and effort used to correct systems and programming errors in relationship to the total maintenance effort. Spending excess time correcting the project's own errors is indicative of a poor maintenance effort.

METRIC WEAKNESS

The metric does not take into account the status of the systems structure.

MAINTENANCE METRICS DESCRIPTIONS

METRIC   METRIC #19

Cost to operate the production system divided by the cost to maintain the system.

DESCRIPTION OF METRIC

The metric attempts to equate the size of the system's operational costs with the costs to maintain it. The lower the metric, the more efficient the maintenance effort; while the higher the metric, the more inefficient the maintenance.

DATA COLLECTION TECHNIQUES

The cost to operate the system can be obtained from either the job accounting system or the departmental budgetary system. And the cost to maintain the system can be gathered from the departmental accounting system.

METRIC STRENGTH

The metric equates maintenance to the dollar amount to operate the system. It relates maintenance and computer operating costs.

METRIC WEAKNESS

The metric does not take into account the importance of the application to the organization.

METRIC   METRIC #20

The assets controlled or processed by the application divided by the cost of maintenance.

DESCRIPTION OF METRIC

The metric equates the importance of the application to the organization maintenance effort. The higher the metric, the more effective the maintenance effort; while the lower the metric, the less efficient the maintenance effort.

DATA COLLECTION TECHNIQUES

The amount of assets or revenue controlled by the application system can normally be obtained from the user responsible for the application. The cost of maintenance can be obtained from the data processing budgetary reports.

METRIC STRENGTH

The metric relates the cost of maintenance to an indicator of the value of the application to the organization.

METRIC WEAKNESS

The assets controlled by an application may not be the best indicator of the value of the application to the organization.

METRIC   METRIC #21

Total maintenance effort divided by total maintenance effort applied to converting the old version of the system to the new version.

DESCRIPTION OF METRIC

Too much conversion time in relationship to maintenance time can mean poor use of maintenance effort. Therefore, a low metric is indicative of poor maintenance practices; while a high metric is indicative of good maintenance practices.

DATA COLLECTION TECHNIQUES

Total maintenance time can be gathered from departmental accounting systems, but the amount of that time expended on conversion may have to be gathered through other methods depending upon whether the conversion effort is broken out in time-reporting systems.

METRIC STRENGTH

The method shows whether or not maintenance groups are expending too much effort on converting from one version of an application system to another.

METRIC WEAKNESS

The metric does not take into account the type of change which can have a significant impact on the conversion effort.

METRIC   METRIC #22

Number of users using the application system divided by the number of programmers assigned to systems maintenance.

DESCRIPTION OF METRIC

The metric is most valuable for on-line applications and attempts to relate problems to the number of users. The higher the metric, the more efficient the maintenance process; while the lower the metric, the less efficient the maintenance process.

DATA COLLECTION TECHNIQUES

The number of users of the system can normally be obtained from the user responsible for the application system, and the number of programmers assigned to maintenance can be obtained from the data processing manager. The number of programmers assigned should be the equivalent of full-time programmers.

METRIC STRENGTH

The metric shows how successful the maintenance programmers are in maintaining an application system used by a large number of users.

METRIC WEAKNESS

There may not be a direct relationship between problems caused and the number of users of the application.

METRIC   METRIC #23

Number of programs in the application system divided by the number of programmers assigned to maintenance.

DESCRIPTION OF METRIC

The metric attempts to relate maintenance proficiency to the number of programs one maintenance programmer can maintain. The higher the metric, the more efficient the program is; the lower the metric, the less efficient the program is.

DATA COLLECTION TECHNIQUES

The number of programmers assigned to a project can be obtained from the departmental accounting system or data processing manager, and the number of programs in an application system can be obtained from the application system project manager.

METRIC STRENGTH

The metric shows how proficient programmers are in maintaining programs. The metric rewards those individuals who maintain a large number of programs.

METRIC WEAKNESS

The metric does not take into account the number of changes made in programs. Thus a programmer may have a large number of dormant programs.

Appendix C
Index and Purpose of
Systems Maintenance Questionnaires and Checklists

Appendix D
Index of and Forms Use Matrix

INDEX OF AND FORMS USE MATRIX

NAME OF FORM	ASSESSMENT OF MAINTENANCE FUNCTION	EMERGENCY MAINTENANCE	RECORD PROBLEMS	ASSIGN RESPONSIBILITY FOR CORRECTION	PROBLEM SOLUTION	PREPARING THE CHANGE	TESTING CHANGES	INSTALLING CHANGES
3-1 Installed Changes Form	✓							
3-2 Change Backlog Form	✓							
3-3 Application System Maintenance Profile	✓							
5-3 Call In List		✓						
5-4 Inventory of Privileged Maintenance Capability		✓						
5-6 Emergency Problem Report		✓						
5-7 Quick Fix Authorization Form		✓						
5-8 Emergency Problem Number Control Form		✓						
5-9 Request to Formalize Installed Quick Fix		✓						
6-1 Anticipated Need Identification Checklist			✓					
6-4 Government Regulation Requirements			✓					
6-5 Documentation of Maintenance Need – Data Processing Version			✓					
6-6 Documentation of Maintenance Need – User Version			✓					
6-7 Need Analysis and Estimation Request				✓				

INDEX OF AND FORMS USE MATRIX

NAME OF FORM	ASSESSMENT OF MAINTENANCE FUNCTION	EMERGENCY MAINTENANCE	RECORD PROBLEMS	ASSIGN RESPONSIBILITY FOR CORRECTION	PROBLEM SOLUTION	PREPARING THE CHANGE	TESTING CHANGES	INSTALLING CHANGES
7-2 Maintenance Solution Control Form					✓			
7-3 Data Change Form					✓			
7-4 Program Change Form					✓			
7-5 Impact of System Maintenance					✓			
7-6 Error Alert Form					✓			
7-11 Cost/Benefit Analysis					✓			
7-12 Maintenance Approval Form					✓			
8-2 Planning the Change Worksheet						✓		
8-3 Access Authorization Form						✓		
8-4 System Change Performance Criteria						✓		
8-5 System Maintenance Test Work Plan						✓		
8-6 System Maintenance Documentation Work Plan						✓		
9-2 Acceptance Test Plan Worksheet							✓	
9-3 Training Material Inventory							✓	

INDEX OF AND FORMS USE MATRIX

No.	NAME OF FORM	ASSESSMENT OF MAINTENANCE FUNCTION	EMERGENCY MAINTENANCE	RECORD PROBLEMS	ASSIGN RESPONSIBILITY FOR CORRECTION	PROBLEM SOLUTION	PREPARING THE CHANGE	TESTING CHANGES	INSTALLING CHANGES
9-4	Training Plan Worksheet							✓	
9-5	New/Modified Training Modules							✓	
9-6	Acceptance Test Checklist							✓	
9-7	Conduct Training Checklist							✓	
9-8	Automated Application Segment Test Failure Notification							✓	
9-9	Training Failure Notification							✓	
10-2	Restart/Recovery Planning Worksheet								✓
10-3	History of Change								✓
10-4	Notification of Production Change								✓
10-5	Source/Object Library Deletion Notice								✓
10-6	Program Change Monitor Notification								✓
10-7	System Problem Caused by Systems Change								✓